THE MUNSTERS

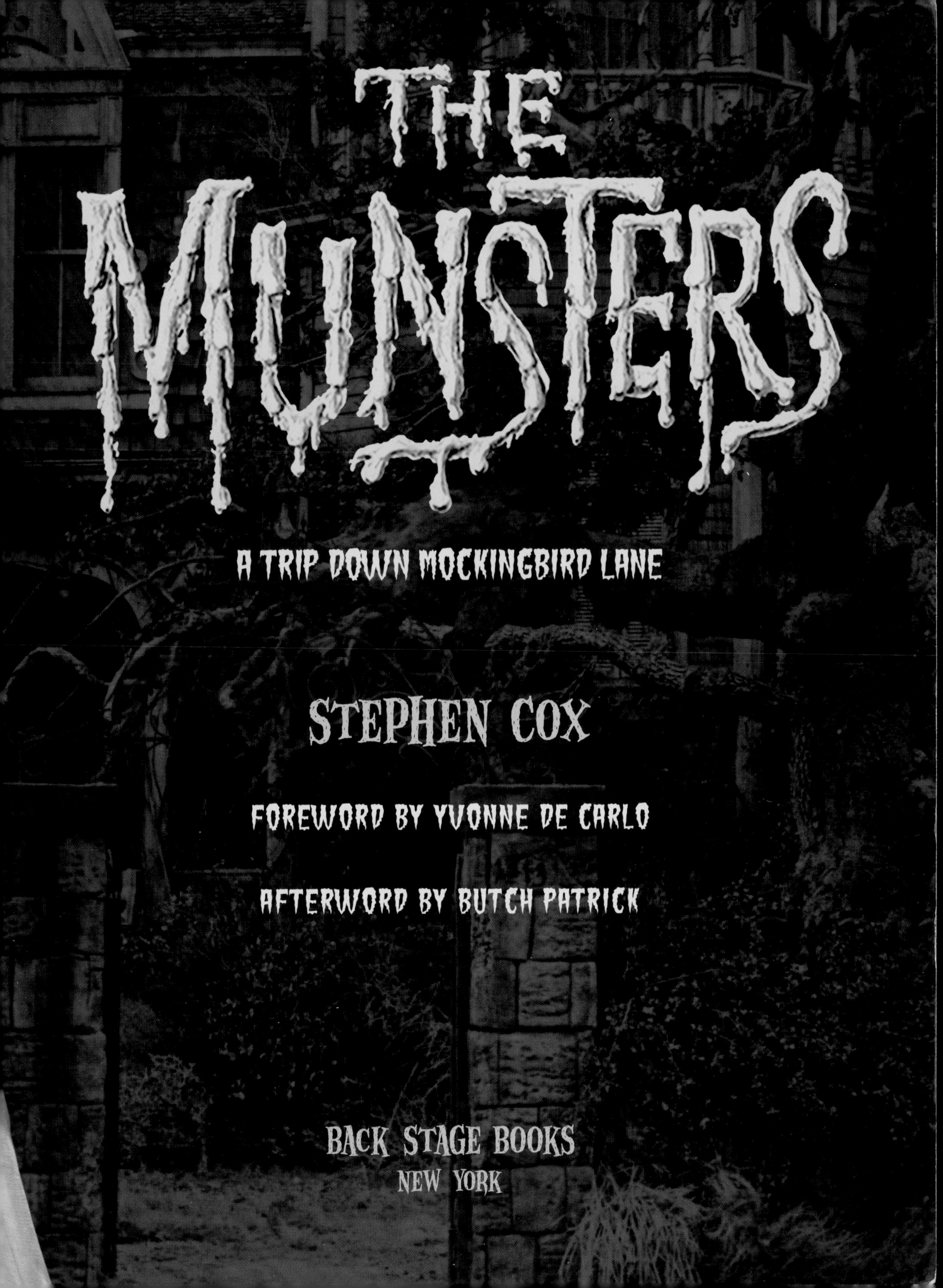

THE MUNSTERS

A TRIP DOWN MOCKINGBIRD LANE

STEPHEN COX

FOREWORD BY YVONNE DE CARLO

AFTERWORD BY BUTCH PATRICK

BACK STAGE BOOKS
NEW YORK

ALSO BY STEPHEN COX

The Beverly Hillbillies

The Munchkins Remember The Wizard of Oz and Beyond

The Addams Chronicles

The Abbott & Costello Story (with John Lofflin)

Here's Johnny!

The Munchkins of Oz

The Hooterville Handbook: A Viewer's Guide to Green Acres

Here on Gilligan's Isle (with Russell Johnson)

Cooking in Oz (with Elaine Willingham)

Dreaming of Jeannie: TV's Prime Time in a Bottle

It's a Wonderful Life: A Memory Book

One Fine Stooge (with Jim Terry)

Executive Editor: Mark Glubke
Project Editor: Ross Plotkin
Senior Production Manager: Ellen Greene
Designer: Jay Anning, Thumb Print
Cover photos © Universal Studios

First published in 2006 by Back Stage Books,
an imprint of Watson-Guptill Publications, the Crown Publishing Group
a division of Random House, Inc., New York
www.crownpublishing.com
www.watsonguptill.com

Library of Congress Control Number: 2006014626

ISBN-10: 0-8230-7894-9
ISBN-13: 978-0-8230-7894-3

Printed in Malaysia

First printing, 2006

4 5 6 7 8 9 / 14 13 12 11 10 09

DEDICATION

My favorite character has always been "Grandpa,"
so I lovingly dedicate this book
to my own grandparents:
Genevieve and John Blessing,
Ruth and Nelson Cox.

I'm glad I got to know them.

CONTENTS

Acknowledgments

Wild applause goes to the following individuals and organizations who helped with the original edition of this book and this expanded version.

First, and foremost, I thank Kevin Burns for his expertise in all matters of Munster. His generosity has made this book a more thorough trip through time, a more nostalgic tribute to this show. I want to thank my research consultants, Bruce Button, Mark Doyle, and Scott Maiko for their patience with my questions.

For a variety of contributions, I sincerely wish to thank: Norman Abbott, Academy of Motion Pictures Arts & Sciences, Joyce Arthur, John Astin, Kent Battle, George Barris, Earl Bellamy, Mel Blanc, Carol Brady, Tom Brown, Susan Buntrock, Allan Burns, CBS-Television, Steven Colbert, Joe Connelly, Richard Connelly, Jerry and Blanche Cox, *Creature Features*, Nancy Cushing-Jones, Mike Dann, Frank DeCaro, Robert Easton, Ted Eccles, Joe Gardner, Tony Greco, Debbie Gwynne, Foxy Gwynne, Abe Haberman, Fred Hansing, Bob Hastings, Chris Hayward, Paul Henning, Karen Ingenthron-Lewis, Pierce Jensen, David Lewis, Marge Lewis, Paul Lewis, Ted Lewis, Ed G. Lousararian, Kevin Marhanka, Charles and Sandra McKee, Scott Michaels, Vic Mizzy, Bob Morris, Robert Morse, Pam and Bob Mosher III, Rose Mosher Perry, Brian Nash, Louis Nye, Peter Petrucci, Prometheus Entertainment, Joel Rasmussen, Ernie Renn, Gene Reynolds, Peter Robbins, Dan Roebuck, Ray "The Red Phantom" Savage, Jack Sheldon, Judy and Karl Silvera, Alan Skinner, Clif Smith, Stephen D. Smith, Dave Strauss, Derek Tague, Debbie Watson-Taylor, Van Ness Films, Mike Westmore, Lennie Weinrib, and Dave Woodman.

Additionally, the astounding photographs and images found within these pages are all due to the generosity of the following individuals: Forry Ackerman, Buddy Barnett, George Barris, Ken Beck, Ron Borst, Kevin Burns, Fred Cooper, Mark Doyle, Fox Broadcasting, Don Glut, Bill Harrison, Marshall Hinsley, Corlandt Hull, Jackhammer Productions, Al Lewis, Tod Machin, James Madden, Jr., Bob Morris, Bill Mumy, NBC/Universal, Mark Offschanka, Gary Owens, Duane Pederson, Phil Potempa, Pat Priest Hansing, Gabor "Gabi" Rona, Karl Silvera, Scott Soly, Michael Tom, *TV Guide*, Inc., Universal Consumer Products Group, and Taylor White.

Naturally, to the cast members, I offer applause and gratitude: Al Lewis, Yvonne De Carlo, Fred Gwynne, Butch Patrick, Pat Priest, and Beverley Owen.

This book wouldn't be possible if it weren't for Cindy Chang at Universal/MCA Publishing; Mark Glubke, Ross Plotkin, Brian Phair, Elizabeth Mendel, Ellen Greene, and the rest of the talented folks at Watson-Guptill Publications; and designer Jay Anning.

FOREWORD
BY YVONNE DE CARLO

My most vivid memories of the two years I spent on *The Munsters* are pleasant ones, mostly. After all, I'm going back plenty of years, so don't count on a day-by-day narration.

The role of Lily was hard work with early mornings and late working hours. The makeup was another burden, especially making personal appearances in makeup. Two hours a day in the chair and the Indian wig that I wore gave me terrific headaches. One good thing did come from the makeup. The bile-green color helped me become friends with Marlon Brando.

I went to the set of *The Appaloosa*, a movie Marlon was making at Universal. I was still in costume and makeup, but stood nearby to watch a scene he was in. After he caught sight of me, he asked who I was. He came over and introduced himself, offering me his chair. Apparently he was fascinated with the makeup and characterization.

Brando was not the only celebrity to meet the Munsters. Liberace stopped by the set, as did Rock Hudson, and many more. Once, while I was still in makeup, Milton Berle shouted to me on the Universal lot, "Hi Yvonne! Working today?" Somebody else asked, "What's wrong, Yvonne, did you eat in the commissary?"

The most rewarding part of working in the series was the new generation of little fans I gained. They all loved Lily. (They were afraid of Herman at times, and they didn't know what to think of Grandpa.) Sometimes children would approach me at the market and ask, "Where's your silver streak, Lily?"

The popularity of *The Munsters*, though not surprising, is most pleasing. The show just keeps coming back. I've had so many roles over the years, in film, on the stage . . . but I guess I'll always be known as Lily Munster.

Enjoy the book.

Yvonne De Carlo

INTRODUCTION "Dead Serious: Some Author Scribble"

HERMAN: *Aren't you going to wish me luck, Grandpa?*
GRANDPA: *Drop dead.*

Directly after *The Munsters* was cancelled, pushed into rigor mortis by the network, many newspaper columnists assumed that it—and programs like it—had done their time after two years. Back then, kids hated the fact that shows like *The Munsters* and *The Addams Family* were not returning.

Batman was blamed. The Associated Press explained it in the newspapers: "*Batman*, who cut heavily into the *Munsters*' audience helped cause the *Munsters*' cancellation . . . also, there's an industry feeling that the monster era has run its course." The critics' vision for shows such as *The Munsters* and *The Addams Family* was nearsighted, and now, three decades later, both programs have been uniquely resurrected countless times on television, in animated cartoons, in print, in feature films—you name it. Let's face it, no other programs in television history have germinated with such breadth. These dark creatures of comedy have not died at all, for monsters never do. They've just been lurking, waiting to emerge again and again.

Does everyone agree that *The Munsters* peaked with seventy shows? Not me. Had I been old enough to voice an intelligent opinion in the mid-sixties, I would have shaken my fist, yelled and carried a fiery torch, demanding to see the creatures back on the small screen. *The Munsters* had at least another good season in them, and it's a shame that never materialized. I've always felt that by the second season, it appeared like the characters were just getting the blood pumping, feeling comfortable in their heavily powdered skin. What we have then, are two seasons, which to me anyway, are shining jewels of television.

The year I was born, CBS ceased *The Munsters*, only to have the show soar in syndication thereafter, so my exposure to it came during adolescence in the seventies. I was a child of television, fed with a continuous, healthy dosage with reruns every single day. It wasn't force-fed—I begged for it. This sitcom in particular pulled me in; not realizing, through the antics of Herman and Grandpa I learned how to appreciate superb comic timing, how to recognize quality in a production, and admire black-and-white television at its purest—where the images *should* be in gray tones rather than "in living color."

There wasn't much to read regarding *The Munsters* back then. No internet. Home videotape was in its infancy; I didn't have the luxury of popping in tapes whenever I wanted. My fascination was stunted. What possessed me then, as a kid, to start dialing the California long-distance directory assistance and hunt for the *Munsters'* stars, is beyond me. What did I know? I thought that any family who had a red phone like Commissioner Gordon, must have a direct connection to the Batcave. I believed anything. I asked directory assistance for Lucille Ball's phone number and the operator laughed and informed me that Miss Ball "probably isn't listed." What did I know?

The weirdest part of it all is that Al Lewis *was* actually listed in the phone book. (Our family's phone bills were never the same since I had learned how to access long distance.) One of my dreams came true when I got Grandpa on the telephone. My mouth turned dry, I couldn't believe it. I remember Al being patient with this inquisitive little fan, answering my inane questions; and eventually he sent me a signed color picture of him as Grandpa, a treasured piece I still have today. He never exploded into that same hardy cackle like he did on *The Munsters*, because, well, that was something he got paid to do, I guess. I wanted to hear it terribly. His robust cackle was my favorite aspect of the character. It was a sobering experience to find out this guy was not the loveable old codger Grandpa, but an actor whose talents I had already respected but grew to appreciate even more over time. Sometimes I'd inadvertently disturb Al from watching his basketball games and time with

his family . . . but I didn't pay much attention to such courtesies as a kid. He was nice to me and that was all that mattered.

Fast forward a dozen years. I picked up the phone to call Al again. This time, I was fresh out of college. During the interim, Al and I had met several times, had lunch, and kept in touch all those years. At least the pestering continued, he might tell you. He always answered my questions and reminisced about showbiz, even doled out advice now and then. Earning a college degree was an all-important encouragement on his part, so when I entered college he told me he was proud of that and when I graduated, he sent me a card.

But in 1988, I was calling Al to tell him I had found a publisher and was writing an authorized book about his series and how excited I was to be able to create a pictorial tribute to one of my all-time favorite television programs . . . and to Grandpa, one of my television idols from childhood. Of course, Al—from the start and without hesitation—was the most supportive of the cast, never doubted my intentions or questioned my qualifications or even displayed a hint of possessiveness toward the show. Any time I asked for help, Al was there.

So, if I wanted to be flip, I could end this story right here by offering a moral: always be nice to little kids, because you never know what the future holds. It's like the old joke: Be good to your kids because they're going to choose the retirement home you live in. But seriously, I'd like to share a little bit more about the cast, if I may.

When I wrote this book in 1989, one of my missions was to reach all of the main cast for an interview. Luckily, they were still alive, all still working, and for the most part, all still in the public eye, but I also knew Fred was going to be the tough one. I decided not to take advantage of Al Lewis's generosity; I didn't want to put him in an awkward position with his old friend, so I never asked him for Fred Gwynne's home phone number. (I figured I'd use that safety hatch only in an emergency, when all else failed.) The only clue Al offered was that Fred lived in the [Greenwich] Village, not far from his Italian restaurant, on Bleecker Street. I would have done anything to meet Fred Gwynne in the process of writing the book. Oh, to be able to sit down across from this imposing man, to take in that deep, beautiful timber in his voice, and quiz him about *The Munsters*, and the makeup and everything. I wanted it so badly I could envision shaking hands with this larger-than-life person. Months went by . . . and it wasn't happening.

I attempted to reach Gwynne through the usual, professional channels: a series of letters shot to his agent; a letter to his home address (which ended up being his ex-wife, Foxy Gwynne), follow-up phone calls. Gwynne's agent said "No thank you" in a quickie phone reply. Nothing worked and I just couldn't reach this guy. I was undaunted. If I was going to get a rejection, I wanted it from the Herman himself.

Finally, one night, maybe three AM, I was up warming my hands with a cup of coffee in a basement office, working on the book and sifting through files of old articles and newspaper interviews and vintage *Munsters* press releases—all of the printed materials necessary for the book's research. I happened upon a small gossipy blurb from a New York newspaper describing Fred's recent courtship with a young lady named Debbie. The article described something about a pair of lovebirds he purchased at a pet store to present to her, and it listed her full name. Hmmm. I wondered, if by any chance, could they now be married and listed in the phone book under her maiden name? I couldn't dial long distance directory fast enough. *Bingo!* There it was . . . on Bleecker Street, in Greenwich Village.

It seemed like an endless span, but in reality, I waited just hours until a decent daylight opportunity arrived to phone New York and speak with Herman Munster—at last. The hunt was still on and I was extremely nervous because I was so close. I didn't want to mess this up.

When I did manage to get Fred Gwynne on the phone, he wasn't very receptive. He wasn't rude, just not sporty about the whole thing. That was a letdown. But first, he wanted to know where I had gotten his telephone number. I hesitated, and said, "Do you really want to know?"

"Oh, I know where you got it," he told me flatly. "You got it from Grandpa."

It really struck me odd that he would refer to his old friend Al Lewis as "Grandpa," but I loved it just the same. He openly wondered how I managed to get his phone number. When I divulged my tactics, he complimented me: "You should've been a private investigator instead of a writer." I thought my honesty might open the door for him to ease up and submit to an interview, but he preferred not to speak about his years as a monster, and gave me a couple of brief reasons. "I don't give many interviews, really." Then I resorted to mild pleading.

"Please, Mr. Gwynne, didn't anyone ever give you a break when you were getting started?"

"Ummm . . . no."

And so, I found him, but found him to be less than receptive to someone unearthing details about a life to which he had waved goodbye. It was a past life for him. But he did say he would like a copy of the book when it

A sketch Fred Gwynne drew
and presented to a fan in 1966.

is published, and he wished me luck. So I promised him a book—provided he personally autograph a few items for me, including one of his illustrated children's books. (What the heck—at this point, why not ask for the world?) He agreed.

Many months later, Fred received his copy of the book and I got my autographs promptly in return. I suspect I treasured my items considerably more than he did his paperback *Official Ghoul Guide*, but the experience was something I'll always remember. I can still hear him concluding our conversation in that deep resonant, "Thank you, you're very kind." For the book, I'm sure he realized I was forced to rely on past interviews from *TV Guide* and the like, but it's nice to know that he did participate in a few in-depth discussions, sparse as they were over the years. He never provided any feedback about the book, but that was okay. Fred Gwynne had a copy on his shelf.

Later on, I would find out from Butch Patrick that Gwynne and his wife had lost a child around those years, so I can only assume that maybe I approached him with this fragile topic at an inopportune moment. I gather the Munster era was a period he wished to forget, and who can blame him? Those who knew Fred well said his relationship with Herman was a love-hate kind of thing, leaning on the hatred. He hated it when people mentioned only the Munsters when discussing his career. He hated it when Howard Stern dispatched "Stuttering John" up to his face with a microphone to pose "Munsters" questions to him at the opening of an art exhibit. He hated it when fans asked him in a restaurant, or in a public setting, to shake his wrists and do that heavy "Herman laugh."

Darn, darn, darn. Fred Gwynne was not the jolly, nostalgic type, even for a historical account. On the flipside, the rest of the cast was more than wonderful, obliging, and positive when I approached them about sharing their memories. Yvonne De Carlo was even gracious enough to compose and contribute a handwritten foreword for this book, a gift that meant so much. The common thread among the cast was that they could hardly believe the show has endured through the decades. Butch Patrick, Pat Priest, and Beverley Owen happily reminisced about their experiences. Funny that to this day, Beverley Owen and Pat Priest—the series' two Marilyns—have never met.

During the past few years I've run into Pat Priest on several occasions and she's always inquired about this book, wishing to see it back on the shelves. Fans have approached her at various nostalgia shows, constantly asking how they could find a copy. I've gotten more letters than I can count asking the same thing: What happened to the "Munster" book? On eBay tattered copies have sold for $75, which astounds me. There really is no good reason for its absence. You see, after a successful run with its original publisher (including a German edition), this book suddenly—and inexplicably—crept back into the crypt, waiting to be revived for another generation of *Munsters* fans. So here we are. And I thank Pat Priest for gently prodding me all these years to finally get this book back in print.

My experiences with Yvonne De Carlo have been brief and nice, only meeting her a few times, once being backstage at Vicki Lawrence's daytime talk show in the nineties. That was among her final television appearances, if I'm not mistaken, and the robust little lady was the picture of an Italian grandma with her gray hair in a bun. Last year, I visited a much frailer Yvonne in a retirement home where she was shockingly thin. I brought her flowers and stayed just a moment. Although she was cogent and remembered me, she was only able to muster the strength to smell the flowers and smile a little and thank me for coming by.

This book has been a long time coming and I am very excited about the opportunity to present a handsome collection of extremely rare, never-before-published images within these pages, as well as updated biographies, and additional interviews. Feast on this Munster chronicle. Hopefully I have assembled a fun representation of the show, a retrospective in which the Munsters will unmask right before your eyes. Trick or treat?

—STEVE COX
Los Angeles, California
March 2006

Postscript

While working on this revised book, the sad news arrived that my buddy Al Lewis died in February 2006 after a lengthy illness; his death was actually a blessing because I think his quality of life had diminished to a heartbreaking degree. He was eighty-three, not ninety-five as most obituaries listed. (He loved to fib about his age and let people marvel at how great he looked for a man in his nineties. That was Al.)

About a year before he died, he gave me a nifty gift in the form of his strained signature on something special. I had subscribed to a series of colorful designer *Munsters* bank checks and some of them featured Grandpa on the face of the check. I got an idea and wrote out a check to him on Halloween day, and filled in the amount for $13.13, neatly made out to the order of: Al Lewis. I thought it was unique. I sent Al the check with a note and told him to most certainly cash it and buy a nice thirteen-dollar cigar on me. Although he was very ill, he scribbled his name on the reverse . . . and I hope he picked up that stogie. The cancelled "Munsters" check, probably the only one he ever endorsed, is a treasure. My treasure from Mockingbird Heights.

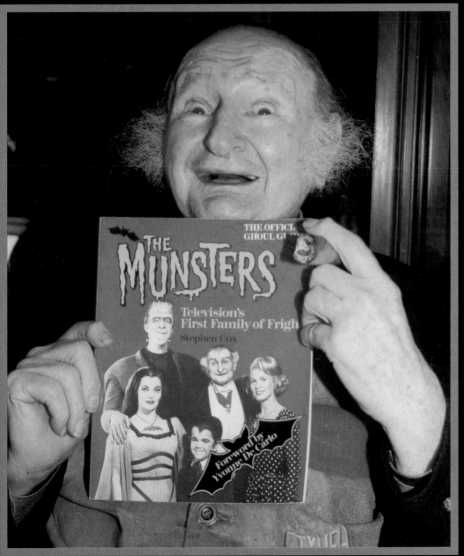

Al Lewis in his eighties and still smoking cigars, poses with the original edition of this book.

MEET THE FAMILY FROM MOCKINGBIRD HEIGHTS, U.S.A.

LET ME INTRODUCE YOU TO THE MUNSTER FAMILY, an unusual clan of monsters that live in a mansion fit for Dr. Frankenstein, Dr. Phibes, or Norman Bates. *The Munsters* derived inspiration from Hollywood's early horror films.

Herman Munster, who greatly resembles Frankenstein's monster (à la Boris Karloff), is the head of the household. His matronly wife, Lily, is a Vampira with the clichéd duties of a housewife. She cooks, cleans the dungeons, and dusts. The world centers on their residence at 1313 Mockingbird Lane, Mockingbird Heights, U.S.A.

Herman and Lily's only son, Eddie, is an eight-year-old in grade school growing up with the normal yearnings of a youngster his age—except he's green and has pointed ears. But his chums don't mind that.

Next in line is Lily's father, affectionately known as Grandpa. He's a cantankerous old vampire from Transylvania who smokes a stogie and enjoys a good laugh. His hobby, performing wild experiments in his basement laboratory, gets him into trouble, but he's always forgiven. Who could stay mad when good intentions are at heart?

The last to be shaken out of the family tree is the most unusual. The bruised banana of the bunch, or so the family thinks. She is the beautiful niece, Marilyn, whom the ghoulish Munsters fret over, worry, and protect, for the cruel trick nature has played is making her so "plain."

As you can see, these are ordinary, upright citizens. By their standards, they are the all-American suburban family that just happens to be monstrous, a detail that has escaped their notice. They do not know they are different in any way and are proud of their monster heritage. "Class. We're dripping with class," Grandpa explains.

Towering in the forefront is the philosophical Herman, always ready to help others with his understanding of life. For example, when little Eddie was bothered about his looks after being called nasty nicknames at school, Herman was there, like any devoted father, to calm him down. "It doesn't matter what you look like," Herman says. "You can be tall or short, fat or thin, or ugly or handsome; or you can be black or yellow or white; it doesn't matter. What does matter is the size of your heart and the strength of your character."

"You know something, Herman?" Grandpa comments. "You're a pretty nice guy. You're no Norman Vincent Peale . . . but you're a pretty nice guy."

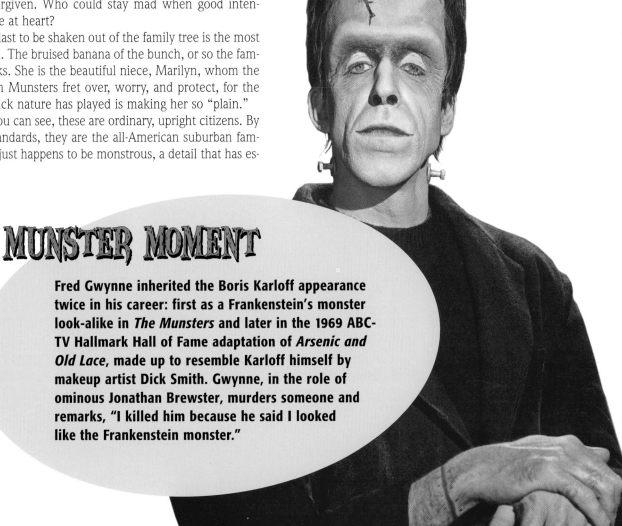

MUNSTER MOMENT

Fred Gwynne inherited the Boris Karloff appearance twice in his career: first as a Frankenstein's monster look-alike in *The Munsters* and later in the 1969 ABC-TV Hallmark Hall of Fame adaptation of *Arsenic and Old Lace*, made up to resemble Karloff himself by makeup artist Dick Smith. Gwynne, in the role of ominous Jonathan Brewster, murders someone and remarks, "I killed him because he said I looked like the Frankenstein monster."

Munster, Her...

Name: Herman Munster

Age: 150

Appearance: Size 26C shoe; seven-foot-three frame; one brown eye and one chartreuse; steel bolts in neck; green complexion; flat head; ears do not match; lantern jaw; five-inch-long, lightning-bolt-shaped beauty mark on forehead

Made (Not Born): "In Germany in a laboratory. Built by a Dr. Frankenstein, whose hobby was putting together do-it-yourself people kits." (Herman left Germany at an early age and was adopted in England by a family named Munster)

Ability: Telling tasteless jokes ("I just invented something to keep the inside of my car quiet. It fits right over <u>her</u> mouth," or "My family is in the iron and steel business. My mother irons and my father steals.")

Education: Matriculated at Heidelberg University Medical School for six years—in several different jars

Occupation: Employee at mortuary, Gateman, Goodbury & Graves (His boss, Mr. Gateman, says: "He's one of the few people at the parlor who don't lie down on the job.")

Preferences: Huckleberry Hound and Pat Boone albums (enrolled in fan club)

Self-Description: "Level-headed"

Name: Lily Dracula Munster

Age: Varies (but more than 137 years old)

Appearance: Vampire-like; silver streak in hair

Birthplace: Transylvania

Siblings: Brother Lester and unnamed sister

Abilities: Reading palms, sewing, and cooking

Preferences: Wears Chanel No. 13 perfume ("the most exotic"); sleeps with a hair bonnet and a white lily clutched in her hands

Noticeable Qualities: Undying devotion to husband and family; sensitivity; strong matriarchal characteristics

Familiar Name: Grandpa

Real Name: Count Dracula (a.k.a. Sam Dracula)

Age: 378

Appearance: Resembles a tall penguin

Birthplace: Transylvania ("the Old Country")

Abilities: Magic (limited); psychic (he can tell when the phone is about to ring)

Marital Status: Currently single (has had 167 wives)

Children: Lily, Lester, and another daughter (no name given)

Occupation: Mad scientist

Habit(s): Sleeps on a slab; hangs from rafters; wears gloves; smokes cheap cigars

Philosophy: "My father and I were very close. He used to give me such wonderful advice. I remember one day he said to me, 'Son, as you go through life, bury your mistakes.' You see, my father never believed in divorce."

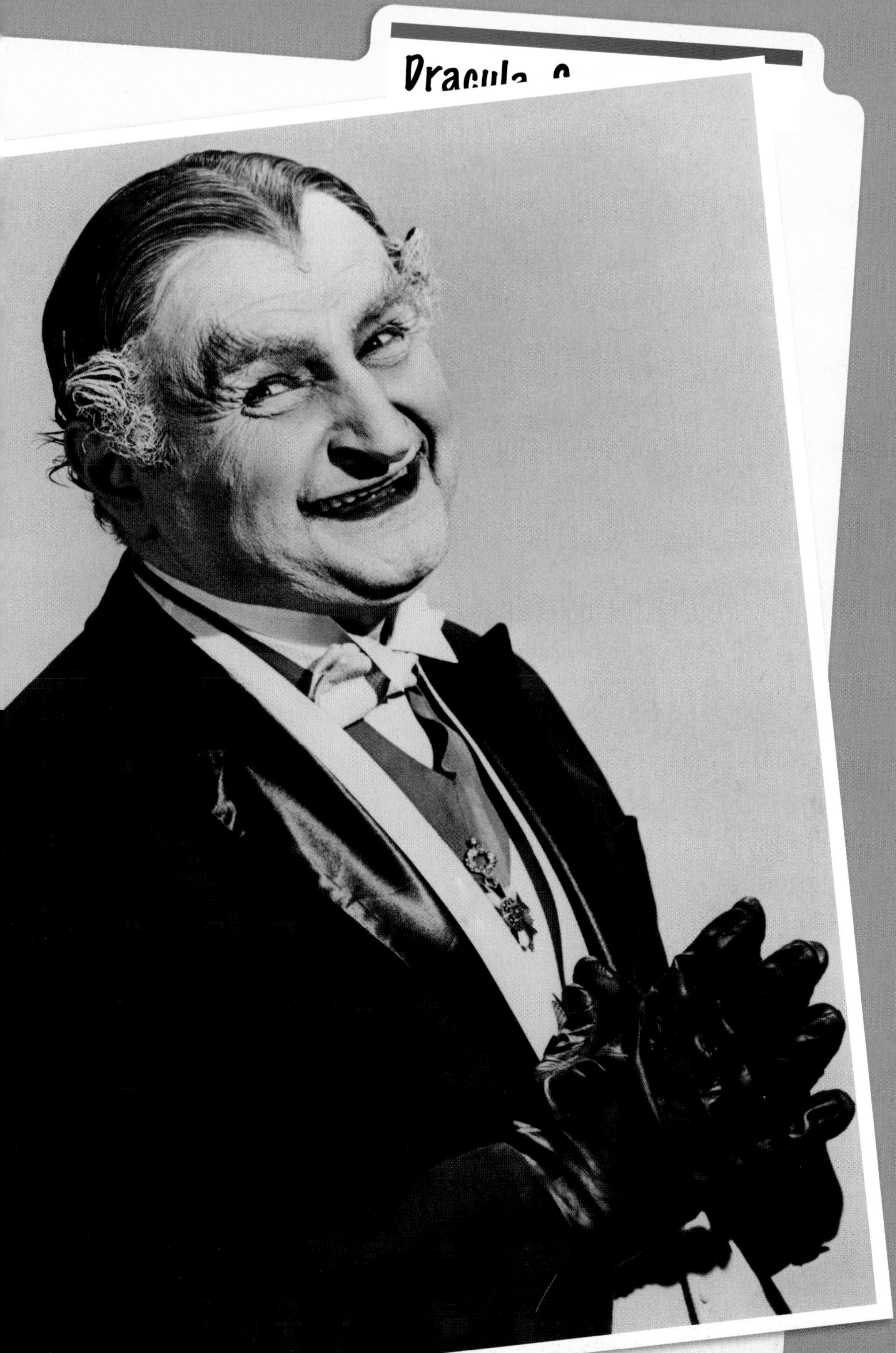
Dracula

Munster, Edward W.

Name: Edward ("Eddie") Wolfgang Munster

Age: Eight, nine, and ten

Appearance: "Ordinary" child who wears a Little Lord Fauntleroy suit (he only owns one) and carries a doll; dark hair with widow's peak, pointed "Spock-like" ears, and mini-fangs; usually green around the gills

Abilities: Opens tin cans with his ears; howls at moon

Education: Enrolled at the Mockingbird Heights Elementary School

Achievements: Wrote school composition titled "My Parents, An Average American Family" (written in blood ink); won several ribbons for track competition at school

Preferences: Carrying Woof-Woof doll and sleeping in a coffin

Name: Marilyn Munster

Age: Varies (anywhere between twenty-three and forty-three)

Appearance: Blond, beautiful, sexy

Genealogy: Daughter of Lily Munster's sister

Abilities: Cooking, chatting, smiling, helping Lily do the dishes

Marital Status: Involuntarily single

Education: Attends Westbury College

Noticeable Quality: Periodic melancholia

Goal: To find a man—any man, and do nothing but good in life

CREATING MUNSTERS

"There is not the slightest doubt how youngsters and probably a good many of their elders will begin their television viewing on Thursday night; it will be with The Munsters *and, more particularly, with Fred Gwynne as the most engaging and amusing Frankenstein monster ever to reach the screen."*

—*NEW YORK TIMES,*
September 25, 1964

STEVEN SPIELBERG WAS NOT THE ONLY KID IN America getting caught up in this. In the late fifties and early sixties, a trend was creeping across the nation. The horror monsters from Universal Studio's vintage library were being released to television in a package they called "Shock Theater." Horror-rific late night TV hosts were springing up all in every corner of the country, in all of the major markets (Vampira in Los Angeles, Zacherly in New York, Ghoulardi in Cleveland, Dr. Shock in Philadelphia, Morgus in New Orleans, and who could forget Count Gore DeVol out of the depths of Kentucky?). It was a Saturday night treat to roll out the sleeping bags in front of the TV set and make some popcorn before watching Boris Karloff in *The Mummy* or Bela Lugosi in *Dracula*. You couldn't keep kids away from watching *Abbott & Costello Meet Frankenstein* on a weekend night. Magazines such as *Famous Monsters of Filmland* and horror-themed comic books were consumed by kids at feverish pace.

"The late-fifties revival was accompanied by the rise of a fascinating subculture of 'fandom' of adolescent and preadolescent males, revolving around the television screenings of the classic films by horror hosts in major cities," explains author David Skal. "Several of today's prominent filmmakers were weaned on these magazines and the activities they generated, including Steven Spielberg, John Landis, and John Carpenter."

Filmmaker Joe Dante was another product of the monster pulp produced at the time. As he told David Skal, ". . . here, all of a sudden, was this magazine [*Famous Monsters*] that was a validation that there were other people out there like us. It was written in a style geared to eleven- and twelve-year-old kids, but in a way it fostered a kind of serious film history study. It talked about films we hadn't seen, and it made them sound very exciting and mysterious. I remember going to the school library and getting all the film books out and trying to find any mention of Frankenstein or Dracula, and there weren't any—the films weren't considered worth studying. How times have changed."

Toys, model kits, games, Halloween costumes, and comic books featuring Universal Studios' creepiest—"Dracula," "The Mummy," "The Werewolf," and Frankenstein's creature—were being marketed heavily to the baby boomers in the early sixties who were eating it up as fast as they gobbled Cap'n Crunch. (Count Chocula and Frankenberry hit stores years later.)

"In a suburbanized, plasticized America, monster culture answered a need among male baby boomers for haunted houses instead of tract houses," added Skal in his book, *Hollywood Gothic*. "The need would find its most popular apotheosis in two television series, *The Munsters*, and *The Addams Family*, in which the nightmarish undercurrents of the American nuclear family would be playfully exorcised."

Meet the Munsters.

As illustrated by this Dell comic book from the early sixties, all of the fantastic horror figures from Universal's stable of creatures were clawing their way back into popular culture in a monstrous way.

MONSTER MISH MOSH

Television veterans Chris Hayward and Allan Burns, credited for creating the "Format" of the series, were a fast-rising comedy writing team in the early sixties. The two men met while working at Jay Ward's cartoon factory in Los Angeles brainstorming material as fast as they could. ("Cap'n Crunch" was born.) In between *Rocky and Bullwinkle* sessions, they formulated a television show titled *Meet the Munsters* a treatment for a sitcom of monsters, and basically sold it effortlessly in the summer of 1963. Here, for the first time, the prolific Emmy-winning comedy writers/producers share their bittersweet, albeit occasionally conflicting, recollections of this period in their professional careers.

Hayward: We were both at Jay Ward, we were periodically let go because we'd complete a production term. Jay would say to us, "Well, hope to see you next year if we sell this or that . . ." I got tired of that and I went in to see Allan who was kept year-on because he wasn't attached to a show. He was producing publicity booklets and such. He had written a script which I admired so much and I asked him if he'd be interested in doing something together. I had come up with two ideas, one of which was a family of crooks and the other was a family of monsters. We tried the monster idea and we wrote a pilot script. We called it *The Munsters*. The Addams Family possibly might have been an unintended inspiration, the books by Charles Addams. We wrote a pilot script and gave it to our first agent.

Burns: *The Munsters* was the first thing Chris Hayward and I did together. We were working at for Jay Ward at the time and we were looking for a way out of the cartoon business, which he had been in quite a long time. I had been in a much shorter time. We came up with a bunch of ideas and this was one of them.

Said Fred Gwynne in 1964: "I'm a smiling monster. CBS wants him jolly. You might be scared for one second, then you discover he's the Santa Claus type."

It's not very far from a cartoon, as you can see. We weren't working together at Jay Ward. Chris was mostly partnered up with a man named Lloyd Turner, who at the time didn't show any desire to change from the animation business. Chris and I had put our heads together and this idea kind of amused us.

We ran this idea by a guy we were hoping would become our agent. He was at the old Ashley-Steiner agency which eventually it became ICM. There was an agent there who looked very Neanderthal, a mouth-breather. Les Colodny. I don't even remember how we met this guy, but we did and we went over and pitched a lot of things to this man. He said he was a little busy to handle us now.

Hayward: While they liked the concept, they didn't think we were capable of writing it . . . they had under contract Connelly and Mosher and they took our concept and assigned other writers for it. They didn't use what we had written.

Burns: What we had written up, to be truthful about it, was closer to the Addams Family or what became *The Addams Family*. We were basing this show on these kinds of characters and we thought it might make an interesting series. Strange, macabre, offbeat characters. Not what *The Munsters* became. I think we called it *Meet the Munsters* and there were many similarities to what it became.

What happened was we gave Les some pages he seemed interested in it. And then we would call once in a while. And then come to find out he no longer worked there when we called once again. They gave us no forwarding address. A month or so later, we get a call from Les Colodny. He tells us he has this job at Universal and "I'm in charge of comedy development here and I've been thinking about that idea of yours and I think we'd like to try and develop it." We would meet with him and talk about it, mostly away from the lot, which was strange to me. It seems we would always meet in coffee shops somewhere and usually we were picking up the checks.

On our own hook, we began to write this thing and send this guy pages. We actually wrote a pilot script. Nothing happened. When we finished, we hadn't heard a word from him. I don't remember if we'd gotten paid for this. By then we had a new agent who I think tried to negotiate some deal for us but it was some low end thing, if there was a deal at all. I can't ever remember getting a check for it but we may have. It simply went away.

Our agent Peter Fleming called us up and said, "Hey, I read in the trades today Universal is gonna do your *Munsters* pilot. Actually, they're gonna start shooting in a couple of days; would you like to go out and see it? The director's a friend of mine." It was news to us.

> Allan Burns, seventy-one, and Chris Hayward, eighty-one, have given television audiences some of the most inspired comedy the medium has seen. And there were a few clinkers, too. After all, they created *My Mother the Car*. The two collaborated also on the sixties *The Smothers Brothers Show* (the sitcom version). *Get Smart* redeemed them, and then came the short-lived *He and She* which brought them an Emmy Award. Eventually, the two writers branched out on their own. Burns went on to write more television (*Room 222*) and co-create a classic, *The Mary Tyler Moore Show* (and spin-offs *Rhoda* and *Lou Grant*.) Hayward went on to write and produce such hits as *Get Smart*, *Barney Miller*, and *Alice*.

Hayward: While they liked the concept, they didn't think we were capable of writing it . . . they had under contract Connelly and Mosher and they took our concept and assigned other writers for it. They didn't use what we had written.

I think we had Mockingbird Lane in our script. Allan, who is a brilliant cartoonist and artist, liked the concept and wrote it with Fred Gwynne in mind. We cut a picture of him out of a magazine and Allan drew the screws out of the neck, and that was what we submitted as part of our idea. They went out and got Fred Gwynne to do it. It was not our idea for Al Lewis. I don't even know if we had a Grandpa. That could be theirs.

We visited the set one day while they were shooting a ten-minute color film and we were introduced to the creators, which shocked us. Two writers, Liebmann and Hass. We all just looked at each other and said, "My god, what happened here?" We wound up sharing credit and that was the end of it. That's where it went.

Burns: Peter our agent takes us over to the director to introduce us and says hey, these are the two guys who created the show. And he says, "No they aren't. Norm and Ed created the show." We were puzzled.

Clearly, this former agent and head of development, was taking our idea and was working with a couple of guys named Norm Liebmann and Ed Hass who were contract writers there at Universal. This guy was passing on our stuff to them as his ideas. Therefore, they were cutting us out of the process, which is what had happened. This was a very naughty thing and they were just going to cut us out. We had brought them the idea and they weren't going to even acknowledge it. We met Norm and Ed at that time and I remember them being as puzzled about it as we were. I was very uncomfortable once we got there and saw that and heard the director, I remember it was

Norman Abbott. I felt like an interloper at that point and I just wanted to get the hell out of there.

Clearly, Norm and Ed had no knowledge of our participation in the thing. Then someone added the extra element with the monsters. I don't know if it was somebody at Universal who said, "Hey we own some of these characters like Frankenstein, let's use those." And morphed it together with our idea. Admittedly, they went into another direction with their pilot script than we had. It was not at all like what we had originally proposed. Ours was very far away from it.

Hayward: We had to sign a disclaimer that we really didn't create it, that we wrote a presentation. I didn't want to sign that. But I was convinced by our agent and Allan himself, that we wouldn't step foot on the lot again, so we did.

Who knows? If we had done it, it might not have become so popular. Got to give credit to whoever was responsible. They saw it done one way and we saw it another. The joy of the whole thing is the fact that both Allan and I, even after we left working with each other, we're attached to things that are popular, in our own way. We grew beyond that, and look back on it strictly as a fun recollection. And the loss of a great deal of money.

Burns: Chris and I, well, to say the least we were perturbed by the fact that we were being pushed aside. We went to the Writers Guild. We were not members of the Guild and this would turn out to be the first job we ever had away from animation, and animation writers are not covered by the Guild. We told Mike Franklin, who was the director of the Writers Guild and told him the story and his eyes glittered and he licked his lips and he said, "Let us get into this."

Long story short, the Writers Guild came down pretty heavily on Universal. We ended up getting some money out of it and getting a credit on it. By that time, Joe Connelly and Bob Mosher had been brought in to executive produce it. They didn't want to have anything to do with us, this was their show.

To me, *The Munsters* is just a cartoon with live actors doing it. To be honest with you, I never much liked *The Munsters*, I didn't watch it much. What Chris and I had proposed was a little more bizarre and a little more sophisticated, I think, than what they had. I think it was actually closer to *The Addams Family*. There was a kind of sexiness to the Addams Family that we had tried for in ours.

I don't list it on my list of credits and I don't really take any pride in it, because why should I? It's not really our work, it was only in protecting our interests that got us a credit on it. Even as powerless as we seemed to be, the Guild really came through for us, and that always impressed me.

I don't recall having Fred Gwynne in mind. I don't think that can be true. Frankenstein was never part of my recollection of what we had contributed. I disagree with Chris on that, but he is older than me, so . . .

THE PILOT: "MY FAIR MUNSTER"

The Munsters were first seen in full color. For years, only a privileged few hardcore aficionados saw the extremely rare prints of this brief film presentation which ultimately sold the show to the network. Underground-TV buffs searched incessantly for anyone who possessed this rare Munster footage—the holy grail of Mockingbird Heights. And now, thanks to Universal Studio's DVD release of the entire series, fans were treated to a beautifully remastered print of "My Fair Munster," the first time the series' pilot had ever been released to a mass market.

The pilot was titled "My Fair Munster," shot late in early 1964, but the format was revamped and re-shot several times until the final black-and-white fleshed-out version aired later in the Fall of 1964 as the program's second episode. The initial pilot was a twelve-minute film, actually called a "presentation." Producers Joe Connelly and Bob Mosher were still in the midst of casting. (Although Connelly is the only one listed as executive producer, Mosher was later added.)

The pilot/presentation was written by Norm Liebmann and Ed Hass, and directed by Norman Abbott. Liebmann suggests today he contributed several of the characters' names, all derived from his own relatives. Fred Gwynne and Al Lewis had been flown in from New York as the stars of the show and made tests at Universal Studios. The two, who had worked together so well on, Nat Hiken's CBS comedy show, *Car 54, Where Are You?*, were the first actors hired on the show. They were not the first choices, however, for the roles of Herman and Grandpa. Aging vaudevillian Bert Lahr, who was still acting in television, stage, and commercials in the sixties, was the original choice for Grandpa. With Lahr's over-the-top delivery and charm he exhibited as the Cowardly Lion in the classic film, *The Wizard of Oz*, he might have been a rather humorous, growly Grandpa. Horror-sci-fi actor John Carradine was originally offered the role of Herman, but his stern delivery would not have won the hearts of children like the magic Fred Gwynne tapped into.

In this brief, color version of *The Munsters*, actress Joan Marshall was hired for the role of housewife "Phoebe" (not Lily) and child-actor David "Happy" Derman portrayed Eddie; and Beverley Owen rounded out the cast as cousin Marilyn, the black sheep of the family.

Joan Marshall, as Herman's wife, Phoebe, was adequate, but her portrayal and image—in retrospect, anyway—hued much closer to that of Carolyn Jones's

Scenes from the 1964 color pilot with Fred Gwynne, Al Lewis, Joan Marshall as "Phoebe," and David "Happy" Derman as a feisty wolf-boy Eddie.

"Morticia" on *The Addams Family*. Marshall's depiction of the Munster matriarch was more vamp-like, slinky, with long straight hair. Think of a young Cher.

Happy Derman portrayed Eddie wildly like a screaming brat, possessed, clawing at his parents and shouting, "Let me go! You always pick on me! You never let me have any fun! That's all you do is pick on me! I hate it!" The scene is reminiscent of something out of *The Exorcist*—much creepier than necessary for a sitcom.

The plot of the presentation is virtually the same as the opening scenes in the episode "My Fair Munster": Marilyn, returning home with her date, asks him if he'd like to come in and meet her aunt and uncle. The frightened fellow gets as far as the porch, takes one look at Herman and dashes off the property hysterically. The camera takes us into the Munster home where the folks are settling in for the evening. Grandpa is playing check-

ers with an invisible friend while Eddie sits up in the rafters, refusing to come down at bedtime.

"The pilot was pretty bizarre," said Fred Gwynne years later. "They hadn't figured out the costumes or the laughs. God only knows how they ever sold it on those fifteen minutes, because it was just awful."

As the film was passed around CBS network executives, notes were made and things began to change: Joan Marshall was cut, as was Happy Derman. Further casting continued and more tests, this time shot in black-and-white, were made as the script and the set was being overhauled. From one film to the next, additional detail is paid to the set—the cobwebs, the music, the costumes—and scripting improves noticeably. Al Lewis had been fit with a nose extension for the pilots (and the first few episodes), however this minor detail was dropped for logistical reasons. (Lewis kept dipping it in his coffee,

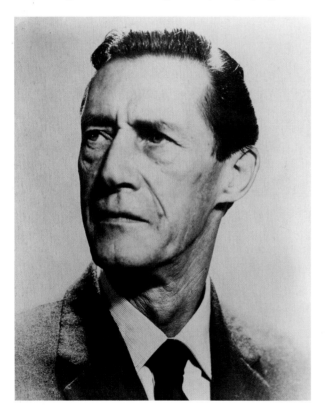

Legendary horror and sci-fi actor John Carradine was originally offered the role of Herman Munster, but declined. He was, however, the perfect choice to portray Herman's morose mortician boss, Mr. Gateman. Carradine, who died in 1988, appeared in more than a few horror classics—*Bride of Frankenstein*, *The Mummy's Ghost*, *House of Frankenstein*, and *House of Dracula* among them. In 1976, Carradine once again played an undertaker in John Wayne's final film, *The Shootist*.

Aging vaudeville and movie comedian Bert Lahr, most known for his trip to Oz in a lion's pelt, was originally tapped for the role of Grandpa.

This is one of the first photographs of Al Lewis as Grandpa taken during production of the pilot presentation; Grandpa is wearing a serpent amulet instead of his usual medallion. Lewis is also adorned with a nose extension, a facial appliance eventually nixed.

ruining the prosthetic-tip appliance.) Besides, Lewis's honker hardly required additional length to be funny.

Director Norman Abbott remembered, "We had everybody from the studio at the soundstage watching the filming. Somebody called the people from the head office and told them to come down to see it. It was wild. Jim Aubrey from CBS bought it instantly."

The presentation was to accomplish just that—a sale to the network and sponsors. Hunt Stromberg, Jr. at CBS wanted the roles of Lily and Eddie recast. (Stromberg loved the horror genre, knew the value in it, and wanted to see *The Munsters* make it on the air. Ten years prior, Stromberg was the man who put local TV host Vampira on the air in Los Angeles which made her a lifetime horror icon. Years later, he would produce movies such as *Frankenstein: The True Story* and *The Curse of King Tut's Tomb*.) Word came down that adjustments needed to be made on the pilot and Joan Marshall, along with Happy Derman, were suddenly axed.

Eddie Munster's role was offered to young redheaded actor Billy Mumy prior to Butch Patrick. Because Mumy's parents did not want him to have to undergo such makeup and hair dyeing, they persuaded the budding young actor to decline the series. Eleven-year-old Butch Patrick (real name: Patrick Lilly), who had already worked in some films and TV commercials, was brought out from Illinois to test for the role of the pointy-eared wolf-boy and the producers liked what they saw in his innocent approach.

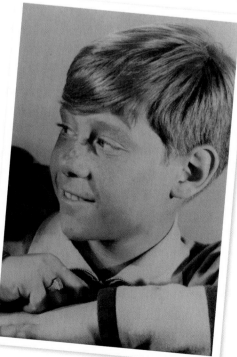

Billy Mumy was offered the role of Eddie Munster.

Connelly and Mosher continued to test women for the role of Lily until they found Yvonne De Carlo an interesting candidate. A filmed test was made in early 1964 at Universal with Yvonne and passed on to the network.

In a CBS interoffice memo dated March 15, 1964 from vice-president Mike Dann to Universal Studio's production executive Hunt Stromberg, Jr., Dann commented: "The Yvonne De Carlo test is completely satisfactory. She overacted a little but obviously that's from inadequate direction. She's just over the hill, but still sexy enough to have some extra interest. . . . As far as the little boy, Butch Patrick . . . is concerned, he's just fine but I think his ears should be pointed not quite as much as in the test, but he should be a little bit different than the ordinary boy."

Eventually, two additional versions of the presentation were shot in black-and-white, with movie-queen Yvonne De Carlo in the role of "Lily," Herman's wife. De Carlo seemed to make the role a more motherly, but firm character. Eddie Munster was recast with young Butch Patrick in the role, only without a widow's peak. That adjustment came later as the series actually rolled. Butch Patrick's performance was toned down a bit, not so over the top as his predecessor, and the new Eddie was a charmer rather than a demon.

The color process was considered for the series but ultimately dropped. "The big thing then was black-and-white," said producer Joe Connelly in 1988. "Networks were just starting to go to color. The Munsters were ugly enough in black-and-white." The cost of color would have toppled the already-stretched budget, so the decision was primarily a financial one. Some may disagree, but Munsters in black-and-white are aesthetically more dramatic, reflective of the old horror films Universal was famous for. This created an appropriately eerie effect which actually worked better in gray tones, and to the viewer, the makeup wasn't as grotesque to grapple with, so the characterizations bloomed with no colorful distractions.

Mike Dann, a former NBC head of programming and now CBS's Vice President in charge of programming, immediately felt a spark with *The Munsters*; Dann knew it was something fresh for primetime, but his choice was not met without resistance. "I was thrilled to find it," he says. "It had the potential to really hit.

"I had no 7:30 show and you can't throw that timeslot away. I had to show the color pilot to Bill

Press Information
Television City, Hollywood, Calif.

February 18, 1964

"THE MUNSTERS," NEW IDEA IN SITUATION COMEDIES, MAKES
DEBUT IN FALL ON CBS TELEVISION NETWORK

Stars Fred Gwynne and Al Lewis

The CBS Television Network has entered into an agreement with
Kayro-Vue Productions for the presentation of "The Munsters," new,
weekly 30-minute situation comedy series starting this fall, it was
announced today by Michael H. Dann, Vice President--Programs.

Fred Gwynne and Al Lewis of "Car 54, Where Are You" fame are
the stars.

A completely new idea in situation comedy, "The Munsters"
deals with a "normal" American family whose physical characteristics
are reminiscent of such famous movie monsters as Frankenstein's creation,
Dracula, and a lady vampire.

But here's the switch: although the family looks like the
famous monsters, its members are unaware of it. In fact, they think
they're just plain folks. For instance, Fred Gwynne plays Herman, the
husband and father, who looks like Frankenstein's monster; Al Lewis is
the grandfather, who might remind one of Count Dracula, and the wife
(to be cast) is a vampire type. They worry about the "normal-looking"

(More)

ADD "THE MUNSTERS". . .looking"

neice (also to be cast), whose orthodox features evoke sympathy.

"The Munsters" will be produced by Joe Connolly, who created
"Leave It to Beaver." Norman Liebmann and Ed Haas are the chief writers.

The new series is tentatively scheduled for Thursdays, 7:30-
8:00 PM, PST, starting in the fall. It will be filmed at Universal City
Studios, Hollywood.

The CBS press release which announced the arrival of *The Munsters* to television in the fall of 1964. Fred Gwynne and Al Lewis were the first to be hired.

Paley, the chairman of the board, he was very active in programming. Bill would never force me to schedule something, but he would give you a hard time if he didn't like it. He was a very elegant and proper man. Everything he did was in a grand style. And he looked at *The Munsters* and said, 'Shouldn't this be on Saturday morning?'

"I said, 'I think it would work very well on Saturday morning, but I don't need it for Saturday morning, I need if for Thursday night at 7:30.'

"He said, 'Well, that's not CBS.'

"Of course, if you're a hit, well, 'that's CBS.' Look at *The Beverly Hillbillies* . . . that's CBS, you bet, as long as it's a hit. Well, the show went on the air and it was an instant hit," Dann says. "I originally felt this show would appeal only to children and I happened to be wrong. It turned out to be an all-family hit. But there was no question in my mind—it would appeal to young people."

By the summer of 1964, the series was cast and set to roll with a season's worth of episodes ordered by the network and already in production.

Eddie Munster, pre-widow's peak for the pilot, with his stuffed Woof-Woof doll. (This Woof-Woof was only used in the pilot and a few initial episodes and was replaced with a more detailed doll.)

THE MAD SCIENTISTS

The meeting of two young creative minds at the J. Walter Thompson advertising agency in New York years ago was prophetic. It foretold enormous success to come; it signified the fusion of two brilliant comedic minds destined to help create a new medium: television.

The team of Connelly and Mosher is nearly forgotten now, but in the late fifties and in the sixties, they proved a powerful union, especially on the Universal Studios lot. This team brought life to these comical monsters for television, and were comfortable with a successful track record even prior to *The Munsters*.
At the time, Connelly

and Mosher was one of the most successful comedy writing teams in the entertainment business.

Between the two impresarios, their television credits read like a history of the medium itself. After working in New York, Bob Mosher moved to Hollywood to begin a career in show business during the days of popular radio comedy. Joe Connelly quickly followed his friend to the West Coast in 1942, and the two found work in radio as writers on *The Edgar Bergen/Charlie McCarthy Show* at the star's request (Bergen's, that is). The team eventually wrote for *The Frank Morgan Show*, *The Phil Harris Show*, and then spent the next dozen years writing for the immensely popular *The Amos 'n' Andy Show* before finally making that all-important transition to television with the same program recast. (The legendary radio show was performed by its creators, two white actors Freeman Gosden and Charles Correll; for the all-black television cast, actors Alvin Childress and Spencer Williams, Jr. became Amos and Andy.) The writing duo reportedly churned out a whopping 1,500 scripts for Amos, Andy, and the Kingfish on radio. The television series lasted just two seasons on CBS Television.

Peter Orlick of the Museum of Broadcast Communications recently commented: "Although *Amos 'n' Andy* now is viewed as a distorted repository of racial stereotyping and segregated casting, Connelly's and Mosher's experience on that program helped them refine a flair for extracting humor from uncomplicated, yet likable characters immersed in unremarkable situations with which the audience could easily identify."

Television's first all-black sitcom, *Amos 'n' Andy* (1951).

It is true that the *Amos 'n' Andy* radio version contained moments of racial stereotyping. It is highly debatable, however, whether the television version of *Amos 'n' Andy* can be labeled racially stereotypical toward African-Americans. It was never intended as a true-to-life picture of black Americana; it was very much a caricature like Ralph Kramden and Ed Norton are caricatures. The situation comedy in *Amos 'n' Andy* was not derived from characters being a minority; the show centered on simple, funny characters, surroundings, and situations, with little regard or reference to shadings of the skin. Moreover, if *Amos 'n' Andy*, as a show, was stereotypical toward black society at the time, then white Americans could claim *The Honeymooners* negatively reflected all Caucasians at the time.

The point being, Connelly and Mosher were foremost writing funny, universal material for and about Americans. It was not racially triggered comedy. The humor did not stem out of black societal situations, nor did it stereotype the characters. The situations could have been interchangeable with *The Abbott & Costello Show* for that matter—a sitcom filmed at the same studio during the same years, with characters getting into similar comedic predicaments. It's about time someone applauded TV's *Amos 'n' Andy*, America's first black sitcom, where comedy was just comedy and race had little to do with it.

Connelly and Mosher next created and produced an anthology series, *The Ray Milland Show* (also known as *Meet Mr. McNulty*) which ran two years in primetime. In 1956, the pair received an Academy Award nomination for their original story for the film, *The Private War of Major Benson*, which starred Charlton Heston. The following year marked a milestone in their career as television auteurs.

On October 2, 1957, the first episode of a family program they had patterned after their own brood, *Leave It to Beaver*, was telecast and became a popular, wholesome show for American audiences—one which lasted six seasons. Connelly, who had seven children, and Mosher, who had two, drew upon their own family experiences to make *Beaver* a family favorite. Although the team created, produced, and wrote most of the shows, they delegated some of the writing duties to other talented individuals—always closely overseeing the productions from every aspect.

During production of *Leave It to Beaver* and even today, actress Barbara Billingsley, known best as the sympathetic June Cleaver, credits the success of this family series to the exceptional writing. She told a reporter in 1962, near the end of the series: "Each story has a sound little moral message for parents and children and each story is true to life. Our scripts are the best in the business," Billingsley explained. "The material written by Joe Connelly and Bob Mosher is always fresh and natural. They not only write the show but they own it and produce it too and they can do what they like. If a situation isn't coming off when we're before the cameras, Joe and Bob improve it right on the spot."

Billingsley continued: "Joe and Bob claim they come up with most of the plots for the shows simply by watching and listening to the antics and questions of their own children. For instance, not too long ago Joe Connelly's seventeen-year-old son, Jay, wanted to buy an old car and repair it. Well, quite a debate ensued over the pros and cons of a car for his youngster, so they did a script about the funny incidents revolving around that real-life family problem. In the show, it was our TV son Wally who wanted the car and I used the same reasoning as Joe did in talking him out of it. In short, Joe's son

Producers Mosher (top left) and Connelly (seated in chair) rarely spent time on the set of their productions; rather, they hunkered down in their office working on scripts. This extraordinary photo on the set of their hit show, *Leave It to Beaver*, shows the writing team discussing a scene with actors Hugh Beaumont, Jerry Mathers, Tony Dow, and director Norman Tokar (right).

didn't get his jalopy and neither did Wally on TV. That made sense for a lot of mothers and fathers, we hope. Seventeen is too young for a car of their own."

Ironically, Connelly and Mosher graduated from many years working on the radio and television versions of the all-black comedy, *Amos 'n' Andy* and went almost directly into a purely white-bread television series, *Leave It to Beaver*—which was about as remote as you could get from the Afro-American experience. And inasmuch as they created comedic situations for black characters for nearly fifteen years, you'd be hard-pressed to find a black character in an episode of *Beaver* or their following hit series *The Munsters*.

The duo moved on from *Beaver* to another series, *Ichabod and Me*, which lasted just one season, and then they dipped their hands into an altogether different and relatively untested area of television: an animated cartoon series in primetime. *The Flintstones* was breaking ground with rock-solid ratings in primetime, so Connelly and Mosher produced and wrote a series in 1962 titled *Calvin and the Colonel*, starring a dim-witted bear (Calvin) and his shrew fox friend (the Colonel). The show was highly reminiscent of radio and television's *Amos 'n' Andy*, complete with vocals supplied by Amos and Andy themselves—the original radio actors Freeman Gosden and Charles Correll. The animated show lasted just one season on ABC-TV, but without a doubt it helped pave the way for more animated programming in primetime.

Individually both Connelly and Mosher scripted some TV comedies and in early 1964, the team (by then working under their own Kayro-Vue Productions banner—"Kay" for Connelly's wife Kathryn, and "Ro" for Mosher's wife Rose) helped fashion a family of monsters which would spark another television hit for them in first run and in undying syndication. By the time *The Munsters* hit the airwaves, the team was labeled one of the most prolific producing duos in television.

The primetime animated adventures of *Calvin and the Colonel* aired on ABC-TV featuring the same voice talents as radio's "Amos 'n' Andy."

Butch Patrick recalls of his employers, "I think I knew Joe a little better than Bob," he says. "Bob was a little more chameleon like. You didn't notice him as much. Joe seemed to be more of the high profile of the two.

"Those guys were not on the set very much," Patrick remembers from his days on *The Munsters* set. "They never interfered with the actual production once filming began. They were in their office working. We'd see them Monday for the readings and that would be about it until Friday night after the wrap. We always had a little party on the set after wrap and Joe and Bob would come around and put some money on the party tree. There was a little tree on the coffee cart and people would put money on it and that would fund the party for the next Friday night wrap party. That was routine. It was a nice time for everybody to let their hair down and sometimes Joe and Bob joined everybody, especially if there was a guest star."

Following *The Munsters*, Connelly and Mosher produced a CBS comedy Western series called *Pistols 'n' Petticoats* starring Ann Sheridan. The show lasted just one season, mainly due to the sudden death of its star. Having partnered in comedy for nearly thirty years, Joe and Bob decided it was time to retire as a team. Connelly continued with a few attempts at series comedy, but with shows that produced relatively little promise.

Joe Connelly, co-creator of *Leave It to Beaver* and *The Munsters*, visits his original cast members when they kicked off a new version for television titled *Still the Beaver* (1985).

As fate thrust both men onto the road of success simultaneously, it also struck both of them down at the same time. In the early seventies, both Connelly and Mosher suffered serious health problems which, ironically, landed them both in the same hospital at the same time. Connelly had suffered an aneurysm while his partner was afflicted with an inoperable brain tumor. Bob Mosher died on December 15, 1972.

Connelly recuperated in a limited capacity but suffered from some memory loss, mostly with respect to day-to-day activities. His memory of the past was intact. A widower, Joe and his second wife, Ann, moved to Pebble Beach, California, in the eighties. Speaking from Pebble Beach, Connelly warmly remembered his writing partner of many years: "He was a very quiet guy. He never said much. But it was pretty much a fifty-fifty relationship. He was a damn good writer and a good guy, God rest his soul."

For Mosher, *The Munsters* represented his favorite accomplishment in television. "He liked the *Beaver* show," said his wife Rose Mosher Perry in 1988, "he had tremendous fun with that show. He was a big fan of the Boris Karloff/Bela Lugosi genre. He thought the old horror moves were rather funny. Never took them seriously."

In college, Mosher demonstrated his proclivity for ghoulish humor with such pranks as swiping a skeleton from the science lab and hanging it from a tree outside the lab building one night. "He always did things like that," said his wife. "He wanted to hang one in our closet one time, but I wouldn't have that. He loved to get people's reactions."

Mosher was, believe it or not, a timid sort. Of the collaboration, most agree that Connelly was the extrovert and Mosher the quiet padding. Over the years, they developed their own formula for working together and creating successful shows on radio and television. While at Universal, they shared a large bungalow office with all the amenities. For some time, they even wrote material at Mosher's home in a special custom-built "glass-brick, fifties-style house," says Mosher's son, Robert. "They had a typewriter back there on the desk and a pool table, and they'd be laughing their heads off." Their humor, often off-color, couldn't be used on television naturally, however from this sprang ingenious material which drove several lasting television series.

"Writers usually get the back end of the stick," said Connelly in 1988. "Bob and I owned twenty-five percent of each of the shows, so we did pretty well over the years." And what with the unending reruns of both *Beaver* and *The Munsters*, and remakes of both series having been produced for television as well as motion picture adaptations, the annuities are likely to roll on forever.

Joe Connelly eventually resided at the Motion Picture Country Home in the late eighties after the death of his second wife. Suffering from Alzheimer's disease, he made very few public appearances, except a rare moment when the aging radio and TV pioneer stood and took a bow at a tribute to *Leave It to Beaver* (part of the Museum of Television and Radio's William S. Paley Festival/Los Angeles) in October 1996. Connelly died at the age of eighty-six on February 13, 2003 from complications of a stroke.

MONSTERS ON FILM

The Munsters, as a television production was an elaborate web, complex from the start. The outcome was certain to be awesome, but getting things sewn together proved to be something akin to murder.

The show was filmed with one 35-mm camera throughout its two-year run. On Mondays, routinely the cast assembled in the offices of Joe Connelly and Bob Mosher for a read-through. The producer's office was a fairly large one, located in bungalows directly across from the studio commissary. Scripts were handed out as everyone marked their lines and sometimes new material was battered about during the morning session.

"In their office were couches and chairs all facing one another," recalls Butch Patrick. "Joe and Bob were at their desks. There'd be a table set up with coffee and munchies and coffee cakes. It was pretty casual; it was just a simple read-through which took just an hour or two, and that would be that for the day."

Tuesdays were relegated for rehearsal and blocking, and occasionally extra wardrobe fittings, a process which sometimes stretched into lunchtime, but it was a non makeup day and the cast could casually run through the script. The rest of the week meant filming the show's precious minutes. Connelly and Mosher were producers who insisted on high-quality performances—from the actors, the crew, and of themselves. The makeup process, an elaborate concern for all, could not be played down for the convenience of the actors and rarely were allowances or shortcuts granted. Because Fred Gwynne evolved as the show's greatest asset, the scripts centered more and more on Herman and this gave Gwynne little rest.

One of the first problems the producers faced was the cast's clashing of egos. Right from the start, even before filming really got underway, the main cast members began pitching fits for one reason or another and it became a constant duty of Connelly (not so much Mosher) to keep the actors placated.

For impassioned costars Gwynne and Lewis, just the casting choice of Yvonne De Carlo itself sent them rushing into the producers' office with fiery torches, ready to do away with the monster. "We went down to the producers and screamed bloody murder," recalled Al Lewis. "Fred and I thought she would not be right in the part at all. Experience told us we were wrong. From the superficial observations, we were dead wrong. She was excellent in the series, the biggest surprise on the show."

Joe Connelly remembered those private, but loud, conferences. "They [Gwynne and Lewis] objected to everything," he said. "We had to put up with a lot of s—t from those two. Fred objected to the makeup and argued with us a lot about that."

It took some time for the cast to adjust to each other's idiosyncrasies and settle into a routine. "We still fought for a lot of things," added Lewis. "We fought to get Fred relief from the script sometimes. It was murder on him. Fred and I fought for the whole show. That's why Connelly disagreed with us so much. I don't think Mosher said five words during the two years we were on the air."

Butch Patrick recalls Fred Gwynne becoming openly irritated with the producers as the schedules and responsibilities increased. "He resented the fact that we had to come in on Monday mornings to read with these guys, which should have been a day off," Patrick says. "Because all they did is sit there and laugh at their own jokes and have coffee and Danish. Fred did not like that because these guys made us all come in. I didn't care. I was on the set for school regardless; even during hiatus I still came in to go to school."

Production initially took place on Universal's Soundstage #7 until the show was relocated on the lot. "It was one of the older stages on the lot from the early days," says Butch Patrick, "and we broke a huge beam and the roof cracked one day. It might have been after an earthquake or something but once they noticed the big crack in one of the beams in the ceiling, they knew something had to be done."

The entire set and production was then moved midseason over to one of the new soundstages, #32, where both the massive living-room set, the kitchen, as well as Grandpa's dungeon/laboratory were housed. Additional sets such as Herman and Lily's bedroom were off in other corners and sometimes made portable

and reused only when necessary. There were mini-dressing rooms and makeup areas behind the scenery, lining the walls of the soundstage. The living-room set and the laboratory set were massive, oversized in order to compensate for Fred Gwynne's hulking stature. The house's two front doors, which looked more like the gates to Jurassic Park, stood proudly at eight-and-a-half feet tall—and solid. The couch was larger than average and the famous stairwell was immense. The door built into the living room floor which opened up to Grandpa's lab actually led to nothing. "It was just a big hole in the ground," says Patrick. "It was like a square bomb-shelter area, about six feet deep. It was big enough for us to go down a few steps, but Fred would have to crouch down to hide. If the door was shut on him, he'd have to hunch over."

Universal Studios called special-effects technician Kenneth Strickfadden out of retirement to work on several episodes of *The Munsters*. Strickfadden's original Tesla coils laboratory equipment which displayed high voltage in motion—or "indoor lightning"—was used in the original Universal Studios classic film, "Frankenstein" (1931). Strickfadden, who developed the whizzing generators and fizzling lightning rods for film, kept much of the original equipment. Much of the complex circuitry seen in Grandpa's laboratory was the very same elaborate setup of glowing coils, transformers, resistors and capacitors that zapped life into the Boris Karloff monster three decades earlier.

Fred and Al with their propman, Eddie Keys, who went way back to silent-movie days. Keys worked as a prop master on the film *Frankenstein* in 1931 at Universal.

Filming the seventh episode, "Tin Can Man," in September 1964.

The furniture was musty and dirty with more dust being added on filming days. Just keeping the house in fresh cobwebs was a chore for the art directors. "I remember these guys had guns which looked like the weapons that were used in *Ghostbusters*," recalls Ted Eccles who appeared on the show. "They were these large devices that had fans built into them and spun the equivalent of rubber cement in front of a fan that when blown would make these long tendrils and catch on everything and essentially re-cobweb the set. I'm sure today, you couldn't do it because of issues with OSHA and other environmental protection agencies. The entire set smelled like a rubber-cement factory.

"With all the people moving around and cameras and cast," he adds, "it was a constant re-webbing process going on just before they'd shoot. They'd usually come in and spritz it all down with fresh cobweb and eventually the lights would melt it."

A rare set still displaying a portion of the Munster living room on Soundstage #32 at Universal Studios.

▲ A rare set still of Grandpa's dungeon laboratory.

▶ Just a few members of the CBS family in 1964. Standing: John McGiver, Sterling Holloway, Yvonne De Carlo, Paul Ford, and Fred Gwynne. Seated: Julie Newmar, Cara Williams, and Tina Louise. (Portrait by Gabi Rona)

Al Lewis said he and Fred Gwynne respected the producer's choice of Yvonne De Carlo for the role of Lily only after they worked with her for a time. "We were wrong about her. She was fabulous," Lewis admitted.

As the cast finally felt cohesion—or began to clot, as Grandpa might say—the production took a hit when Beverley Owen left after her thirteenth episode. Owen was so unhappy during the production, all the while wanting to return to New York, that she begged and literally cried to be replaced until producers finally granted her request. Although Owen added a warm and poignant touch to the show, the producers felt they could bandage the situation and replace her without causing a hemorrhage. Enter: Pat Priest.

"I had a little run-in with Yvonne De Carlo almost immediately," recalls Pat Priest today. "I remember Yvonne saying to me one day, 'There's one thing I want you to know, young lady. Don't you ever upstage me!' At that point I didn't know what I had done. The director had asked me to step forward."

Priest and De Carlo eventually became good friends during the production, says Priest, but the ground rules had to be set. Gwynne and Lewis found out that ground rules needed to be set for De Carlo herself.

"Yvonne played better-than-thou for a while," Fred Gwynne told a reporter in 1984. "She stayed in her wagon while we were outside seating, waiting for her. But once she knew we were just as tough as she was and that we were there to do the job, we got along like gangbusters. I think we had to. It was so difficult a show, that if we didn't, it would have been a disaster."

"Eddie,
don't just sit there . . .
wolf down your food."

Filming the episode "Tin Can Man" with director Earl Bellamy (in front of the car) on September 25, 1964.

In the beginning, De Carlo was holding up production with her constant adjustments to makeup, hair, and nails, all done in her trailer outside the soundstage. She began dictating which scenes would be shot, all from the vantage of her convenience. Gwynne and Lewis became enraged as production would halt at times and the crew would be waiting. Finally Al Lewis had taken enough and pulled aside the beauty queen and confronted her about her demanding attitude. He then informed her exactly what scenes, according to the production call sheet, would be shot that day and in what order, thereby making it plausible for the entire ensemble—not just her. He explained that this was the way a company works together. De Carlo recoiled and understood Lewis's stern admonishment and according to Lewis, it never became a problem again.

De Carlo had been one of the queens of the Universal Studios lot during her heyday in motion pictures in the forties, so her appearance on a TV sitcom was somewhat of a comedown for her. She was a former glamour girl now in her forties and life was changing quickly for the actress. "I did the show in the beginning for one reason only," De Carlo explains. "Money. I needed money at the time. I thought the makeup would make me look horrid, but it wasn't so bad after all. Eventually, I liked the work."

With time and some exerted patience, the cast began to work well together and the production as a whole gradually ran, well, smoother. Not *smoothly*, but smoother. *The Munsters* was such an unconventional set that it took an enormous amount of time and extra preparation to get the scenes on film. Thankfully there was no live audience because it would have made the entire process impossible. The days spent on location could be miserable and exhausting for everyone involved, especially when times taking special effects or stunts were introduced.

Just from his solo guest appearance, former child-actor Ted Eccles took away a vastly different experience while shooting an episode of *The Munsters* versus working on other shows of the day. A seasoned child actor when he appeared in the first-season episode "Herman the Great," Eccles recalls vividly his visit to Mockingbird Heights:

"I remember an enormous amount of time involved in the makeup process. As a little kid, they were pretty strict in those days that kids could only work four hours on the set, and Butch might have had a tough time juggling it all," he explains. "So when you had these huge makeup issues that would always play havoc for the assistant directors trying to figure out when to pull the kids out of school and trying to time it so they got them out

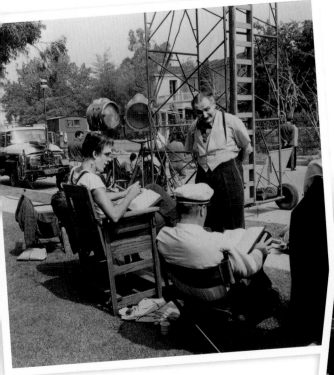

Fred and Al run through their dialogue. On the set, Fred's personal perch was a lofty custom-built wooden chair, made to accommodate his height while in the giant boots.

MUNSTER MOMENT

Just ask Julia Gnuse, the world's most tattooed lady, if she likes *The Munsters*. Examine her over-inked body and you'll fine prominent images of the Munsters cast (along with artwork of the Three Stooges and Lucille Ball). She says on her website: "Growing up in the fifties and sixties, I was exposed to some of the classic American television show, movies, and cartoons. Along with my favorites I tattooed events from my life, such as a picture of my face as a blank slate, a picture of my first tattoo artist, and the name of my old cookie business, Sweet Temptations." Featured on TV's *Larry King Live* and *Ripley's Believe it or Not*, the fifty-year-old mother and businesswoman has been officially listed in the *Guinness Book of World Records* as the most tattooed human female.

to do whatever scenes they were going to do and do this when everybody's makeup was ready.

"Fred's makeup application would come off and you'd have pulled a kid out of school and somebody's makeup is sideways and there goes thirty minutes. I'm sure that was a challenge because the time that Butch spent in makeup was counted as working time."

Eccles also recalls the inordinate efforts on the set to keep Fred Gwynne cool under his heavy makeup, headpiece, and padded wardrobe. "Between takes, it was tough because if you rehearsed a scene with Fred, you then had to wait about five minutes from rehearsal until they actually did a take. And he was good for two or three takes before he had to be cooled back down. If it was tough to cool Fred down inside, I can imagine what it would have been like outside."

The process of keeping Gwynne cool and comfortable in his new skin required some ingenuity. Because the show was being shot with relatively slow-speed film, an overdose of light was required to be pumped onto the stage to properly capture the scenes. Huge carbon arc lamps threw off oppressive heat and caused Fred Gwynne to swelter. That, combined with his heavy padding, created limitations. It got to be where Fred knew just when to stop for breaks and many times called

those shots—not the director—out of sheer survival. It was the smart director, a flexible type, who understood this and went with the flow to get the job done on time.

Naturally, the soundstage was equipped with industrial-sized air conditioning, but a more concentrated solution was required to assist Gwynne. To combat the heat, set workers designed and constructed a rig made out of two-by-fours, sort of a leaning device, for Gwynne to take breathers. It was like a slanting board which he could step up on, lean back, and prop up his arms. There were three or four openings built into his inner suit and padding and while Gwynne leaned back to take the weight off his feet, set workers would plug air hoses into his padded wardrobe and blast him full of air. This would happen frequently on the filming days.

Ted Eccles recalls the scene: "Keeping Fred cool was a huge part of the process because if he started sweating, the headpiece would come loose. And if the headpiece came off, that was another hour in makeup. It was hysterical to watch even as a little kid because normally you'd go in and run your lines, block the scene, shoot the master, and then do the close-ups and you're done. But when you worked in this situation, it was a whole lot more involved and it moved a lot slower. Frankly, I don't know how they got it all done.

Fred Gwynne sweltered under his wardrobe—especially outdoors in the southern California heat—and shed the thick, padded garments at every opportunity.

"Between trying to cool Fred Gwynne down in the suit and trying to keep cobwebs on the set, I don't know how much compressed air they had to have, but it was a hell of a lot. That operation ran on things being blown."

Achieving some of the special effects on *The Munsters* also took great time and care, especially when it came to the pyrotechnics involved with their pet named Spot. (Was Spot a dragon? A fire-breathing throwback from the dinosaur age? Who knows? All we *do* know is that the rest of his species was extinct.) The show boasted some of the most experienced special effects supervisors the studio had to offer. Filming the dropping beams, explosions, and moments of Herman's fits (with collapsing furniture or breakaway doors and props) all took extensive preparation and timing to capture on film. No one can say it wasn't worth it.

The cast eventually became accustomed to the rigors of filming this particular television show—a program which, in time, emerged as a priceless jewel of the decade.

With time, the cast became better acquainted with their characters and let loose. Notably the best Herman shtick emerges late in the first season. By the second season, the characters were off the charts and over the top; these episodes include some of the cast's best performances. "We became not only a family on film," says Pat Priest, "but a family of actors. We learned to rely on one another and things got a lot better in time."

Meantime, Al Lewis was the one on the set who ribbed everyone and kept the atmosphere lively.

Yvonne enjoyed it, and Gwynne counted on it. While Gwynne passed time playing the guitar or just napping on the set's living-room couch, Lewis was the prankster and the laugher on the set, letting loose a loud breathy cackle he'd go into at will. It was a memorable guffaw with gusto, as infectious as Paul Lynde's laugh.

"I remember Fred and Al joking with me constantly," says Pat Priest. "It got to where I couldn't believe anything they said to me. They lied to me always. It was really funny. As a matter of fact, they lied about their ages until just recently when I found out the truth."

It's hard to believe that Gwynne was just thirty-nine when he started *The Munsters*. Yvonne De Carlo was forty-two, and Al Lewis—supposed to be Lily's father—was a year younger than De Carlo. For years, Lewis fibbed about his age to keep the press on its toes. Because of the convincing makeup, most thought Lewis was actually into his geriatric years. Another misconception for audiences was the adult cast's actual height. Most people assumed Al Lewis was short. He was far from short, standing at a respectable six-foot-one. Yvonne De Carlo was the petite one, standing five-foot-four. And Gwynne towered over them all, standing six-foot-five in stocking feet and seven feet tall in the giant Herman boots.

Herman finds his old baby bonnet in the episode "Eddie's Brother."

#27031

- 10 -

17 INT. MUNSTER LIVING ROOM - DAY   17
    Herman is still sitting on the floor as Lily ENTERS.

                    LILY
    Herman Munster, what are you doing?

                    HERMAN
    Lily, don't you get the picture?...
    Da da...goo goo!

                    LILY
    Yes, I get the picture -- the
    picture of you being hauled off
    to the flaky farm.

                    HERMAN
    That's not the picture at all. I'm
    just hinting to you in a subtle
    manner that Eddie wants a baby
    brother to play with.

                    LILY
    Herman, let's be logical about this
    thing.

                    HERMAN
    Yes, let's be logical.

                    LILY
    I can't be logical when you're
    wearing that stupid bonnet.

                    HERMAN
    Oh.

    He takes the bonnet off.

                    LILY
    First of all, Eddie is nine years
    old.

                    HERMAN
    I'll go along with that.

                    LILY
    If we had a baby now, by the time
    it was nine years old, how old
    would Eddie be?

                    HERMAN
    Well, he'd be...almost...around...
    There's only one answer, isn't
    there?

                    LILY
    Yes. He'd be eighteen.   CONTINUED

WHERE DO MUNSTERS COME FROM?

It took pains, but they did it. The cast actually took simple roles that were merely printed on paper and added a texture of their own invention and created icons.

"The role of Grandpa is not complicated because you're wearing odd makeup or bizarre costumes," explained Al Lewis. "That's not what complicates a role. What makes Grandpa a little odd is the fact that he had no prototype. When I approached this role, I knew that whatever I was doing was original. So no director could say to me, 'Listen, remember how he did it, this is how I want it done.'"

A book could be devoted on just the intricacies of Herman and Grandpa alone. Gwynne, Lewis, De Carlo, and Patrick displayed fine acting by creating not just monsters but lovable creatures. For the adult cast anyway, every movement, utterance, sentence, and eye twitch was for the character. Grandpa's memorable hesitating line delivery was a grand touch added by Lewis.

"I worked very hard creating that character," admitted Lewis. "I made those lines work. The walk and posture all fit the character."

Gwynne attributed his conception of Herman Munster to his mother—

not in appearance, but in manner and characterization. "I told my mother, God love her, that I used her voice. I used her inflections," Gwynne noted on TV's *Dick Cavett Show* in the seventies.

In some of the initial episodes, Gwynne noticeably mimics Boris Karloff's Frankenstein monster with his walk, stiff stance, and all. Granted, some of the stiffness was due to the makeup; in an effort to keep the headpiece in place, Gwynne could not fully twist his neck and was constricted by this. So effective, however, in some shots he can almost make the viewer believe it is Karloff's monster. Later, Gwynne toned down that particular aspect, loosened up, and made the character all his own with a completely disarming and humorous flavor that utterly charmed audiences.

In *TV Guide*, co-producer Bob Mosher praised Yvonne De Carlo for her portrayal and progress as a vampire/housewife. "She has never done anything like this before," he said in 1965. "But she has picked up the idea wonderfully fast and has given the character, Lily Munster, warmth and charm. And to date, she has been uncomplaining."

"Grandpa was kind of a Dracula-type Major Hoople."
—AL LEWIS

For decades, TV fans assumed it was some *other* couple who were first shown sharing a bed together on primetime television. Actually TV's most unlikely couple transcended that taboo when, on *I Love Lucy*, Fred and Ethel Mertz slumbered together in a saggy double bed in a memorable on-the-road episode. Maybe censors overlooked it because everyone knew sex wasn't going to enter that equation. Over the years actress Florence Henderson has frequently proclaimed that she and Robert Reed—as Carol and Mike Brady— were the first to break the bedroom barrier in 1969 on *The Brady Bunch*. Not so, lovely lady. Let it be known, the first wedded pair to *routinely* appear in bed together on a hit sitcom were Fred and Wilma Flintstone, drawn together in the early sixties on ABC-TV. Maybe censors looked the other way since they were animated characters. The real mystery is why Rob and Laura Petrie on *The Dick Van Dyke Show* remained nocturnally separated while Herman and Lily Munster, on the same network, slept cozy in bed together—like any average, American married couple.

IT ISN'T EASY BEING GRAY

"We weren't exactly green. Kind of a faded, shipwrecked gray. Not a distinctive color. It looked like a ship with too many barnacles on it."

—AL LEWIS

A GREAT IRONY ABOUT THE MUNSTERS HAD TO DO with their extensive makeup. While the public adored the characters who arose from the makeup chairs, most of the cast despised the tedious daily routine they had to endure for two seasons. Hated it. Even though it became a chore, all of the actors eventually agreed that getting made up and wearing costumes was a necessary evil—even a fun one—to create such an illusion. It was all very clown-like, but they realized it was a pure exercise in acting that ultimately proved quite pleasurable and addictive. Discomfort and all.

Fred Gwynne was inflicted with the most pain, you might say; however, the actor looked at it as a challenge and he basically knew what he was getting into. "In fact," he said in 1966, "that was one of the reasons I took this show. I don't think there are that many chances in TV to submerge beneath a mask." For Gwynne, it was a domino effect: the makeup process was drudgery, but the costume situation was even worse. The outfit was hefty and made him sweat profusely, which in turn would ruin the makeup and necessitate that he be touched up constantly. Gwynne's greatest problem was staying cool on the set in order to preserve the makeup and his own health.

The Munsters' makeup artists have gone uncredited for years, mainly due to the fact that Bud Westmore's name was the only one in the show's credits. Westmore was the head of the makeup department at Universal Studios, but contributed very little to the day-to-day activity or even the original facial designs for the Munsters. The team of veterans who transformed the actors into monsters are truly unsung television heroes. It was Karl Silvera who applied the greasepaint to Fred Gwynne; Perc Westmore who transformed Al Lewis into Grandpa; Abe Haberman who usually made up Yvonne De Carlo, and, with Mike Westmore, also prepared both Pat Priest and Butch Patrick.

For the makeup process, the work started right from day one. Each of the cast members (except the women playing Marilyn) needed to have a mold cast from their face, subjecting them to a wet-plaster application process involving their entire visage—and sometimes entire head. Some people have found the experience quite smothering. For one reason or another, Gwynne had the procedure performed several times throughout the show's progression. (You'll notice the second-season headpieces are a little wider than the narrow ones used during the first season.) There were at one point several molds of Gwynne's head in the Universal Studios makeup department. From those molds and casts came the foam latex headpieces he wore, as well as life-size busts with which the makeup men could experiment. One of those life-size busts was eventually used in an episode where Marilyn sculpts her Uncle Herman for a college art-class project.

"At first, they didn't know what they were getting into with the makeup," says Butch Patrick today. "They had made up some gray greasepaint, but after we actually started doing the show, this greasepaint would crack and then break off about two hours into the day. They had a hell of a time. They would have to redo the entire makeup, shoot for another hour, and redo again for another hour's shooting."

Yvonne De Carlo, right from the beginning, said she had reservations about this job. She knew it was a far cry from playing Mary Magdalene. "I must admit that I thought very carefully before deciding to do this show," she told the *Los Angeles Times* in December 1964, "because once you sign the contract, you're stuck. I called [the makeup department] to find out just what they were going to do to me. When they said I would have a green face with sunken cheeks, I began to worry.

"But as it turned out, they decided to glamorize me. I do have exaggerated eyebrows, but nothing more than a ballerina uses on stage. And gradually, I'm getting away from the witchy streak of white in my hair. Actually, my makeup doesn't take longer than a complete glamour makeup for the movies."

De Carlo even went so far as to compare herself with Carolyn Jones on *The Addams Family*, the "rival" eerie sitcom. "I'm not too far removed from that Morticia look . . . and I'm not too far out," she said.

▲ The earliest makeup test photos of Gwynne proved a little too grotesque. Gwynne told the *L.A. Times*: "It was a matter of sticking with the original property, which was Frankenstein's monster. There was some talk of taking the scar off my forehead, but they decided to leave it. And I think they were right. You should stick with the character."

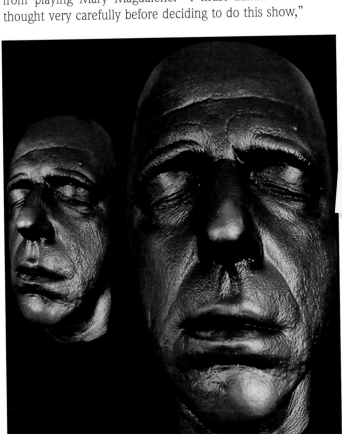

◄ A close-up view of Fred Gwynne's eerie life-cast, used to mold the Herman headpieces and additional facial appliances when needed.

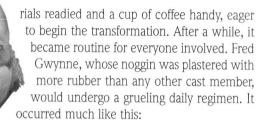

THE SECRETS REVEALED

"'Now I'm seen and heard, but in that getup, who's to recognize me?' That getup is his costume and makeup for the role of 'Grandpa,' the venerable, chalk-faced, beady-eyed practical joker of the Munster clan who walks around the house in black gloves, tuxedo, a voluminous swirling cape, and high Ming collar."

—UNIVERSAL CITY STUDIOS PRESS RELEASE, 1965

It didn't turn out the way Al Lewis expected. More and more, Lewis accepted the fact that fans and viewers *did* recognize him under all the makeup. His transformation wasn't that drastic. When Gwynne and Lewis would go to basketball games together, Lewis was always recognized and surrounded by the kids and fans, while Gwynne, towering over the crowd, could slip away almost unrecognized. It was his voice that gave him away.

The skilled makeup artists on *The Munsters* were highly inventive craftsmen who evaluated the actors carefully and jointly created each character appearance by accentuating each actor's existing features. For instance, Al Lewis's natural puffy cheeks were dabbled with makeup, creating the exaggerated appearance of an old man's wobbly jowls. His naturally receding hairline remained, yet became a devilish point. His cheeks were sunken with the aid of precisely detailed shadings and highlights, and his nose jutted out just a bit farther with the addition of dark lines that circled and seemed to draw back his nostrils. In the end Lewis, though still recognizable, became a cartoon version of himself.

Arriving in darkness at the makeup department each morning, the cast would scatter to their respective makeup rooms, where their personal artist was waiting with mate-

rials readied and a cup of coffee handy, eager to begin the transformation. After a while, it became routine for everyone involved. Fred Gwynne, whose noggin was plastered with more rubber than any other cast member, would undergo a grueling daily regimen. It occurred much like this:

Half awake, Fred Gwynne drove through the morning mist, arriving at the studio around 6:00 AM He proceeded down a long corridor in the makeup building on the Universal lot to Room 23, where he changed into a T-shirt and trousers, threw on a barber's smock, and seated himself in the chair for the ride. Gwynne and Lewis were simultaneously transformed in one big, brightly lit makeup room with two barber chairs. While Gwynne was being made up on one side of the mirrored makeup room, Lewis sat in the chair on the other side. Gwynne's makeup artist Karl Silvera had everything assembled: a new headpiece, a pile of bolts, all the makeup and brushes. He flipped on the radio, took a sip of coffee, and began the two-hour plastic surgery.

Most of the time, Gwynne was freshly shaven. Silvera began by applying mortician's wax to Gwynne's eyebrows to coat and protect them. "I used a trick system when I glued down Fred's headpiece," Silvera admits. A foam latex top was molded and fitted onto Gwynne's head, then fastened and gently secured with tweezers. The flat top, combined with the lower humped-over section of Gwynne's forehead, gave him a Neanderthal brow. The headpiece was glued in a special way to Gwynne's scalp. Silvera further explains:

> I'd put a little pan stick on his face, or wherever the appliance was gonna go, and I'd powder it well and stipple it with pure latex rubber and powder again; and then I'd glue the headpiece onto that so that the glue was not ac-

tually touching his skin. When you take if off, the rubber gives and pulls right off; however, it would [otherwise] stay on all day. I glued a little flap in the rubber to the back of his neck to keep the headpiece in position because it would shift during the day—or he would knock into something, and it [w]ould move; or somebody would hit it. This flap in the back stabilized it some.

The headpieces changed sizes slightly over the years; about three times, Silvera recalls. Not every headpiece made was in perfect shape for use on Gwynne. "If they handed me a lousy one, I'd sometimes repair the one from the day before and use it," says Silvera. "When these rubber headpieces are shot into the mold, air gets into the rubber and creates weak spots that might give in. I'd have to strengthen them so they didn't cave in."

Silvera then rubbed the battleship-gray greasepaint across Gwynne's nose, cheeks, chin, ears, and neck, drying the paint with a blow dryer. "I whipped up those colors out of rubber grease," he says. "I'd make the gray tone from black and white and put a little green in it. And then I'd brush his face with new pastels I would rub off on sandpaper, and brush that on to bring out the green and the blues and so forth.

▶ Hair stylist Jeanne Bodel fixes Fred's flattened coiffure.

▼ Makeup artist Karl Silvera applies the finishing touches to Gwynne.

"They ended up making some pan stick over at Max Factor's to match the color," Silvera says. "They probably still have Munster gray, which came from the colors we originally whipped up."

Strategically, the rest of Gwynne's makeup consisted of color-blending to fill in the hollows of his cheeks and darken the sockets of his eyes. The eyelids were given some depth, and a mascara pencil outlined Gwynne's steel-blue eyes. Then yellowish-green hue was applied over the gray and blended. The lightning-bolt scar across Herman's forehead was painted (but never too realistically) like an open wound.

"His eyelids were almost like a clown's," Silvera explains. "We wanted that heavy-lid look without putting stuff on his eyelids. Fred was a very fine artist and a lot of the ideas were things we worked on together. We'd

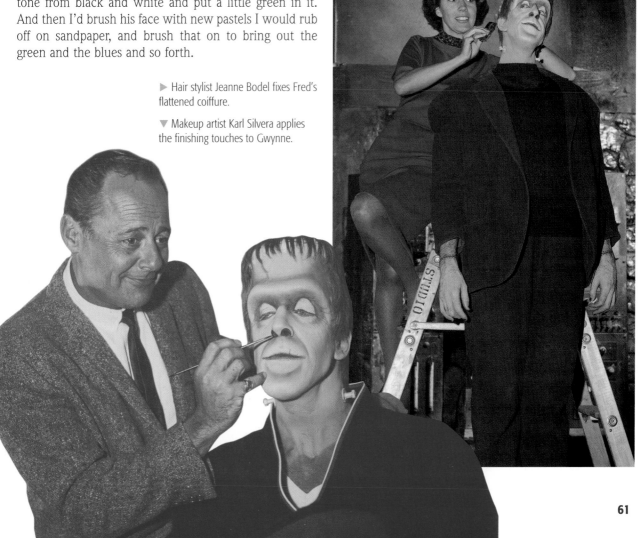

Fred and Al were not only costars whose talents complemented each other beautifully, but the men were the best of friends at the time.

bare. One of the greatest problems facing Gwynne on a daily basis was the inadvertent smearing of hand makeup all over his wardrobe, especially Herman's favored dark knit, collarless shirts. Their fabric took on powder effortlessly and his shirts needed to be dusted time and again during production.

Right atop the crown of Herman's head was a small hole where the finely woven wig of human hair was affixed to the latex headpiece. To provide a salt-and-pepper texture, the hair was streaked with the same green color used on his face, and the hairpiece was delicately combed and set with hairspray. Herman was built. ("It's alive! . . . It's alive!")

"The makeup is a very good sleeping pill," Gwynne said at the time. "It'll knock you out while you wait two hours."

Gwynne resigned himself to the makeup process and trudged through it. "We got along great," says Silvera. "He had a booming voice that was very nice to listen to, and he was an entertaining person. He was a quiet kind of guy in the makeup chair unless he got antsy from sitting there. He'd get up and go and chase some gal walking up and down the hallway, or some kid would come in and he'd pretend like he was gonna scare them—which he never did. They all loved him."

Seated in the opposite chair, being made up by Perc (pronounced "purse") Westmore, was Al Lewis. "I sat there and had wonderful times with my makeup man," Lewis says. "We'd sit and tell jokes and stories, talk about kids and wives. Fred would always sleep in the chair, but I rarely slept."

Since his makeover was not as extensive as Gwynne's, Lewis perceived the chore as routine and not necessarily painful.

"After a while it just became the normal thing to do," he said. "You'd just go in and do it because you knew you had to. There was some tightening around the eyes. It got itchy sometimes, but overall it wasn't too bad."

For the most part, the makeup was consistent with each member of the cast. There were subtle alterations, like the size of Herman's headpiece, or Lily's disappearing gray streak. Grandpa's nose extension was eliminated after the first few episodes.

"In the beginning, I was doing Al's makeup," remembers Karl Silvera. "I used to watch Al on the set and I'd

discuss things and come up with the ideas." Silvera recalls Gwynne drawing out certain features he wanted to accentuate, like using highlights to create the appearance of a rounded, bulbous, chimp-like mouth. It achieved an airbrushed, shadowing effect that photographed perfectly in black-and-white.

Remember, all of the particular colors applied to the Munster faces were strategically blended and applied—not for the amusement of the actors on the set, but for the appearance it ultimately burned on black-and-white film.

Silvera's final steps with Gwynne involved powdering his face to give his makeup some protection from periodic perspiration. His lips were outlined with black pencil, creating a wider smile than Gwynne actually possessed. (A similar trick was used to create Cesar Romero's broad happy-lips when he portrayed the Joker on TV's *Batman*, although Gwynne's appearance was not quite as pronounced.) Gwynne lastly had his fingernails painted black, and scars drawn around his wrists. In the beginning, Gwynne's hands were made to appear very hairy, but that detail was abandoned after a few episodes. Most of the time, his hands were lightly covered with a base makeup; on occasion, they were left

Veteran makeup artist Perc Westmore takes us step-by-step through Al Lewis's Munster metamorphosis. These rare stills, from Al Lewis's personal collection, illustrate how Westmore's use of shadings and highlights skillfully hollowed the actor's cheeks, elongated his nose, and created heavier jowls for a properly aging vampire. In one image (shot into the mirror) you can spot Fred Gwynne on the other side of the room undergoing his own two-hour treatment with makeup artist Karl Silvera.

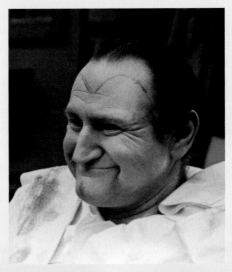

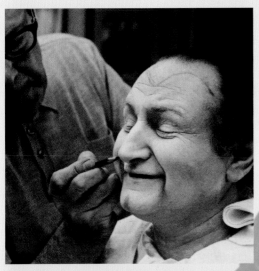

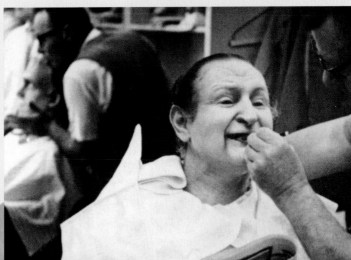

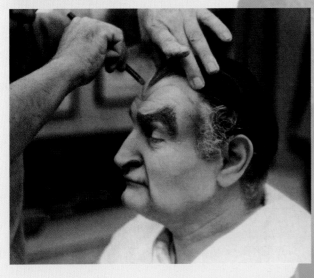

have to keep drying off his nose. I thought, *What the hell is going on here? Is he sweating through that?* And then, finally, I saw him drinking coffee. His nose was dipping into the coffee."

But that wasn't the reason the nose extension was eighty-sixed. "I'll never forget it as long as I live," Silvera says, "when someone from the front office told me we weren't going to use the nose anymore because 'he looks too Jewish.' I couldn't believe they were serious." The description infuriated Al Lewis as well, but hey, it was one less hassling detail to deal with each day.

Al Lewis was given an artificial widow's-peak overlay on his forehead, and his frilly sideburns were frosted. In the beginning, Perc Westmore played around with applying bushy sideburns to Lewis, but that was abandoned after only a couple episodes in favor of Lewis's natural hair (and the actor rarely trimmed his sideburns short since). The rest of Lewis's metamorphosis occurred with the help of greasepaints and powder. Oddly, though, bushier false sideburns were reintroduced and applied to Lewis's temples in the 1966 feature *Munster, Go Home!* No one quite knows why this alteration was made, but the new appearance proved a distraction.

Yvonne was garnished with a pallor of green and gray and a heavier green tint on the eyelids; she wore securely glued half-inch false eyelashes each day. Her swooping black brows were expertly drawn, and eyeliner and lip-lines were applied with precision. Yvonne wore a long, black, heavy Indian wig which fell to her calves and caused her headaches.

At least one or two of the makeup men were on hand during filming for touch-ups and repairs, especially after the lunch break. Gwynne attempted to keep the white powder and the makeup from flaking off onto his dark sweater during the course of the day, using bibs at lunchtime or otherwise wearing tissues around his neck, but nothing really prevented it. If you watch closely, many scenes reveal a dusting of powder on Gwynne's chest.

After many hours in front of the camera, the cast couldn't have been happier when they could at last rush to the washbasin, tear off the artificial appearance, and clear their smothering pores with a washcloth. In 1965, Gwynne told *TV Guide*: "The only problem is, I usually itch around lunchtime, especially in my nostrils. The most delightful thing is blowing my nose at the end of the day."

▲ Pat Priest is serenaded by makeup artist Karl Silvera. Look closely in the mirror behind Silvera—you can spot Al Lewis and Fred Gwynne talking.

▶ Fred enjoys a smoke while Karl Silvera picks the guitar to pass the time. "Fred played the guitar very well," says Silvera, "and he bought me one, just like his. I've still got it. We used to horse around with the guitars. We had great times."

ABOUT THE MAKEUP ARTISTS . . .

Universal Studios had the best in their makeup department. The studio, remember, was known for their expertise in the field, unleashing such classic creatures as the Phantom of the Opera, Frankenstein's monster, Dracula, the Hunchback of Notre Dame, the Wolfman, and the Creature from the Black Lagoon, just to name a few. Universal has always been monster-central in Hollywood. And like most of the major studios in Southern California, Universal had a Westmore or two.

Although Bud Westmore's name appears on the credits of all *Munsters* episodes, he did not directly work on the series. Westmore supervised Universal's makeup department at the time. The hands-on work was accomplished by four main makeup artists—Perc Westmore (Bud's brother), Karl Silvera, Abe Haberman, and Mike Westmore (apprentice and nephew of Bud and Perc)—

who took their powder and pancake and created Munsters out of actors. In the sixties, the original Westmore dynasty in the film-and-television makeup field was beginning to dim as most of the Westmore brothers were nearing retirement; and due to mounting jealousy issues among them, the brothers' fighting prevented any long-term or serious collaborations of expertise. A new generation was emerging, as young nephew Mike Westmore and several cousins began to break out of the rivalry-driven mold and step into new territory in a new age of filmmaking and television.

Abe Haberman, designated as the artist for Yvonne De Carlo and occasionally Butch Patrick and the two Marilyns, worked in film-and-TV makeup for many years before retiring in the eighties. Appearing in the field in

Yvonne De Carlo poses with some of the crew who helped maintain her ghoulish figure. Makeup artist Abe Haberman explained, "I had them print CANS OFF on my studio chair because I hated it when someone else was using my chair. I wanted others to keep their cans off my seat."

Makeup artists Karl Silvera and Perc Westmore have applied the finishing touches, and Herman and Grandpa are prepared for another day of filming. Gwynne told an interviewer in 1966: "Actually, my makeup man and I did a stint on *The Red Skelton Show*, and they wanted a very quick rehearsal to see what the makeup was like. This was in color. The makeup man said, 'Here, I'll just put the headpiece on you, slap the hair on.' Fine, fine. I went out and he looked at it on the monitor, and he said it was terribly good. 'But Karl, I've spent almost a year-and-a-half sitting in that chair for two hours a day!' He put it on in something like five minutes. It was done much better than it need have been done for black-and-white."

1933, Haberman honed his talents at Max Factor in Hollywood and was an early member of the Local 70s, the makeup-artists union. He went on to make up Gene Autry, Roy Rogers, John Wayne, Ronald Reagan, Abbott and Costello, and many other actors. In the fifties he worked as the makeup man for Abbott and Costello's television cast, later joining the long-running series *Bonanza*.

Said Haberman of *The Munsters*: "The hardest part was getting to the studio at six in the morning and being in Yvonne's dressing room. I would greet her with a smile and she'd say, 'I love what you do, but you don't have to be so damn happy in the morning doing it!' I'd say, 'Well, one of us better be.'

"Yvonne was a little difficult for other people. She fired five hairdressers. She hated the green makeup and wanted more beautifying makeup, but the network refused. When we did the feature in color, we had to use it.

"For Lily, Yvonne didn't want to wear black nails, and there wasn't any black nail polish around. So my wife Dorothy went to her manicurist, got a formula, and mixed up a black polish and tested it on her own toenails. I got some false nails and we put some polish on those and lightly glued them onto Yvonne's nails. When she'd lose them in the shots, the crew used to help me find them while production was stopped.

"It drove me a little crazy trying to keep ahead of her with those nails," said Haberman, "but she was a wonderful woman to work with, really."

Abe Haberman died on December 30, 1997 at age eighty-eight.

Karl Silvera was the artist who transformed Fred Gwynne into Herman. Silvera started in the prop department at RKO, then dressed the sets of films including *Bringing Up Baby* (1938), *Stagecoach* (1939), and *Gunga Din* (1939). After the war, Silvera began his apprenticeship with makeup and eventually landed at Paramount Studios, where he was on staff for thirteen years before moving to Universal Studios.

"People are cognizant of *The Munsters* more than any other thing I've done," says Silvera with no hint of distress. "I can name things, but *The Munsters* they know right away." Some of Silvera's favorite working experiences involve the films *Sorrowful Jones* (1949), *Fancy Pants* (1950), *Sunset Boulevard* (1950), *Julius Caesar* (1953), *White Christmas* (1954), *The Desperate Hours* (1955), and *The Night Walker* (1964). His efforts also bettered Hope and Crosby's "Road" pictures, and he applied that trophy-winning shiner to William Holden's beaten eye in *Stalag 17*. He has fond recollections of making up Sophia Loren, Barbara Stanwyck, and Humphrey Bogart, with whom he frequently played chess during breaks.

Naturally, discussing *The Munsters* leads to the trail of Westmore, and Silvera does not hesitate to speak candidly of his fellow artists. "When Bud was on my side, he was friendly," says Silvera. "And it seems like it took a turn when I asked for screen credit and more money. A little recognition. Bud got mad. A lot of things I did over there at Universal, Bud liked to stand up and have his picture taken with them, like he'd done it. That happened for years, until we started getting recognition for what we did. That happened after *The Munsters.*"

For years following the show, Silvera kept in touch with his pal, Fred Gwynne. It was Gwynne who requested Silvera step out of retirement and personally

apply his makeup for the TV reunion movie *The Munsters' Revenge*. Silvera's final work included doing makeup for the 1982 films *Two of a Kind* and *Personal Best* and for six seasons of TV's *Falcon Crest*. Now in his eighties, Silvera is retired from the greasepaint biz, and regards his time with the Munster crew as some of his favorite memories.

The Westmores of Hollywood: The Westmores were comprised of six brothers: Monte, Perc, Bud, Wally, Ern, and Frank. Their father, George Westmore, began as a wigmaker in Europe. Originally from England, the Westmore family immigrated to the United States in 1909 and settled in the Los Angeles area in 1916, where George became a makeup artist on silent films at MGM. He died in 1931, and the sons carried on the craft, dominating the profession for more than half a century.

Son **Perc Westmore** started young, learning to be a wigmaker while going to school. He helped his father in the various wig shops and salons he operated. By age fourteen, Perc (pronounced "purse," short for Percival) was a skilled wigmaker and employed by the Paris Hair

Perc Westmore shows his handiwork, the result of the two-hour routine transforming Al Lewis into Grandpa.

Company and Hepner's. Later, at Maison Cesare, Perc experimented in the fields of cosmetology and makeup. He painstakingly developed his talents and honed his natural ability. In 1923, Perc conceived the first makeup department of the First National Studios, which later consolidated with Warner Bros. For the next thirty years, Perc was under personal contract to Jack Warner, working with First National and serving as head of the makeup department at Warners. He became a respected name in the business, just like his brothers.

Perc Westmore entered into an agreement with the Max Factor Company in 1929 (with consent from Warner Bros.) whereby he served for six years as an advisor. Many revolutionary improvements in the cosmetic and wig fields were the result of his years there. The hair-lace feature of wig-making was created by Perc, for instance. One of his most impressive contributions was the founding of the Hollywood Art School of Makeup.

Perc's abilities to draw, sketch, and paint, combined with his knowledge of sculpting, served him well in creating character makeup and hairstyles. Like most of the Westmores, Perc had his fans, like Bette Davis, who loved his artistry and how he made her look on film. Perc became an authority on feminine beauty techniques, and proved he could apply his knowledge to other businesses. Working in conjunction with his brothers, he founded both the House of Westmore, a beauty salon that operated from the mid-thirties to 1965, and a House of Westmore cosmetics company. At age sixty, Perc was urged out of retirement by his brother, Bud, and assigned to do makeup on *The Munsters*, specifically Al Lewis.

"There are makeup people who didn't work if they wronged Perc," says his nephew, Mike. "Perc was a powerful guy in the business. Very creative and nice, but you didn't cross him. He was a tidy guy. I remember he used to wear these white suits and never got anything on them."

Perc, like his brother Ern, was a drinker, and it became a hindrance in his life and undoubtedly at work. Perc was eventually relieved of his duties with Warner Bros. He had worked on many films in his career, most notably *A Midsummer Night's Dream* (1935), *The Private Lives of Elizabeth and Essex* (1939), *Casablanca* (1943), and *Mildred Pierce* (1945). *The Munsters* kept Perc busy during a fragile period in his life, and he put in some fine artistry on the show. Perc's final work was on the 1970 Kirk Douglas film *There Was a Crooked Man*. He died on September 30, 1970.

"Perc and I got to know each other later in life," says Karl Silvera, who worked with or knew four of the Westmore brothers. "When Perc was fired from Warner Brothers, he lost his confidence. He kept getting lower because nobody would hire him. One of those things. He even tried to commit suicide a couple of times. Bud put him in the studio and I was on good terms with Bud at the time. Bud asked if I would mind if Perc would 'work here with you' and I told him, 'Hell, no, I don't mind.' In the beginning, I was doing Grandpa's makeup as well."

"I loved Perc," Silvera says. "He was one of the finest people I ever knew, and probably one of the most talented. I only wish I had known him earlier because he was, without a doubt, one of the most creative people I'd ever seen. We had great times together."

Perc's equally talented brothers all carved out niches in the industry as well. Monte, who worked in the field for just a few years, contributed to makeup on *Gone With the Wind*. Monte died early on, in 1940. Ernest "Ern" Westmore, a longtime film makeup man, died in 1968. Wally Westmore served as Director of Makeup for Paramount Studio for many years. His first films, *Dr. Jekyll and Mr. Hyde* (1932) and *Island of Lost Souls* (1933), featured some innovative makeup and film techniques. Wally built a strong reputation in Hollywood and worked on more than 300 motion pictures. He died in 1973. Brother Bud (real name: Hamilton) was affiliated with 20th Century-Fox and then Universal, eventually becoming the latter studio's makeup supervisor. Bud's impressive credits include *Abbott and Costello Meet Frankenstein* (1948), *Creature from the Black Lagoon* (1954), Jimmy Cagney's *Man of a Thousand Faces* (1957), and *Spartacus* (1960). Just days following Wally's death, Bud died too, with 1973's *Soylent Green* proving his final film work. Frank began in the forties, and eventually contributed to a long line of films including epics like *The Ten Commandments* (1956). Frank, the quiet one, who had worked in films and with the art school early on, put the story of the family down on paper in his 1976 book *The Westmores of Hollywood*. The last surviving member of the Westmore brothers, Frank, died in 1985.

"If they had stuck together, they would be as big as any cosmetic company today," Karl Silvera surmises. "They just couldn't pull together, and they competed against each other. At times, they'd stick together; then they'd go back to fighting." Despite the rivalry and bitter betrayals between the famous brothers over the years, the

Makeup artist Mike Westmore measures the ears on the life-cast molded directly from Butch Patrick's head.

Westmores collectively launched a tradition of excellence that anchored the beginnings of Hollywood filmmaking.

Mike Westmore, son of Monte Westmore, was in his late twenties when he began working with his uncle, Perc Westmore, on *The Munsters* and *McHale's Navy*. Mike's duties were to make up Butch Patrick and sometimes Beverley Owen or Pat Priest.

Butch Patrick's makeup was nothing extraordinary: greasepaint, ears, and the widow's peak overlay on his forehead. "I remember having my legs and knees painted with wet body paint," Patrick says, "and it was cold some mornings getting that stuff painted on you."

Recalls Mike Westmore: "Every morning while I was gluing on Butch's ears, we'd talk about what was going on in our lives and such. I was like a big brother to him. I also worked in the lab on the new makeup pieces for the next day's work, and on any new materials needed for productions. Butch loved to watch that.

"I think that Al and Fred got one hundred dollars extra because of their extensive makeup jobs. Back then that was a pretty good bonus, besides their salary. They'd order steak for breakfast from the commissary, and other foods that the commissary wouldn't ordinarily have. The kitchen had problems running smoothly because of Fred and Al, I remember."

Mike Westmore has worked at Universal ever since, creating some extraordinary makeup visions for megahits like *Raging Bull* (1980), *First Blood* (1982), *Rocky* (*I, II, III, V*), and *Mask* (1985), for which he took home an Academy Award in the newly established Best Makeup category. Westmore has supervised all of the *Star Trek* television series since 1992.

The Westmores of Hollywood have left an impressive beauty mark—and a few scars, too—in the field of makeup for films and television; and a more cohesive, family-oriented version of the tradition continues today with another generation of the famous family.

KILLING TIME

IN TELEVISION, MUCH LIKE MOTION PICTURE PRO-duction, a lot of time is consumed waiting for a scene to be prepared by the crew and all of the elements assembled and readied for the moment it's put it on film. What to do with the extra time?

Fred Gwynne spent what little time he had (he was virtually in eighty-five percent of the scenes) physically relaxing in his oversized wooden chair—upright, so as not to damage the makeup. Or he did things that were soothing to him, like doodling. Gwynne brought giant artists pads and pencils and pens with him sometimes and sat and quietly sketched out these odd concepts swimming around his mind's eye. Sometimes he'd stand isolated, with the pad held like a nurse with a clipboard, sketching . . . looking. Looking. Sketching. People gathered sometimes, marveling at his style and ease in drawing, but Gwynne could be shy with his talents, outwardly anyway.

Gwynne was known to just approach people he worked with on the set and ask to draw them, in caricature, just to do it. And then he'd apply his signature at the bottom and hand it to them as a gift. He could create inspired, well-executed cartoons, worthy of ink in the *New Yorker*. The artwork was a deep-seeded passion for Gwynne, who truly took his talents to task and doodled often to keep his skills sharp—usually enjoying it and the expressions of those he would share it with. Gwynne knew he had a specialty in capturing just the right curves when drawing people's profiles. Loved unconventional profiles, like his own. He told *TV Guide:* "If I doodle on the sides of my script, I remember the doodles, not my lines."

One visitor to the set was reporter Gene Handsaker, who caught a glimpse of Munsters for a day while working on an Associated Press story. In it, he's fixated on Al Lewis, sitting quietly by himself off camera on the wooden electric chair, munching on sunflower seeds. Lewis, Gwynne, and De Carlo routinely gave interviews on the set because the atmosphere was a stunner, an impressive background that intrigued every outsider. Or they went to the commissary to get gawked at. De Carlo had a couple of eateries near Universal Studios who accommodated her wacky looks with a quiet table during lunches and noontime interviews with reporters.

Al Lewis was a social type, joking opposite Gwynne most of the time, triggering each other into hysterics. But for this pair, the task of creating comedy on film was taken seriously, and the result is something unique in television. Al Lewis sometimes headed outside the soundstage on a sunny day and tossed a baseball with Butch Patrick. Once a Frisbee tournament got going with some of the cast members. Butch Patrick remembers flashes of things like that.

"I spent a lot of time in the makeup department," says Butch Patrick. "Most of the makeup men were free during the day. I'd spend time in the lab making rubber masks and designing new stuff."

◄ Butch, Al, and Beverley try to entertain themselves in between scenes.

▼ Beverley Owen was one to knit while waiting to film her scenes. Here she enlists the help of Fred Gwynne.

Patrick was like a kid let loose in a candy store. The Universal lot was a vast play land for someone his age and for a while he was the studio mascot. Patrick scaled the hill to the *Psycho* house and explored the haunting shell that stood stately atop a little Universal back-lot bluff. "I wandered everywhere," he says. "Makeup and all."

When Patrick wasn't in a scene or rehearsing, much of his time was spent on schoolwork with his teacher, Eleanor Petrie. "I think kid actors have it harder than adults do because their time is always taken," Patrick says.

Beverley Owen and Pat Priest (who succeeded Owen as Marilyn) coincidentally both used to knit while waiting to be called for their scenes. "I used to do little sewing projects or talk with guests on the show, or my stand-in, Marilyn Bell. I was a great talker," Priest says. Priest's soft, sexy voice could sometimes be a friendly alternative to Gwynne's loud boisterous tones and Al Lewis's wonderful wheezy cackle that dominated the volume levels on the soundstage.

Oh, to have been a spider on the wall just once.

Munsters on the Mend

Rarely was the cast asked to perform stunts which could endanger them. They were too valuable to the show's quaint cast. Besides, that's what stunt persons were for. The special effects—especially those involving fire and smoke bombs and dropping beams—were well orchestrated by the crew and the cast for safety. Considering the amount of gags in the show, the set ended up being a safe one to be around.

Fred Gwynne had a double throughout the series named Bill Foster (who adopted the professional name Jefferson County). Foster took a few pratfalls for Gwynne when the camera angles warranted. Many times, however, both Fred Gwynne and Al Lewis performed their own faintings or knockouts where they fell straight on their faces or backward without a bend in their bodies.

For these instances, there were protective mattresses placed on the floor for the actors, but occasionally an actor would land wrong and bruise his noggin.

"I took a few lumps in the show. I had a couple things happen to me accidentally," says Butch Patrick. "I bounced off a few lights one time when I was yanked through the ceiling. They had me not do dangerous stuff, but minor, minor things.

"One time, in that episode where Herman and Grandpa built me a go-cart ("A House Divided"), I'm supposed to fall into a pit outside the garage. Well, after I fell in I was standing in the pit and Fred and Al rushed over to see what happened and they kicked about a pound of dirt right into my eyes. They caught me with my eyes wide open and packed my eyes with dirt. So I had to go to the hospital to get my eyes washed out."

Hours later, Butch returned to the set. "My teacher said, 'Well, I guess you won't have to do any homework tonight.' I just thought to myself, 'Wow, what a lady.'"

Al Lewis remembered the episode in which Grandpa turned into a bat and infiltrated a sorority house to rescue Herman. "I jumped down from a perch where Grandpa turns back from a bat into a human," he said, "but someone forgot to put the mattress down. They put a cover down but no mattress, and I scraped the side rail of the bed on my shinbone. It wasn't too bad, but boy it was painful."

A rare photograph of Fred Gwynne and his stand-in/stunt-double Bill Foster, who worked under the professional name Jefferson County.

OGRE HERE, OGRE THERE

A SPECIAL APPEARANCE BY ANY OF THE CAST MEM-bers was an extraordinary experience, because this was not simply someone with a mask on . . . it was Herman Munster, in full regalia, shaking your hands and taking pictures. The in-makeup personal appearances were a rarity because of the time and effort involved in preparation, so Fred Gwynne was not fond of the duties. And because he was the show's star, he got wrangled into it more than he preferred. Al Lewis, who toured with Gwynne much of the time, had a little more fun with the job, and no doubt, eased Gwynne's pain while in tow. Makeup man Karl Silvera boasts about the royal treatment he received—insisted on by Gwynne and Lewis—when he was brought along to prepare the cast.

"Kids were usually afraid of monsters, but Fred made his character into a big, lovable oaf. At personal appearances, kids couldn't wait to meet him," says Silvera. "On all the appearances, I was hired to go along to make him up so he looked the same. One time, I made up Fred and Al on the plane going to Seattle. We had a plane full of reporters who watched. When we landed, the actors stepped off the plane made up for the network's appearance tour."

All of the cast made appearances to hype the show, and even visited children's hospitals and participated in charity events. That was one of Al's favorite things. The cast made appearances on other TV programs, like Al and Butch on Art Linkletter's *Hollywood Talent Scouts*,

▲ Fred films a cereal commercial.

▶ Fred Gwynne does his patriotic part in hawking U.S. Savings Bonds for Uncle Sam in July 1964.

which took place onstage at the Hollywood Bowl with the Munster Koach revving up behind them.

The award for the most unique personalized promotion of the show might go to Yvonne De Carlo: during the show's run the actress proudly sported around the Los Angeles highways in a customized black Jaguar Mark X. "It has coffin rails on the tope and spider-web hubcaps and handles on the back of the boot. Of course they call it a trunk here," she described to a reporter in 1966. "It has a Lily Dracula crest on the side which I designed, and a lovely vampire wolf on the front of the car."

De Carlo hired George Barris, who designed the show's autos, to transform her own personal wheels. "Yvonne was the one who really had fun with the part once she got going with the series," says the famed car-customizer George Barris. "We put some intricate Munster detailing on the car, and she loved to parade around town in her own personalized Munstermobile."

Fred Gwynne couldn't possibly fulfill the amount of requests that came in for personal appearances, and remained selective with regard to these duties. Connelly and Mosher wanted to squeeze many more personal appearance dates out of him, but Gwynne reserved his energies and refused. His hesitance mainly was the time and effort it took to get into makeup for such extra appearances and pushed his makeup artist Karl Silvera to skimp and invent shortcuts with the facial appliances when possible. Gwynne, however, found it fun to work on variety shows and agreed to perform regular sketches as well as Herman Munster sketches with Red Skelton, on his show, and a particular favorite to Gwynne was his appearances on *The Danny Kaye Show*. In addition, the cast participated in commercials for Cheerios and in spots plugging a U.S. Savings Bond campaign. Not all of the promotions went off flawlessly.

In November 1964, *The Munsters* was the hot new television show and the network specifically invited Gwynne and Lewis to fly to New York and ride in the Macy's Thanksgiving Day Parade, on the back of the Munster Koach, no less. George Barris had the vehicle flown to the Big Apple and drove the vehicle in the parade route, and makeup man Karl Silvera was brought along.

Perched up in the back riser of the Munster Koach, out there exposed to the elements, Gwynne and Lewis greeted the crowds which lined the city streets . . . *their* city, mind you. It took a lot of energy for Gwynne to do this, and required special nerve medicine, so Gwynne prepared. Karl Silvera recalls the event.

"Oh God, the Macy's parade." Silvera can't help but laugh out loud. "I was in the Koach handling the loudspeaker and radio

Pat Priest posed for a series of auto-magazine layouts featuring the Munster Koach . . . but who noticed the car?

The Munsters were riding a wave of popularity at the 1964 Macy's Thanksgiving Day Parade in New York City. This photo was taken as George Barris steered the Munster Koach (with makeup artist Karl Silvera riding shotgun) past Macy's department store on 34th Street.

Fred Gwynne and Edie Adams joined Danny Kaye on his popular CBS variety show in the sixties.

Kaye, a fan of *The Munsters*, loved having Fred Gwynne as a guest on his show. Gwynne was frequently invited to appear on the myriad of variety shows in the sixties, but there were strings attached. Everyone wanted Herman Munster in the deal, too.

system that was playing the Munster song. Fred had brought along a bottle with him, wrapped in a paper bag, and he got fractured. And Al was mad at him. Fred was cussin' at people. I just kept the music up so nobody could hear him.

"We turned the corner there at Macy's," Silvera recalls. "And there was the media box with, I think it was Betty White and Lorne Greene up there describing the parade. Fred looks up at the camera and yells 'F—k you!' We told him this later on, when he was sobered up and he was so embarrassed. I thought Betty White and Lorne Greene were gonna fall off the platform. But I have to admit, it was funny."

TV Guide hinted at the Macy's escapade when they featured Gwynne in a cover piece: "This time, [Gwynne] came properly fortified for the chill and the children. He waved to throngs on both sides of Broadway with one hand while taking slugs from a bottle concealed in a paper bag that he clutched in the other hand. 'I had to get bombed so I could say hello to the little kiddies for forty blocks,' he explains."

Needless to say, Al Lewis was more receptive to in-makeup appearances than the rest of the cast, and directly after the series premiered, he made promo appearances around the country at press conferences for local affiliates. His stops included the National Association of Broadcasters convention in Chicago and the annual St. Paul Winter Carnival. If kids were involved in the press events, Al could count on being swarmed.

But it was the Munster home base which topped them all. During the Munster years at Universal, the studios began treating vacationers and tourists to southern California with something extraordinary when they introduced an unparalleled studio tour. The attraction became Hollywood's newest theme-park event, which, during one portion, transports you through the back lot on a driven line of trams. Remembers Butch Patrick: "When the trams drove by, they actually took precedence over the filming. We'd have to stop and wait for them to go by. Sometimes we'd go over and shake hands with the tourists and sign a few autographs. They were always thrilled with that."

On a CBS publicity tour, Al Lewis steps off the plane camera-ready. In the foreground is *Gilligan's Island* star Jim Backus and Bill Bixby from *My Favorite Martian*.

▲ The Universal Studios tour in 1965 took guests on a trip down Mockingbird Lane.

◀ This must've been a bizarre sight: Having lunch in the studio commissary with Fred Gwynne and Al Lewis is their former *Car 54* costar, Charlotte Rae, and famed British actor Harry Secombe.

Teammates from the Los Angeles Rams visit the set in January 1965.

Exhibiting the Munsters at the Studio took on a new meaning once when a gang of tourists were being escorted around the studio. The tourists took home a real treat. "Swede Munden was Al's wardrobe man," remembers Karl Silvera. "Al was in his dressing room outside on the back lot, and Swede says, 'I gotta go get something.' Well Al had all of his top on, and didn't have anything else on except shoes and socks, and this long shirt. So he bent over doing something, or picking something up off the floor and all of a sudden he hears laughing and he turns around. The door to the dressing room is wide open. Al hasn't got any pants on and his ass is bare. I asked him what he did and he said, 'I turned around and waved.' You couldn't embarrass Al. Nothing bothered him."

That fact never became more apparent than during the nineties when Al Lewis made several appearances on the controversial Howard Stern radio show. At one New York City rally protesting constraints imposed by the Federal Communications Commission, an angry Lewis grabbed the microphone from Stern and shouted "F—k the FCC! F—k 'em!" Well, there's something to be said about free speech and the medium of television, and where we have all landed after several decades of domination by the tube.

MUNSTER MOMENT

In 1991, radio shock-jock Howard Stern dispatched his stooge Stuttering John (John Melendez, now the *Tonight Show* announcer) to a New York art exhibition featuring the work of Fred Gwynne. As was the trend, Stern's typical goal was to instigate a scene in any way possible and pose the most embarrassing questions. With a cassette recorder in hand, Stuttering John cornered Gwynne and began asking him if he thought Van Gogh ever dressed up like Frankenstein's monster. "Do you sign your artwork 'Fred Gwynne' or 'Herman Munster'?" he kept pestering. Gwynne politely declined to comment.

Decades after the show left primetime, the surviving cast members of *The Munsters* were still in great demand for personal appearances, especially during that mad month of October. Jay Leno, a fan of *The Munsters*, flew Al Lewis out from New York to Los Angeles for a special Halloween appearance on *The Tonight Show* and the pair teamed up for a hilarious sketch. In the nineties, Butch Patrick surprised Yvonne De Carlo on the daytime *Vickie!* show, hosted by Vickie Lawrence. Unimpressed, De Carlo actually showed little to no emotion about being reunited with her little Eddie now all grown up. "That wasn't one of our better reunions," Patrick admitted.

Even today, wherever George Barris tours and exhibits the Munster Koach—whether it is a car show or a nostalgia convention—it's an awesome crowd pleaser. At Universal Studios, where the immensely popular tour continues today with more adventure than ever, the overhauled Munster house still sits comfortably on Colonial Street, however recognized more these days as an integral part of the impressive *Desperate Housewives* real estate known as Wisteria Lane. Despite the fresh paint and manicured grounds around the property, it is still a highly recognized Munster attraction for fans on the tour. It might as well be the *Psycho* house on the hill, it's that popular and recognized by sight. Cameras click away every time, mementos for visitors of Universal's back lot to share when they return home. The stately Munster abode remains a pearl on the studio's back lot and tourists still point and gawk. Let's just pray it never suffers the same fate as Gilligan's lagoon (now a parking lot) at CBS studios in the San Fernando Valley just a few miles away.

The Munsters were unlikely guests at Marineland of the Pacific, with one "porpoise" in mind—a new pet for Eddie. Fred Gwynne expressed to a reporter his initial hesitation to appear on this aquatic TV special unless the storyline was good. "Just so we don't look like monkeys in funny clothes pulled in from left field," he said. The Easter Sunday holiday TV special, titled "Marineland Carnival," aired in color April 18, 1965 on CBS.

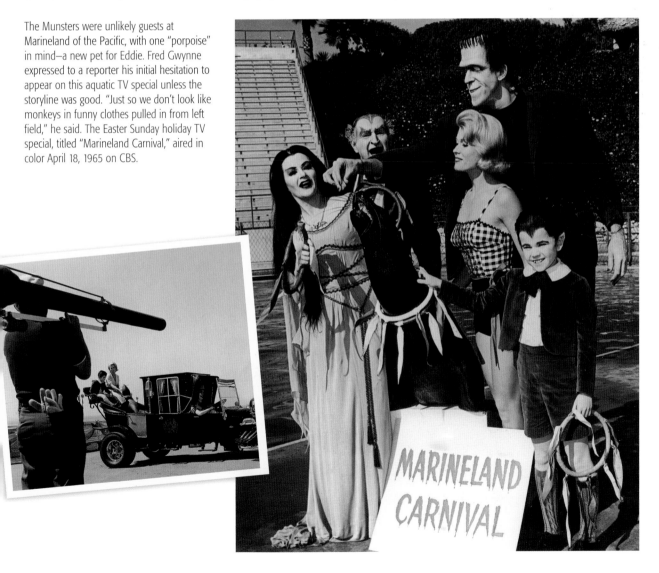

THE MORE THE MARILYN

"I do not believe we should push Marilyn's romance along. . . . If Marilyn's clock of romance has begun to tick, it does not behoove us to over-wind her mainspring."

—HERMAN MUNSTER

FROM CONCEPTION MARILYN MUNSTER WAS A blooper. At least her name was. (Who would dare steal the initials of Marilyn Monroe?) As the *Munsters* episodes explain, this "poor unfortunate" freak in the Munster clan, is the daughter of Lily's sister. If that is her heritage, then her last name would not be Munster. Herman and Lily never spoke of adoption.

Regardless of her origin, Uncle Herman and Aunt Lily—being the kindhearted ghouls they are—took the family embarrassment under their wing when she was but a child and gave her a loving and supportive home.

Marilyn is the family enigma. She can't understand why she fails to build a relationship with the opposite sex. Plenty of men look but never touch—because they get a glance at the rest of the family. Lily plays Yente the matchmaker, while Grandpa assists the young lass with his potions and magic. Still, nothing works.

Still, Marilyn is the sweet cousin, the gentle, thoughtful, beautiful cousin always in optimistic spirits. The Marilyn prototype is blond, stands about five-foot-six, and is approximately eighteen to college age, although this fluctuated over the years. "I think Marilyn thought she was ugly, too," says Beverley Owen, who originated the role. "That's how the family saw her. Wholesome is what they tried for in Marilyn. *The Munsters* is a lot like that *Sesame Street* song, 'It's Not Easy Being Green.' You may not look like your neighbors, but at heart, we're all the same. I think it's fascinating. Someone could do a real study of history on how Marilyn has evolved."

The role was originally played perfectly straight, just the way it should have been. Beverley Owen, a competent television actress with a rising career in television and theater on the East Coast, created the role in the pilot and the show's first batch of episodes. Just prior to being cast in *The Munsters*, Owen had appeared on TV's *Wagon Train*, *The Virginian*, and *Kraft Mystery Theatre*, and a motion picture entitled *Bullet for a Badman*. Soon after, she was put under contract to Universal Studios. Owen was featured in a February 1964 *TV Guide* profile, wherein she admitted she'd be happiest staying and working in New York rather than the West Coast. "California already has plenty of Iowans," she told *TV Guide*, "but it has no New England and no New York Giants football team." And then, the *Munsters* entered her life and everything turned it upside down for her.

When she arrived in California, she and Fred Gwynne's family all had rooms at the Park View Hotel. Soon thereafter, Fred Gwynne and his wife rented a large house in Los Angeles and Beverley shared the house with them, "chipping in on the rent," she says. Beverley also helped baby-sit Fred and Foxy's children on weekends. "I'm the motherly sort," she says. "I loved working with Butch Patrick. He was a sweet kid. I took him to Grauman's Chinese Theatre to see *Mary Poppins* when it first came out. I think it was his first 'big date.'"

The Munsters got rolling and every day seemed a drudgery for Owen, but she says she tried to make the best of it, constantly calling her fiancé back in New York at every chance. Owen says she recalls one day's shooting in particular. "It was my most truthful acting," she laughs. "They were shooting a scene where I was asleep ["Sleeping Cutie"] and it was right after a rather large

lunch. It was a hot day. It takes a while to set up the shot and shoot it, you know. I fell asleep for about an hour laying there on that slab. Al said he wanted to be the one to wake me—something devious I'm sure. Talk about your method actors."

Owen went to work every day very early each morning with Fred Gwynne, all the while discussing her unhappiness with her costar in the car to and from work. The press printed many rumors about the actress's discontent, but Owen says she does not regret her choice in the end. Beverley Owen explained her entire ordeal in a 1988 interview:

About a year before *The Munsters*, an agent named Eleanor Kilgallen (Dorothy Kilgallen's sister), who was the East Coast Universal talent recruiter, saw me on a *Camera Three* TV episode. They flew me out and I had to sign this seven-year contract. Oh, I should've gotten a lawyer. My agent said, "Don't worry, we have good lawyers!" Sure, for *them*. I asked what would happen if I wanted to get married and have children, something

While filming this scene, Beverley Owen actually dozed off waiting for the shot to be set up and filmed.

that I figured would be happening in my future. They said that because that was an act of God, I could then get out of my contract. Totally untrue. They told me anything so I'd sign.

I kept commuting for about a year between New York and Los Angeles and I got leads on *Wagon Train*, *The Virginian*, and some other shows. The more I saw of Hollywood, the more I hated it. I thought I had done something really stupid.

Then Monique James called and said [Universal Studios] had a pilot that they wanted me to do. I told her I didn't want to live in California. She said, "Just do the pilot and we'll talk about it later."

I remember doing the pilot test. On the next sound-stage I was getting ready to do the test and I picked up the phone and called Wayne Rogers. He was a friend of mine. He said, "Don't blow that screen test. If you ever want to work in this business again, go in and do the best you can." So I got into the wig and I did the test and I couldn't have cared less. I wasn't nervous. The edge was off and I guess I did well.

When Monique called me at the end of June and told me they picked up the pilot, I told her no, I didn't want

to do it. She said, "Well, we couldn't have you doing the pilot in tears, could we? You be out here on this date or we'll sue you."

I saw a lawyer about it and it was decided to go ahead and do it while we were working on getting out of it. The studio could have sued me.

I was terribly unhappy doing the show. You can bet I was a lot of fun to work with, bursting into tears and running to the ladies room constantly. I kept talking to Joe Connelly about it, since he dealt with people more. Mosher was more in the background. Joe, however, kept putting me off.

After a couple months of this, I walked into Connelly's office one day and tried to tell him how I felt, and I just came apart at the seams. I sat there sobbing and he stared at me and said, "You really wanna go back and marry that man, don't you? You don't want to do this show, do you?" He assumed that I wanted more money.

So he told me to finish up the thirteen weeks and I'd be gone.

Beverley Owen's hair color was actually light brown, but she was asked to wear blond wigs for the series.

MUNSTER MOMENT

When a tearful Beverley Owen was reluctant to test for the Munsters series, out of desperation she called her friend and fellow actor, Wayne Rogers, for advice. Thirteen years later, Rogers (fresh from *M*A*S*H*) filmed a movie titled *It Happened One Christmas* at the Munster house with costar Marlo Thomas.

It appears that Marilyn Munster was to be patterned after Marilyn Monroe. "I think they were certainly trying to go after that image," professes Owen. "They tried for the look. I think I was more of a cross between Marilyn Monroe and Sandra Dee."

Owen usually wore a headband with a blond wig, since in reality she was a brunette with long straight hair.

"That wig with the headband is one that Doris Day wore in the movie *Pillow Talk*, they told me. Most of the time I wasn't recognized outside the show because of the wig," she says.

After Owen completed her thirteen episodes, she packed her bags and returned to New York, determined to never look back. (That number of episodes might seem superstitiously unlucky, but for Owen it meant good fortune.) "Some newspapers or magazines reported that I left the show because of migraines," Owen laughs.

"I'm not sorry about leaving the show," Owen admits. "Unfortunately, like a lot of other marriages, after ten years we ended up separating and getting a divorce, which I *am* sorry about. But I have two fantastic daughters, Kate and Polly, who are my best friends in the world."

Actress Pat Priest quietly assumed the role of Marilyn in the first season.

Pat Priest and Fred Gwynne share a laugh
on the set as they page through a new
Munsters pocket paperback.

Meanwhile, in order to fill the role, producers Connelly and Mosher took a week and searched and tested girls who resembled Owen. The hunt led them as far as beautiful young actress Pat Priest. Until a decision had been made, the search was kept low-key and the transition was to be just as quiet and smooth as possible. Producer Bob Mosher told *TV Guide* in April 1965: "Ten girls tested for the part of Marilyn. We chose Pat Priest because she had a matter-of-fact, utterly composed manner that we needed for Marilyn, who, after all, has to remain unmoved by her weird surroundings."

Writer Erskine Johnson reported on the ol' switch-the-actor-in-the-middle-of-the-show trick and interviewed both the producer Joe Connelly and the new choice to assume the role of Marilyn, Pat Priest. The new Marilyn was a sexy twenty-eight-year-old at the time, a mother of two, and an actress anxious to delve more into television.

"Producer Connelly made the switch to avoid a fight with Beverley over her performances," wrote Johnson in his January 1965 news story. "She reportedly was bored with the role and eager to give up her acting career for marriage." Connelly confessed that due to Owen's attitude, the character had been subdued, but since Priest was enthusiastic about the role, the character would hence take on a new importance.

Unfortunately, that never really materialized. Not to the liking of Pat Priest, anyway, who would have loved to have played the role with more depth and been given more activity in the scripts.

"I had never seen the *Munsters* show, so I had no idea what the role or Beverley was like," says actress Pat Priest today. "When I tested, they put me in one of Beverley's dresses. I tested on Wednesday, signed on Thursday, rehearsed on Friday, and started on Monday. It was that quick. The only other girl I remember testing was Linda Foster who'd been married to Vince Edwards."

The swap was made and the public was none the wiser. Priest's height, weight, and even her voice were similar to the Marilyn Munster image already instilled. Priest finished the first year and promptly signed for the second, having enjoyed the work so much.

"The role didn't require any great acting ability to say, 'Gee Uncle Herman' or 'But what are we gonna do now, Aunt Lily?' No training or schooling for that—it took blond hair," Priest says. "The character really had nowhere to go. Occasionally they'd have an episode centered around me or something I did. But basically it was just reactions. Just standing, looking, and reacting."

After six months in the role, Priest was getting a little restless and jokingly told the *L.A. Times* in June 1965: "Usually I am stuck with paisley prints, checks, and stripes," said Pat Priest. "I've worn so many full skirts, you'd think I had a hip problem. I'm not allowed to wear any solid colors—nothing that might outline the figure. Sweaters? Are you kidding? I'm not allowed to wear anything that might be the least bit sexy."

Priest, an actress hungry for experience, fit right in with the cast and finished out the second year smoothly. Her innocence was perfectly played in the series by Priest, who knew how to restrain the performance enough and not go over the top. That was for Gwynne and Lewis. "It's an education to be working every day with three pros," she told a reporter at the first season's end.

All was well until midway through the second season, when the announcement of the motion-picture production of *Munster, Go Home!* was made. Naturally, the entire cast looked forward to the film's production and the chance to shoot in color. Slated for filming at the end of the second season, the movie was inspired by the popularity of television show, a successful stunt the studio had pulled with *McHale's Navy*. At first it was to be a television movie, but later the decision was made to make it a big-screen feature. Universal Studios naturally signed the principals to act in the new color feature film—strangely, all except Priest.

"Someone came on the set and informed me in front of everybody that they weren't going to use me in the movie," Priest says. "That really hurt me. I was devastated. Here I'd played the part for almost two years and they decided I was too old. They wanted to use a young contract player, Debbie Watson. What a slap in the face . . . and the way they did it, too.

"Al [Lewis] consoled me. He was the comforting one, explaining how the business can be cruel sometimes. All that stuff. By then I just wanted to be out of Universal. Get out of there altogether."

Universal handed actress Debbie Watson the part. Watson was a perky eighteen-year-old who had starred in a couple of short-lived television series, *Karen* (1964) and *Tammy* (1965), when she was given the role of Marilyn for the feature film. Both Priest and Owen were well into their twenties when they worked on the show, but the studio decided they needed an even younger beauty for the feature to grab the attention of the teenage demographic.

After all these years, it's amazing that the two actresses who portrayed Marilyn in the series, Beverley Owen and Pat Priest, have yet to meet. "Can you believe it?" says Pat Priest says today. "Beverley and I have never met. Isn't that funny? You'd think some show would have brought us together or surprised us by now."

Postscript

After the movie's release in 1966, the Munsters retired and were not heard from again until 1981, when Universal gathered the cast for a television reunion movie titled *The Munsters' Revenge*. Producers signed Gwynne, Lewis, and De Carlo to reenact the roles they had created, and despite the ages of the principal three, the characters of Eddie and Marilyn would be timeless. Neither Butch Patrick nor any of the previous three actresses who played Marilyn were asked to return. Instead they chose child-actor K.C. Martel, an Eddie look-alike, and actress Jo McDonnell as Marilyn.

McDonnell, noticeably older than the character in the original series, was adequate as Marilyn, but she played the role with a little more spice and allure, than her straight-laced predecessors. "In the TV movie, [McDonnell] was blatantly sexy, with long blond hair," observed Beverley Owen.

After another several-year hiatus for the Munsters, MCA, in conjunction with the Arthur Company, decided to re-create the Munsters in the new 1988 series called *The Munsters Today*. It surprisingly survived through three seasons, producing sixty-six episodes that were not received well with fans. Marilyn was played smartly by teen beauty Hillary Van Dyke, the niece of entertainer Dick Van Dyke.

In 1995, the Fox Network revived the family once again in a Halloween TV movie, *Here Come the Munsters*, which featured actress Christine Taylor as Marilyn. Fans of *The Brady Bunch* can recall Taylor as a mirror image of Maureen McCormick's Marcia in the bizarre big-screen re-creation, *The Brady Bunch Movie*. (Taylor later married actor Ben Stiller.) Fox ushered in another holiday Munsters TV movie the next year, with *The Munsters' Scary Little Christmas*, with Elaine Hendrix in the role of Marilyn.

GRANDPA'S POTIONS

"Oh Grandpa, why can't you experiment on white mice, like any other normal mad scientist?"
—LILY MUNSTER

Only once did Grandpa resort to the most powerful weapon known in hypnotism . . . the Transylvanian Brain Freezer. To cure Herman's hiccups, Grandpa puts Herman in a trance. "I learned it from Svengali when the poor fella was down and out. I got it from him for a cup of coffee and a sweet roll," Grandpa says.

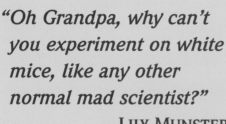

LOVE POTION

A Recipe *From Grandpa*

To give speed to Eddie's athletics

Form: Vitamin pill

Ingredients:

A derby flown in from Kentucky

A feather from the world's fastest bird, the ostrich

A bit of lint from the pouch of a kangaroo

A bit of greased lightning (from Grandpa's fingertips) to top it off

Notes: Success. But after one pill, Eddie only pretended to take the doses and hid the pills because they taste awful.

A Recipe *From Grandpa*

To improve Eddie's trumpet playing

Form: Liquid, slipped into his lemonade

Ingredients:

Three strands of Leonard Bernstein's favorite sauerkraut

A glass of water from the "Blue Danube"

One chopped photograph of Ludwig van Beethoven

Stein o' beer from the "Whiffenpoof song"

A bucket of bilge water from the HMS Pinafore

Notes: Success (though brief). The second batch was not made correctly and Eddie turned into a jazz-playing hep cat. ("Cool, man. Like what's groovin', Daddy-o?")

Items in the Chest

- Rabbit's foot carried by General Custer
- Mother's Day card from Lizzie Borden
- Compass off the Titanic
- Radio direction finder (transistorized)

Assorted Spells

To aid Herman's wrestling abilities:
"Abracadabra and asee dosee, Alakazam and Bela Lugosi!"

To hold a criminal frozen while police are summoned:
"Ibbidy-bibbidy, rinkidy-dink, make like a statue and freeze, you fink!"

To transport Marilyn to the Old Country momentarily:
"Don't let time or space detain ya, off you go to Transylvania!" *(Instead, he accidentally sends the rest of the family to the Happy Valley Motel in Kansas City.)*

Other Inventions/Potions

- A pill that turns water into gasoline

- A medicine for which there is no disease

- A machine that takes electricity from the air and stores it. "We'll never have to pay another light bill!" *(He zaps Herman unconscious)*

- A cough medicine. "One teaspoon and you'll cough for three days."

- Alarm clock pill that can be set to make you sleep and wake at chosen times

- Grandpa accidentally invented athlete's foot—to his delight!

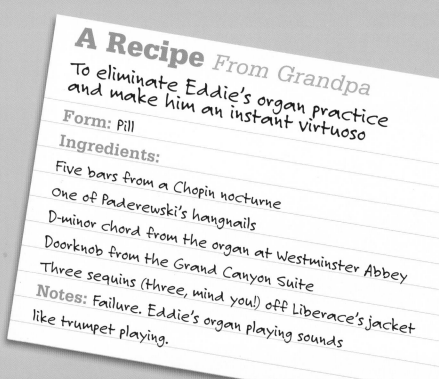

A Recipe From Grandpa

To eliminate Eddie's organ practice and make him an instant virtuoso

Form: Pill

Ingredients:

Five bars from a Chopin nocturne

One of Paderewski's hangnails

D-minor chord from the organ at Westminster Abbey

Doorknob from the Grand Canyon Suite

Three sequins (three, mind you!) off Liberace's jacket

Notes: Failure. Eddie's organ playing sounds like trumpet playing.

MUNSTER MAESTRO

ABOUT JACK MARSHALL

JACK MARSHALL'S MOST FAMOUS THEME WAS HIS perfectly pounding Munster opening, which still, after thirty-five years, never fails to grab an audience with a hint of just the first few notes. As a veteran studio-guitarist, Marshall trusted no one else to perform the electric guitar on the show's opening, and so he picked it himself when he and his small studio ensemble recorded the main theme on August 17, 1964, at Universal Studios. Simply titled "The Munster's Theme," Marshall's infectious, instantly recognizable theme song has been recorded by many musicians and orchestras over the years, including Milton DeLugg, Dick Jacobs, Jimmy Smith, Warren Schatz, and Billy Strange. Arthur Fiedler conducted a Boston Pops version of the show's theme and it ended up a popular track on the LP album, *Highlights from An Evening at the Pops* in 1965. Marshall's own orchestra recorded a jazzed-up, extended version in October 1964, and this excellent version can currently be found on the CD *Prime-Time Tunes from the Tube* (Ultra Lounge series, 1997 Capitol Records).

Jon Burlingame, author of *TV's Biggest Hits* described Marshall's Munster piece, noting the composer "wrote the theme and scored the episodes in a cartoon[ish] Halloween fashion, with organ brass and twangy electric guitar for a kind of Bernard-Herrmann-meets-Duane-Eddy sound."

Marshall wrote the Munster theme as an instrumental, and it never included lyrics until a children's long-playing album was released in 1965, featuring the television cast in song and narration. Titled *At Home with the Munsters* (Golden Records, 1964), the album included songs like "It Takes All Kinds of People," sung by Herman, and "I Wish Everyone Was Born This Way," performed by Eddie (Butch Patrick was dubbed by someone else). Lyrics written by the show's co-producer, Bob Mosher, were added and sung by a children's chorus for this album.

Jack Marshall was a versatile talent: a guitarist, composer, author, and teacher. When he died at the age of fifty-two, in 1973, the relatively young musician had already racked up a handsome résumé of work in the entertainment industry. Born in El Dorado, Kansas, Marshall moved to California as a youngster and later graduated from UCLA. He became a recording artist for Capitol records, and became a staff guitarist for MGM Studios just before he worked with Universal's Revue productions. Later, he lectured on guitar technique at the USC School of Music, and wrote two books about guitar.

Among his film work were scores for *Thunder Road* (1958), *Munster, Go Home!* (1966), *Tammy and the Millionaire* (1967), *Kona Coast* (1968), and *Stay Away, Joe* (1968). Additionally, for television he scored such programs as *The Deputy*, *The Debbie Reynolds Show*, *Laredo*, and *Have Gun, Will Travel*. Marshall also composed and arranged music for singers Peggy Lee, Vic Damone, Judy Garland, and Dinah Shore.

Psychobabble and *The Munsters*

Long ago tucked away in Universal Studio's production files for *The Munsters* is a typed document specifically exploring the television show, composed and submitted by George Horsley Smith, Ph.D., the chairman of the department of psychology at Rutgers University. Titled "A Psychological Discussion of *The Munsters* Audience Appeal," the six-page essay, written in 1965, explored the success of the show. Although the author makes some relevant points, such as a viewer's inherent need to escape reality with fantasy, his essay is not without error and pomp—he repeatedly refers to Herman as "Frankenstein" rather than the scientist's monster. Recently dusted off for your pleasure, reprinted here are a few of the professor's more relevant analyses:

"In psychological terms, turning the TV dial to The Munsters *is a defensive reaction to the insecurities and threats of the real world. The viewer escapes into a fantasy where the traditional symbols of his fears are converted into nice as pie neighbors. It is like falling into the clutches of supposed cannibals—who turn out to be friendly natives. But even as anxieties are assuaged, enough humorous symbols of malevolence remain in the show—the subterranean laboratory, the howling winds, the inadvertently fiendish ploys of the characters—to satisfy omnipresent aggressive feelings."*

"The magnetism of the show can be explained this way: it suburbanizes what used to be macabre. In effect, King Kong becomes the organ grinder's monkey. Demons and fiends become hail-fellows. The most arcane topics become the stuff of jest. (In fact, homeliness via Munster alchemy becomes beauty and anybody who has ever felt insecure about his appearance—which means everybody—is delighted.)"

"Novelty, of course, is also linked with laughter. The unexpected and the incongruous are frequently comic and because The Munsters *consistently innovates and surprises, every episode is laced with laughter . . . The deployment of fantastic characters in real-life situations provides endless possibilities for the scriptwriters and at the same time guarantees the novelty so cherished by the viewer. There are only so many ways to write a 'Western,' but how Frankenstein and Dracula adjust to life in suburbia has hardly been tapped."*

"Consider the problem of getting rid of hostility or aggression. The Munsters *provides a wonderful solution. The viewer can identify with the specter-of-his choice and enjoy it while his surrogate scares the breath out of people—much as we all like to do when in a foul mood. There is also a tidy sum of aggression released . . . Just as the peasants lived for the moment when they could drive a wooden post through Frankenstein's breast, the viewer secretly harbors a hatred for all the denizens of darkness, no matter how comic their guise. The more searing the demolition of the Frankenstein image, the more the audience enjoys it."*

MUNSTER MOTORS

ALMOST AS RECOGNIZABLE AS THE CHARACTERS themselves, the family cars, known as the Munster Koach and Drag-u-la, became instantly associated with the family who drove them.

These two objects of automotive artwork that whisked the Munsters around Mockingbird Heights were the creative inventions of the "King of Kustomizers," George Barris, whose cars of the stars are still in production at Barris Kustom Industries in North Hollywood. (For his trademark, Barris replaces the *c* with a *k* for a nostalgic, "kustom" look, which has proved serviceable in his business for over fifty years, he says.) Barris was a kid growing up in Sacramento, California, and loved cars. He carved balsawood car models when he was seven years old and by the age of thirteen, he was customizing old Fords into hot rods. (He reshaped his mother's 1925 Buick, welding knobs and handles from her kitchen cabinets onto the car's grills and bumper.) Is it any wonder Barris took his fascination—actually a passion—for atypical autos and built a successful career?

In the mid-forties, Barris moved to Los Angeles, and ten years later he started customizing autos for television and motion pictures. (One of his first was a customized Ford for *Dragnet*.) With the burst of the wacky-television era in the sixties and the United States in the midst of the space race, the need for unique vehicles skyrocketed and his shop was busier than ever. Barris built custom autos for an A-list of celebrities during the fifties and sixties: Clark Gable, Dean Martin, Frank Sinatra, Bob Hope, Liberace, James Dean, Elvis Presley, and even Barry Goldwater. During this period, he customized for several television shows, *Dobie Gillis*, *Batman*, and *The Munsters* among them. The Munster cars and the Batmobile became—and remain—his most popular creations.

"A fellow at Universal licensing, Dave Hammond, came to me with the idea of a family car for the Munsters," Barris says. "I felt that something should be put together for the family, not just an old hearse. Something humorous that would have more character instead of a plain, stock vehicle."

An original blueprint design for the Munster Koach.

"Grandpa, how could we scare anyone off?" "Lily, we're dripping with class—it frightens the common man."

Custom-automaker George Barris and his wife, Shirley, pose with Fred Gwynne and Al Lewis outside the Munster house.

After Barris talked with Hammond at length and got a feel for the show, he and his team of kustomizers drew up designs for what they would christen "The Munster Koach" and made a proposal to producers Connelly and Mosher. Producers went for the concept immediately. The Munster Koach would have incredible detail, right down to the spider webs in the windows and casket rails on the sides of the engine. Barris credits his wife, Shirley, with co-creating some of the details. Bob Mosher, also a car enthusiast, loved the Barris's vision and knew the value of pulling in an audience of car buffs, an audience that would increase the popularity of the show.

According to his book, *Barris TV & Movie Cars*, George Barris set Les Tompkins and Bud Kunz to work building the Koach immediately after getting the plans approved: "They fabricated a custom-built, hot rod–styled 133-inch wheelbase chassis, then made the six-door body from several fiberglass Model T bodies by stretching a 1927 touring car with an upright landau coach at center and a footman's seat in the rear."

After the Munster Koach first hit America's television roadways and became such a popular icon within the show, Mosher and Connelly decided to give Grandpa his own sporty little vehicle for the second season. Something fitting, as usual.

A vintage comic-book ad for the Munster Koach model kits by AMT.

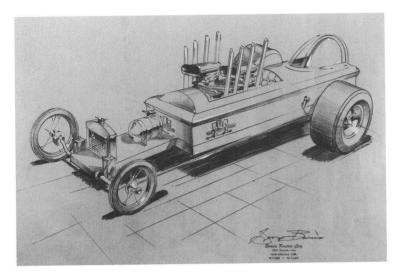

Herman: "I really got to hand it to you, Grandpa. This is quite an attractive vehicle. Detroit could take a lesson from this design. And the organ pipes are a very nice exhaust." Grandpa: "Nice? I'll have you know, Herman, that this is the only dragster in America that can play 'Oh Promise Me' in second gear!"

"I went to several funeral parlors because I wanted to buy a real casket for this car, but they wouldn't sell one unless you were dead." Barris says, laughing. "Finally, one place had a broken one in the corner, but the owner wouldn't sell it. I had a fellow put some money in an envelope and leave it while the owner and I took a walk out back. My guys picked up the casket and walked out. We literally spooked off with the casket."

Barris designed the dragster and named it "Drag-u-la" with Grandpa in mind. It was a stretched, nine-foot-long casket with antique gold-leaf ornamentation and a dragster styling that would whip any design of its day. The actual automobile consisted of a Dragmaster chassis, a real casket, and a 350-horsepower, 289 Ford Mustang V-8 engine with a four-speed stick. The Drag-u-la featured eleven-inch Firestone drag slicks mounted on polished

Rader five-spoke alloy wheels at the rear and English Speedsport wire wheels capped with Italian motorcycle tires up front. It too became a trademark of the show—and of Grandpa, even thought it was used only in a handful of episodes during the series.

Al Lewis said he didn't know if it was going to drive like "a go-cart" or what, but he remembered the first time he nervously climbed into the contraption, lowered the dome top, and actually took the Drag-u-la out for a spin: "George took the damned things up to the back hills on the lot for a test drive. I got in and started to drive. In one second I was choking to death. It didn't have a floorboard! The bubble started filling up with smoke and dirt and sand. I threw off that damned bubble and said, 'George, I'm gonna kill you.' It was fast, but I almost asphyxiated."

A 1984 *Car and Driver* article adds: "Butch Patrick fondly remembers the time Fred Gwynne hijacked the Koach and drove it down the freeway into the heart of Hollywood with the whole cast on board." Butch loved it, later adding, "Fred just took us out on the road driving the car down Lankershim and I think we got on the freeway. It was incredible, the looks we got, and to be out on the road with that car."

For Gwynne, who stood about seven feet tall in full Herman wardrobe, it was not the most comfortable car he'd driven. "Whoever designed that car did not have me in mind," Gwynne said during the series. "They had Butch Patrick in mind. I cannot get into the Munster car and get out again easily."

The car's size cramped Gwynne's awkward stature while filming, so entries and exits from the vehicle are rarely seen in episodes. Gwynne occasionally drove the car without his heavy Herman boots, and wore simple footwear to be able to manage in the driver's seat. Many times, the cast had trouble keeping the car running. "We had to pull it into a scene with a black cable sometimes," said Al Lewis in 1988. "I love ya, George Barris, and I hate to say it, but the thing never ran."

Nevertheless, the six-door touring roadster (seats eight) quickly became identified with the popular television series and requests started pouring in from far stretches of the country. America wanted to see the cars in living color.

Al Lewis takes the customized dragster out for a spin.

Fred Gwynne and Al Lewis test-drive both Munstermobiles through the hills of the Universal Studios back lot which overlook Los Angeles's San Fernando Valley.

"I built the car and rented it out to the studios," Barris says. "So I still retained ownership," Barris explains. While the filming took place, Barris left a Koach at the studio. When not filming, Barris took the roadster on tour at car shows and conventions around the country. They quickly became an extremely well-traveled attraction, and a beautiful promotional tool for the show. Well aware of the popularity of the cars, Barris convinced AMT Corporation to mass-produce the Munster vehicles. The line of model kits soon became one of the hottest television items on the market.

"The sixties was a strong kinky car era," Barris says. His other creations reflect this, such as the Batmobile (there are five), the Monkeemobile (with collaborator Dean Jeffries), the star of *My Mother the Car*, and automobiles from *Daktari*, *Mannix*, *Starsky and Hutch*, *The Dukes of Hazzard*, *Knight Rider*, and *The A-Team*. Barris helped create autos that became characters themselves, or at least trademark images, on their programs. And for most, the cars proved great sellers in the model-kit market.

During the primetime run of *The Munsters* on CBS, the height of the show, Barris toured the autos around the nation occasionally with some of the cast. The auto was transported on a United Airlines cargo jet which flew from city to city. Butch Patrick and Al Lewis (in costume) appeared on *The Art Linkletter Show* with the coach parked onstage at the famous Hollywood Bowl. Both Al Lewis and Fred Gwynne were perched atop the backseat of the Koach and road for miles in the chilly weather for the Macy's Thanksgiving Day Parade. When the Koach was exhibited at the Sacramento State Fairgrounds in California, a nearly forty-percent raise in attendance was reported. At the new Concourse Center in San Diego, one newspaper reported the doors had to be closed for the first time in history due to the overflow crowds inside and the many thousands waiting outside. When *Munster, Go Home!* premiered in the summer of 1966, both Munster autos embarked on an additional tour for the fans.

"I remember one particular visit to a crippled children's hospital," George Barris told a reporter in 1966. "Herman, Grandpa, and I got out of the car and waved to the many smiling and curious faces pressed against the hospital's windows. Some of the children were waiting for us out front, in wheelchairs and on crutches, with braces and such. We talked to them for a while and showed those that could walk what the inside of the Koach looked like. Then we went into the hospital and chatted with the other boys and girls."

Over the years, four identical Munster Koaches have been built, with the original remaining in the possession of Barris. In 1984, Barris put several of his most famous cars up on the auction block and one of the Munster Koaches sold for $36,000. The most recent Koach replica was built by Barris with Keith Dean for the Fox TV-movie *Here Come the Munsters* in 1995.

What is Barris's approach to car design?

"The purpose of customizing is to make your vehicle look prettier," he told Emmy magazine in 2004. "After all, the designers at the car companies design these cars to be the best. So for you to take their car and make it look prettier is a challenge. A car is really an expression of the person. You want something more inspiring, more original and more conducive to you—something that's not the same as anybody else's."

For most of Barris's cars, their originality and detail are the most astonishing features. Even today, crowds snake around arenas and convention center auto shows just to view the Munster Koach—and if they're lucky, they hop aboard. In February 2006, parked outside the Riverside Church in New York City for Al Lewis's memorial was one of the original Drag-u-las. (And no, he was not buried in it.) Both Butch Patrick and George Barris occasionally make personal appearances with the autos at car shows around the country to answer questions and pose for snapshots. These cars are stars.

Features of the Original Munster Koach

- Eighteen feet long, made from three Model T bodies.

- Handmade frame

- A headstone-styled Model T radiator

- Rolled out on a set of Ansen Astro wheels trimmed with knockoff hubs and walnut-wood inserts, with a set of Mickey Thompson eleven-inch-wide slicks fitted to the rear wheels

- Engine is a 300-horsepower, 289 Ford Cobra V-8; ten cylinders

- Four-speed transmission and power rear end

- Wide slicks for the rear

- Hand-formed brass radiator

- Hand-formed fenders

- Square headlamps powered by Autolite 110 electrical system.

- Rear tires: double width

- Wheelbase: 133 inches

- Plush blood-red velvet upholstery, curtain windows, coffin handles with antique lights

- Built in less than thirty days

- The original model cost slightly over $20,000 to build

Actually, the stuffed raven from the clock was brought to life by none other than the most famous "voice characterizationist" ever to utter a syllable or sound . . . the late great Mel Blanc. He became famous as the "Man of a Thousand Voices," and the man who probably verbalized more cartoon characters than any other. Blanc carved out a unique and legendary career for himself starting in radio; he was *the* legendary voice talent in the entertainment business, a genuine performer who emerged from radio shows and later dominated a cartoon business for years, all the while inspiring multitudes of voice actors who are working in the animation business today. Blanc was best known as the voice of such diverse cartoon icons as Bugs Bunny, Daffy Duck, Porky Pig, Yosemite Sam, Sylvester and Tweety, Barney Rubble, Dino the Dinosaur, and countless others. Looney Toons was his game, but for this network show he spouted the flippant dialogue which made the raven character one of the most memorable of the series. (The Raven was not his only non-animated character voiced for television. Blanc was the voice of the diminutive shiny robot Twiki on TV's *Buck Rodgers in the 25th Century* for years until producers replaced him due to cost-cutting measures which swept the final season of the hit NBC show.)

Although Blanc was extremely versatile with his vocal cords, the Munsters' raven was somewhat typical of the avian vocals he relied on in his repertory. If you listen closely, Blanc supplied a voice which closely resembled the wisecracking parrot on Jack Benny's radio show for many years. The parrot often squawked, "Raaahh! Benny's a cheapskate! Benny's a cheapskate! Raaahhh!"

Oddly, Blanc had an affinity for this particular animal assignment because instruments of telling time really yanked his chain, so to speak. Blanc was a longtime clock and watch aficionado, with many antique museum-quality pieces in his vast collection. One of his most prized was a rare "carrying time piece," one of the earliest known surviving instruments of time, made in 1510 by Peter Henlein of Germany. That one he kept in a safety-deposit box, but he prominently displayed hundreds of other watches and clocks in the den of his Pacific Palisades home until his death in 1989.

But that's not all, folks. The voice of the Munster raven changed on occasion. For eighty percent of the raven's lines, Blanc is heard. When Blanc wasn't available, actor Bob Hastings stepped up to the mike and read the raven's rap, but he did not attempt an impression of Blanc's inimitable sound. Hastings delivered it a slightly different tone, void of the personality Blanc was able to infuse in

Legendary voiceover talent, Mel Blanc, supplied the vocals for the irreverent Raven. The man behind the voice went un-credited, his identity a mystery for years . . . *"Nevermore!"*

the sassy winged black bird. (Hastings, by the way, later appeared in the 1981 TV-movie *The Munsters' Revenge* in the role of the Phantom of the Opera.)

For a more "traditional" house pet, instead of a doggie, the Munsters kept a massive reptile or dinosaur—you never quite knew which—a pet that barely fit in the house. The reptilian denizen who resided in the unseen bowels of the Munster manse, usually stayed near his little cove in a secret passageway located under the main stairwell. Spot, or "Spotty" as they affectionately called him, had a nasty habit of breathing fire and smoke and tracking up the house with mud, but that was okay. They loved him anyway. Spotty liked to chase cars, eat manhole covers, telephone poles, or any squirrel that happened to wander into their yard. He once buried the mailman in the backyard.

A temperamental pet, Spotty hated to get his weekly bath at the local carwash and wanted to be left to do what he wanted around the property and the neighborhood. When Herman reprimanded him with a slight

swat on the tail with the newspaper, Spotty ran away. Grandpa promptly composed an ad for the newspaper's lost-and-found section:

LOST

Family pet. Green with yellow scales. Friendly. Affectionate. Answers to the name Spotty. Breathes fire when hungry. Has battleaxe scar on left shoulder.

Butch Patrick remembers a little trivia regarding dear ol' Spot: "What the studio had was a Tyrannosaurus rex model that was used in the movie *One Million B.C.* We only showed the head and the tail. The tail had air hoses in it and was wheeled around the set."

Donald Glut, author of books on creatures both large and small (*The Frankenstein Catalog, The New Dinosaur Dictionary* among them) speculates that Spot's head was actually "a massive fire-breathing prehistoric reptile," created by reusing a revamped prop dinosaur from Universal's 1957 film *The Land Unknown.* Add a scaly prop tail, a little fire, and what have you.

Al Lewis remembered it a little differently in an interview: "Fred [Gwynne] and I designed Spot," he said. "We were the ones who decided the family needed a pet. Fred's a great artist, so we got together and came up with Spot. The prop department built him for us. What does Butch remember? He was twelve!" Lewis said it was his and his costar's concept of having Spot breathe fire, a detail he clearly recalls contributing.

Rumors have it that Fred Gwynne actually supplied the roar for Spot in a sound studio, literally recording it by letting out a blood-curdling yell into a megaphone—which was then amplified, of course. Or was it simply a random roar chosen from Universal's sound-effects library? No one quite recalls.

But for the grandfather of the house, man's best friend was his bat—mainly because upon choosing, Grandpa could *become* one. As the saying went, "Curiosity killed the bat . . . but satisfaction brought him back." Grandpa had a soft spot for his pet, Igor, the honest-to-goodness temperamental Transylvania-born bat which nested in his dark laboratory rafters. Igor was the one sole reminder of the Old Country which Grandpa so longed for.

"You're nothing but a rat with wings," Grandpa would say lovingly. Igor squeaks around the house, mostly objecting to Herman's escapades. Once, as Eddie was about to take Igor to the school pet fair, Herman insulted Igor, and the crazy bat flew away. Grandpa to the rescue: He turns himself into a bat, but Eddie doesn't realize this and trades Grandpa off to a classmate for a "really neat squirrel." The story has a happy ending when Herman retrieves the aged vampire bat from a testing laboratory that would've sent Grandpa into orbit on a space shuttle.

MUNSTER MOMENT

In the 1991 film *Pet Sematary*, based on the Stephen King novel, actor Fred Gwynne gives one of his best performances as white-haired Jud Crandall, an old codger who possesses knowledge of a special Indian burial ground for animals. In one scene Gwynne leads the main character, Louis, to the cemetery and explains that he buried his own family pet named "Spot" on the very grounds they stood. Was this Stephen King's nod to *The Munsters*? Actually, no, since "Spot" was named in his 1983 novel, eons before the film was made. Regardless, it makes for a rather funny moment in the movie.

THE MUNSTER HOUSE: VAMPIRE VICTORIAN

"This house offers everything a family could want. And we're close-in and we have a beautiful yard with a kidney-shaped swamp."

—HERMAN MUNSTER

NORMAN BATES WOULD'VE KILLED TO LIVE IN the Munsters' house. And yet at the same studio, just ten years prior to Norman's inhabitance in the eerie mansion alongside the Bates Motel, a house destined for equal stardom was built on Colonial Street on the back lot of Universal Studios.

Freelance designer and decorator Diana Friedman dubbed the house of Munster "Vampire Victorian." In her book, *Sitcom Style*, she described the famed residence: "The view from the street offers a

stone wall decorated with gargoyles, a bat weathervane, nesting vultures and piles of dead leaves. Good thing few neighbors ever see inside. There, amid drapes of cobwebs, they'd find a casket phone booth, a pet dragon that lives under the stairwell, a dungeon laboratory, and a cuckoo clock with a raven that pops out and chirps 'Nevermore.' Furnishings with medieval flare like a heavily carved mantel, swags of brocade drapes, and a large, detailed player organ are made spooky with layer upon layer of dust, a few cracks here and there; likewise iron and brass chandeliers become gloomy with the bulbs exposed."

The Munster house exterior, located on the back lot at Universal Studios was constructed in the mid-forties; it was originally designed and built for production of the motion picture *So Goes My Love* starring Don Ameche. Eventually, the same home won its place in the unofficial architectural Hall of Fame as one of the most recognizable structures of our time. (Such an honor for just a two-year television series!)

It was constructed like a shell, with a front and a back but virtually no interior. The Bates home was built much the same. Despite popular rumor, the Bates house and the Munster house are two *separate* residences but only yards away from each other at the studio. Next door to the Munsters' house is another Victorian mansion— most recognizable to cult film fans as the *Ghost and Mr. Chicken* house which was used extensively in the popular Don Knotts feature film.

Universal spent a whopping chunk of the show's initial budget to dress this house in a manner befitting a Munster. Bare trees were planted in front, dead leaves were blown around the yard, the house was "roughed up" and the number 1313 was placed on the right tier of the stone entrance gates. A custom vampire-bat weathervane was made and is situated atop the roof half-cocked. In other words, the house is a disaster, but a meticulous one. This dreary, frightening half-acre is a haunted nightmare with tumbleweed and dust drifting across the front yard.

"We rarely used the house," said Al Lewis. "Only for exteriors and that wasn't too often. There's nothing inside at all."

TV's hit family-sitcom *Leave It to Beaver* was filmed just down the block and the Munster house was seen in several episodes, but *Beaver* was cancelled a year prior to the start of *The Munsters*. The Munster house originally sat just four doors down from the residence of June and Ward Cleaver in Mayfield, U.S.A. Imagine, with a few magical television steps, you could be in Mockingbird Heights with Herman and Lily. Strolling in the other direction, you might spot the Beaver and Wally building a go-cart on the driveway. (The *Beaver* house has been uprooted and moved to different areas of the lot several times in the past four decades. Today, the Cleaver home is across the street from the Munster home.)

The Munster residence is still located on Universal's Colonial Street on the back lot but it has since been street-smart sanitized, manicured, and modernized a tad. The surrounding stone and wrought-iron fence is gone, and now only a tiny front yard and a few pleasant live trees line the front. Occasionally, when not in use, Universal Studios displays a MUNSTERS sign planted in the front yard, just so the tourists on the Studio Tour tram don't miss the photo opportunity. The Munster house can be seen in these films and TV shows:

- *So Goes My Love* (1946), starring Don Ameche and Myrna Loy (one of the earliest uses of the house).

- *Abbott & Costello Meet the Invisible Man* (1951); seen in the opening as the physician's stately home and laboratory.

- *All I Desire* (1953), starring Barbara Stanwyck.

- *Monster on the Campus* (1958), starring Troy Donahue.

- Seen in the television drama, *Alfred Hitchcock Presents*, in an episode entitled "Bang! You're Dead," guest-starring Billy Mumy. The episode, which aired on October 17, 1961, was directed by the master himself and is considered one of the most suspenseful episodes of the series.

- *Leave It to Beaver* (series); look for the house in random episodes. Check out the episode where Beaver goes collecting door-to-door for a Community Chest charity (and loses the money).

- *The Brass Bottle* (1964), starring Tony Randall and Burl Ives. Filmed just before the eerie Munster transformation of the house in 1964.

- *Dragnet* (series), starring Jack Webb and Harry Morgan.

- *The Ballad of Josie* (1967), starring Doris Day, Peter Graves, and George Kennedy.

- *Coogan's Bluff* (1968), starring Clint Eastwood and Lee J. Cobb.

- *It Happened One Christmas* (1977), starring Marlo Thomas and Wayne Rogers.

- *Shirley* (series), starring Shirley Jones and Peter Barton (used as her Lake Tahoe home). The series lasted less than one season in 1979.

- *The Incredible Hulk* (series), starring Bill Bixby and Lou Ferrigno (frequently used as backdrop).

- *Dragnet* (1987), starring Dan Aykroyd and Tom Hanks (used as Aykroyd's mother's house).

- *The 'Burbs* (1989), starring Tom Hanks. The street on which the action takes place is titled Mayfield Place, referring to the town of Mayfield, where the Cleavers of TV's *Leave It to Beaver* once roamed.

- *Murder, She Wrote* (series), starring Angela Lansbury.

- Now known as one of the primary houses on Wisteria Lane on TV's hit series *Desperate Housewives*, the Munster house has been brightly painted and beautifully manicured. In one memorable episode of the series, Oprah Winfrey guest-stars as a buyer of the house—but vacates quickly because she's spooked by the neighborhood. (Winfrey featured behind-the-scenes footage of her *Desperate Housewives* appearance on her own daytime show, noting of course that it was Herman and Lily's former residence.)

▲ A rare peek at a portion of Herman and Lily's bedroom set.

▶ For several years following the series, much of Grandpa's laboratory set was kept intact and guests taking the popular Universal Studios Tour were invited to walk through and browse on one of the soundstages.

THE MCKEES' SCREAM HOME

It's one thing to build your dream home. It's another to build a $350,000 dream home inspired by your favorite television show. But that's exactly what mega-Munster fans Charles and Sandra McKee did in Waxahachie, Texas. Where? It's thirty miles south of Dallas in a rather remote area, but just ask the owners—the traffic's picking up. The couple built a massive 5,825-square-foot replica of the Munsters mansion, complete with stone fencing in front and crooked weathervane on the roof.

"Not a day goes by that we don't hear people's brakes screeching, or see people pulling over gawking. I guess some people think we're crazy," owner Charles McKee told a Knight-Ridder reporter in 2002 when the monstrosity was being built.

In an attempt to echo the very mansion used in the television series, the McKees worked closely with their builder (no blueprints, just plans) to re-create the Victorian mansion from the television show. "We used pictures, books and videos to closely match the design of the interior and exterior from the show," says Sandra McKee. "We used one builder and after he left, we built the rest. It's our retirement house. I plan to be here the rest of my life. It really is a dream home and I'm such a fan of the show . . . I figured, you only live once."

Cast alum Al Lewis, Pat Priest, and Butch Patrick have all stepped foot inside, impressed by the manse and the detail put into the decorating. "Butch stayed here with us briefly," says Sandra McKee. "We have used the house and the two-and-a-half-acre property to host an an-nual children's charity event every Halloween and one year we drew over 1,500 people. There are so many Munsters fans, you can't imagine. We get people stopping by all the time wanting to look inside."

The house features four bedrooms, two-and-a-half baths, a fireplace, gargoyles, doorknockers, and a trap door built into the living room floor which leads down to their storm shelter. "We get a lot of tornados down here," says Sandra. "We searched on the internet for furnishings and the clock, the organ, chandeliers, and really everything to match the interiors. But we keep our house clean, no cobwebs. At Halloween, we dress it up perfectly. It's taken years to really finish the house and we're still working on it."

And yes, even the grand stairwell opens up. No fire-breathing reptiles, though. They're still searching eBay.

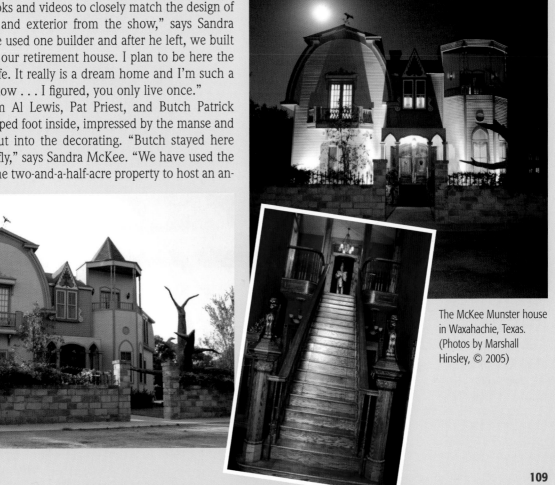

The McKee Munster house in Waxahachie, Texas. (Photos by Marshall Hinsley, © 2005)

The Beatles
Meet the Munsters

"*The Munsters* is Paul McCartney's favorite show," professed Al Lewis. He should know. When the Beatles were scheduled to appear at Dodgers Stadium in the sixties, production on *The Munsters* was well underway. Naturally, neither the Beatles nor the Munster cast suspected a meeting might occur, but it happened.

"It was chaotic in Los Angeles," remembered Al Lewis. "For insurance purposes, no hotel would take [the Beatles] in. "I remember someone coming to me from the front office asking to use my number one dressing room. You see, on the series we had a portable and a permanent dressing room with a couch and all. I rarely used it. With the makeup and hair, I couldn't lie down any place."

Lewis allowed his private cove to be used as a sanctuary for "someone," but no names were discussed. As it turned out, Universal was bedding down the Fab Four in a number of bungalows and dressing rooms on the lot.

"Mine was next to the infirmary. As I walked up the two steps, I heard noise. 'Someone's in my quarters!'" Lewis thought. "So I opened it up and there they were. That's how I met them. We talked for half an hour and I went back to work. Nice guys."

The Beatles never guested on the show; however, another popular musical group of the sixties, the Standells, did appear as themselves for a guest shot, singing the Beatles' hit, "I Want to Hold Your Hand."

Guest actors on the show were almost a constant. Most of the guest stars were either established television actors already or performers who went on to successful series themselves: Pat Buttram (*Green Acres*); Richard Deacon (*Dick Van Dyke Show*); Bonnie Franklin (*One Day at a Time*); Frank Gorshin (*Batman*); Pat Harrington (*One Day at a Time*); Harvey Korman (*Carol Burnett Show*); Paul Lynde (*Bewitched, Hollywood Squares*); Gavin MacLeod (*Love Boat*); Billy Mumy (*Lost in Space*); Gary Owens (*Laugh-In*); and Don Rickles (*CPO Sharkey*), just to name a few.

"The best Dr. Dudley we had was definitely Paul Lynde," affirmed Al Lewis. "He was a perfect comedian. Fabulous. I don't care how famous others who played Dudley went on to be." One of the "others" Lewis was referring to was Dom DeLuise, who took over the role for an episode in the second season. DeLuise did not try to impersonate Lynde's Dr. Dudley at all; however, Lynde was so good as the myopic physician that his presence was missed.

The *Munster* set on the Universal lot was extravagantly decorated, a sight to behold on the soundstage. Many actors who were working on the Universal lot at the time wanted to take time to stroll over to the *Munster* soundstages or the outdoor Munster house and take in the beauty. Yvonne De Carlo recalls Liberace, Dick Van Dyke, Ernest Borgnine, and Cary Grant stopping by (not together) to see the Munster living room. As Lewis remembered, the Munsters set was not completely closed. "All the Chrysler execs were at the set with their kids, wanting to meet the Munsters. It was a fun set and great just to look at," he said. "I remember Jack Paar and his daughter stopping by." For Lewis, probably the most revered celebrity to grace the stage was baseball hero Jackie Robinson, who brought his wife, Rachel. Lewis was so extremely honored to meet the sports figure that he turned the tables and asked Robinson for *his* autograph, which Robinson gladly obliged. "Anything for Grandpa," he said.

MEET THE **MUNSTERS!**

REFERENTIAL TREATMENT

FRED GWYNNE ONCE SAID, "*THE MUNSTERS* IS REALLY *The Donna Reed Show* with monsters." It was an astute comparison as his show was situated in a time to be the first generation to ably poke fun at television and the monster *it* had become. The sixties celebrated television, still a budding phenomenon—and with all its might, gave us an unparalleled era in the history of the medium. With a wink and a nod, *The Munsters* were inventing the era while constantly jabbing the new generation of TV fans in the ribs with fast references about TV shows peppered in the dialogue. They thought, why not poke fun at the ordinary, because they were, after all, part of that hoi polloi. That was the gag. And it worked time and again. The fact that the Munster family had become couch potatoes was the ultimate mirror image of the masses in domestic American society.

Whether it was Grandpa rubbing his hands together in anticipation of seeing his favorite operation on Dr. Kildare, or mere mention that Herman is a charter member of the Pat Boone fan club, *The Munsters*, as a show, adopted a sharp edge while commenting on popular culture. Writers Connelly and Mosher, in particular, loved to insert these TV gags because they knew by this time how to entertain on television, and that what they produced was not quite an actual reflection of reality. So why not take a jab at their own handiwork, their own profession? Butch Patrick says, "*The Munsters* was writ-

> ## *"It's times like this I'm glad I'm a Lawrence Welk fan!"*
> ## —HERMAN MUNSTER,
> ### dancing with Russian sailors

ten with that down-home wholesomeness like *Leave It to Beaver*. In fact, I always thought many of the lines, like 'Gee, pop' could have been interchangeable with the Beaver."

In retrospect, *The Munsters* provides us with a comical, yet historical, view of the decade, that almost no other program exhibited. Not with the same flair, anyway. The show's often funny take on the popularity of television was a cultural comment on the nation's desperate need for escapism and how it was achieved vicariously through television during the sixties. Here are some of the best TV references from the series:

Herman, after the family tells him how much they love him: Now look what you've gone and made me do! I haven't cried like this since they cancelled *Kukla, Fran & Ollie*!

Lily urging Herman to have a father-and-son talk with Eddie: Anyone who's watched *Father Knows Best* for nine years ought to know that.

Herman: All right, but Donna Reed always handled these things on her show, you know.

Herman: I just don't understand what went wrong with my child psychology; it always worked on *Leave It to Beaver*.

Herman: Where were you on the night of August twelfth?

Grandpa: What does that have to do with it?

Herman: Well . . . I don't know, but that kind of junk always seems to work on *Perry Mason*.

Lily: What's wrong with that crystal ball, anyway?

Grandpa: I don't know, all I keep picking up are the reruns of Molly Goldberg from Tel Aviv.

Herman: What am I gonna tell Lily? She's been counting on a raise and if she finds out I've been fired she might get mad at me and stamp on the floor and say mean things to me . . . she might even break my Huckleberry Hound records.

Grandpa: Will you be quiet, Igor? Oh, he hates television ever since Bat Masterson went off the air.

Lily: Eddie, you should always listen to your father because under that sweet, boyish countenance he has the wisdom and understanding of an Art Linkletter.

Herman: Come on, hurry up Grandpa. We're all set to go to the drive-in. They're having a Porky Pig cartoon and I want to get there for the beginning so I can follow the plot.

Lily: Why Herman, you're so gullible. This is even worse than the time you went to that television show and almost wound up as "Queen for a Day."

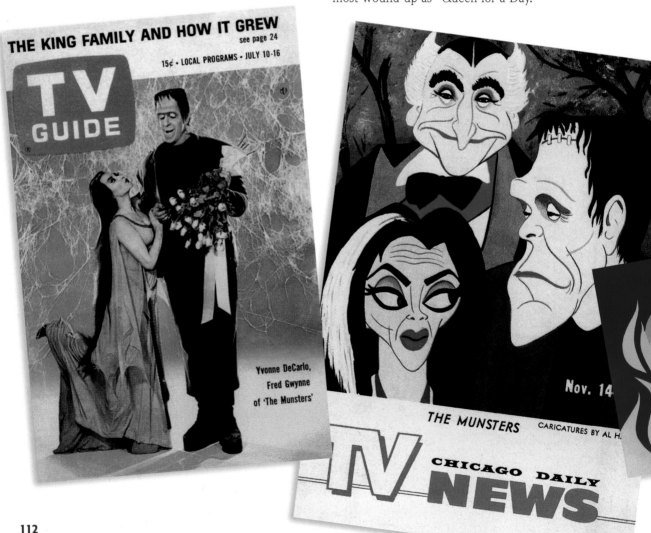

THE KING FAMILY AND HOW IT GREW see page 24

15¢ • LOCAL PROGRAMS • JULY 10-16

Yvonne DeCarlo, Fred Gwynne of 'The Munsters'

THE MUNSTERS CARICATURES BY AL H.

Nov. 14

TV NEWS CHICAGO DAILY

Herman, on the perks of being a major-league baseball player: Oh, it's not just the money, Grandpa. What I'm looking forward to is the fringe benefits. I'll be able to endorse breakfast foods and shave on television. I'll be able to sit in the audience on *The Ed Sullivan Show* and have him mispronounce my name.

Lily to Herman: We look up to you to guide us and protect us against the trials and tribulations of life. You have made, right here at home, our own Ponderosa.

Grandpa: Eight-thirty! Ha ha ha! It's time for my favorite TV program. Oh, it's all about that crazy mixed-up family that's always having those weird, fantastic adventures. [Strains of *My Three Sons* theme is heard coming from the TV.]

Herman: Oh, but remember, Grandpa, as the man on television said . . . You Asked For It!

Herman: Where did you learn [English]?

Russian Sailor: On the TV—we watch the Russian reruns of *Dobie Gillis*.

Herman: I'll be darned. TV—it sure is a great medium for cultural exchange.

BLOOD RELATIVES

A KID'S-EYE VIEW OF THE MUNSTERS

THE CHANCE TO MEET HERMAN MUNSTER WAS something many children wished for back in the sixties. For many who got to visit the set at Universal Studios, or saw any number of the cast at a personal appearance, it was a wish came true. They were amazed how tall—and how green—Herman was. And even today, grownups are surprised that Al Lewis is six-foot-one. (Next to Herman, he appeared short. Fred Gwynne stood six-foot-five and a whopping seven feet with the boots on.)

Children were the Munsters' biggest fans, without a doubt, and much of it was geared toward young audiences. Fred Gwynne had a theory about the Munsters, and how they aren't overly scary at all to kids.

"The only time a child is scared is if there is no movement," he said in 1965. "A little girl came up once and said, 'You can't scare me.' I didn't move. I just said in a deep voice, 'Oh, really' and she was 300 years away in one second. It's not moving that gets them."

Occasionally, the cast received letters from thankful parents who enjoyed the fact that the Munsters single-handedly disarmed the children of their fears of monsters under the bed.

One child, David Lewis—who happens to be the oldest son of Al Lewis—got a personal peek at the Munsters when he was all of seven years old. To top it, he got to have Grandpa tuck him in every night. Unfortunately, one of David's most vivid memories is not the most pleasant, by his own account:

When I was on the set, my big challenge was to be quiet. Butch Patrick and I had a run-in one day. We were running around the place and he kicked me real hard. He was probably just fooling around, but he really hurt me. I didn't tell anyone because I thought it would get him in trouble.

He kicked me right in the shin when I was running away from him. I fell down into a pile of microphone stands and one hit me on the head or something. It was kind of traumatic.

I came back and dusted myself off, and when Dad saw me he said, "What happened to you?" because I had been crying. I just told him I fell and so he grounded me to the chair. That made it worse.

For the most part, David Lewis recalls, hanging out on the set was great fun. "Everyone on the set was great to me," he says. "I slept while Dad was in the chair getting makeup. I remember wondering why we were going to the studio in the middle of the night, because it was dark out. It was really six in the morning."

Another happy recollection was when he got to steer the Drag-u-la car for a while. Even having Beverley Owen baby-sit him was a big thrill. "She was terrific. I got to stay up late and do whatever I wanted."

Poppa Al left the Grandpa persona at the studio, however. "For my benefit, he kept the Munsters very low-key," David remembers. "I learned very early that people would be my friend because my dad was Grandpa Munster. Not because I was a nice guy. Dad didn't subscribe to a lot of the Hollywood baloney. At home he was just a dad."

Remember, vampires rarely see the light of day, but this one did. Al Lewis emerged from the makeup chair daily at eight AM. When the sun set, he hung up his cape

Al Lewis brought his children to the set to see what their ol' man did for a living. "My son David said, 'Hey Dad, I can do it better than you. Here's how you scare people!'"

Butch Patrick: "After a while, you wore that makeup around so much that you forgot you had it on. It was strange . . . you just started talking to Fred or Al in their makeup and it didn't even faze you. They're more familiar to me with the makeup on than without the makeup. It became second nature."

and returned to his home, which was *not* decorated in Transylvania chic. Only a few times did he bring items from work that represented Grandpa. He never saved his scripts, and publicity photographs and Munster collectibles weren't in abundance in the Lewis household, probably because of his kids.

"I wish I had a nickel for all the stuff I ruined," says David. "I remember once he brought home this larger-than-life plaster bust of Grandpa that was painted bronze. It was in the house for a while, but it spooked Mom. We kids were putting hats on it and drawing on the face. It ended up in the storage shed and from there it went to the battlefield. A rock fight started and that was about it for the bust."

Al kept the Grandpa Munster medallion he wore around his neck on the bright red ribbon—an essential part of the costume. "I think I lost that. I was famous for losing things," David laughs. "If he really wanted to save those things, he could have. He's just not a collector when it comes to his career."

David Lewis is now in his forties. Years ago he and his wife, Pepper, gradually began collecting Munster artifacts for their own son, Bryce. "When he was born, Dad

was really proud. Bryce made him an honest grandpa," he says. "Dad was proud of all of his grandchildren."

Maureen Murphy is the granddaughter of Munsters assistant director Dolph Zimmer. She remembers being afraid while visiting the set when she was eight years old.

"I stood behind my grandfather because Fred was so big and green. Fred was naturally big, but to a kid, he was huge. He had to coax me out, but he was wonderful with kids. They all were. I think they knew how much the show appealed to the younger ones."

Murphy went on the set just a few times with her grandfather. "We watched a scene where the steps open up and Spot breathes fire. I was petrified. I thought Spot was gonna come out and get me," she says. Her grandfather, known for having a pipe in his mouth, had also worked on *Leave It to Beaver* as well as many motion pictures before his death several years ago.

"Dolph was a funny guy in person and very well-liked," Murphy says. "I guess that's why he was a natural for *The Munsters*. A very funny show, even today."

Al Lewis takes a moment to please the tourists who are taking the Universal Studios Tour. The comprehensive studio tour and tram ride began in 1965 and continues today as one of southern California's most popular tourist attractions. Munsters not included.

What the History Books Left Out

For centuries historians have distorted stories about the famous, the infamous, in fact, everything—that is, according to Grandpa. He's gotten around in his day and, naturally, influenced the course of history. Just ask him, and he'll tell ya it *really* happened like this:

On Columbus: "So, eh, Eddie, I said to Queen Isabella, 'Why not give this Columbus cat the jewels? I mean, after all, they're not doing any good lying around the top drawer. And besides, he might take a cruise and find something good.' And that, Eddie, is how Columbus discovered America. Over the centuries, you could say I got around."

On King Arthur: "He was mad at the Saxon gang for stealing the hubcaps off his chariot. Boy, there was some rumble down at the stone bridge!"

On Pompeii: "We had a backyard barbecue. Things got a little out of hand . . ."

Grandpa is eager to share his wisdom with all of the family. He's wise beyond his hundreds of years. He claimed to have started the French Revolution, among other historical heroics. "Herman, just learn to mind your own business. That's what I've been doing ever since I told that Napoleon fellow to take a shortcut through Waterloo," he admits.

As a matter of fact, Grandpa was shooting home movies 300 years before the camera was invented. "That must have been hard," an impressed Eddie asserts. "Of course it was, and I'll tell you something else. There wasn't even a drugstore to develop the film!"

He once made Nuthin' Muffins—one bite turns anything good into nothin'. Grandpa recalls: "Thirty years ago in Detroit, a fellow ate a batch of 'em. Next day, he sat down and designed the Essex." And for King Richard, he quickly whipped up instant Bravery Pills. "I made these in the Middle Ages for Richard the Lionhearted. I'll have you know that before he took these, he was known as Chicken-Dickie." (Note: The recipe is good only for crusades.)

TO KILL A MOCKINGBIRD LANE

"Shoot all the blue jays you want, if you can hit 'em, but remember it's a sin to kill a mockingbird."

— HARPER LEE,
To Kill a Mockingbird

NOBODY KNOWS EXACTLY *WHY* THE MUNSTERS were shot off the schedule after just two years in prime-time—only that it happened and that it was a shame. In 1966, the CBS network drove a stake through the hearts of millions of *Munsters* fans by cancelling the show.

Mike Dann, CBS programming head during the sixties says he loved *The Munsters*, and respected its popularity, but felt it had served its early-evening purpose. "I think it just wore itself out quickly," says Dann, who put the show on the air. "That's the children's form. Kids don't stay with things very long sometimes. I don't regret just running it for two years. For two years? Two years at 7:30 is a lifetime for a program head."

Looking in from the outside, the show's cancellation still seems to be puzzling: If a show has good ratings, and it's not broken, why discontinue a good thing? A decent program gathers audiences over time, not dismisses them. *The Munsters* was just gaining strength and it seems the program could have lasted at least one more season, but things didn't click. Confidence in the show failed somewhere.

In 1988, producer Joe Connelly candidly revealed the demise of the show, at least from his own perspective and that of his partner, Bob Mosher. "The actors were a pain in the ass. Fred and Al objected to anything. Fred hated the makeup and caused a lot of trouble about it on the set. We could not stand Fred Gwynne. The sponsor had it, and we had it. We were happy with what we had done. And the show got to be quite expensive. We went into the hole big. Maybe the network didn't want to pay anymore. Bob and I had just had it."

Veteran television director and producer Gene Reynolds, who guided a couple of episodes nearing the end of the second season, noticed the tension between the producers and some of the cast. "Fred was difficult, you know,"

Reynolds says, "and the problem was he was very unhappy with Connelly and Mosher. There was a lot of discord there. God knows what it was. I was walking into a situation where there was a lot of retaliation going back and forth and you're in the middle. The itinerant director is always very much of a shuttlecock in the middle of two badminton players."

Most likely, the final decision came from high up at CBS; the network did not want to spend the additional funds to produce the series, and especially not in color. Strange, because, it's likely that *The Munsters* would have easily attracted a sponsor with big pockets. Merchandising the series was still a strong point in its favor. But the whole thing fell apart early in January 1966. In the fall of 1966, a show called *Jericho* aired instead in the timeslot. *Batman* over at ABC-TV had been blamed for cutting into the show's audience on Thursday evenings. Industry brass felt that the monster phase had run its course, with *The Addams Family* strangely being cleared from the shelf at the same time.

Fred Gwynne and Yvonne De Carlo were both getting restless at the end of two seasons. In fact, De Carlo had it in mind to retire the long black wig as the first season came to a close. She made that fact apparent when she told a reporter for the *Boston Sunday Advertiser* in May 1965: "Now I have this recognition, I think two years of *The Munsters* will be enough for me. If I were sensible about it, I should decide that it would be more practical to go on and on, but I prefer to switch to other things. What I'd like to do is a Western series with strong emphasis on the woman character. I'd also like to do a suspenseful psychodrama movie, something along the lines of *Hush . . . Hush, Sweet Charlotte.*"

Gwynne was just turning forty when he removed the Herman bolts from his neck for the last time. He looked at the little rubber pieces in the palm of his hand, put them in his pocket, left the studio, and didn't want to look back. Gwynne says he felt his creativity stagnating under the greasepaint and rubber headpiece. He told writer Bill Byers in 1966, "I'm not really tired of acting, it just doesn't seem to be enough," he said, expressing much more interest in a life of painting and inventing. "As Herman, I was beginning to feel like a robot. I used

Nevermore!

to be an actor, now I don't know what I am. I just can't make up my mind. Perhaps at forty-one it will be easier."

Associated Press writer Gene Handsaker visited the set of the film *Munster, Go Home!* during the next-to-last day of shooting. It signified the last days for the cast to work and be together as an ensemble. Yvonne De Carlo expressed sadness, but not gloom. "The show has meant security, and it gave me a new, young public I wouldn't have had otherwise," said the actress. "It made me 'hot' again, which I wasn't for a while.

"It's been nothing but good for me and I'm very sorry to see it go," she added. "Still, I can't be too sad now because now I can do other things. I was getting disinterested, and that's bad."

Butch Patrick recalls the end. "The final shot of us driving away from the house at the end of *Munster, Go Home!* with the street wet down and soap suds substituting for snow, that was the last time we appeared together in costume as the Munsters," he says. "Isn't that weird? That was the last time I sat in the back of the car. After that, we were never together again as the Munsters. I was thirteen, old enough to know what was going on, and I was kind of bummed. I had never liked working, but by this time in my life I was just starting to enjoy it and really understand. But now the film was completed and the series was over. It was really an emotional moment."

Al Lewis recalled no anguish or sorrow from that period in his life, or at least he didn't want to admit that he missed it. "I don't remember being mad or sorry that the show was cancelled. You go on to other things and that's that. I have to say that I thoroughly enjoyed the two years."

Immediately after the Munster family was axed from the network schedule, Universal Studios rushed the series into syndication, and the show has not left the air since; this fact is amazing since there are only seventy episodes—typically a paltry offering for syndication. It is still offered in an exploding media market not only in the United States but also in more than fifty countries around the world. Ask any Australian about Herman Munster or Gomez Addams. Can't get enough of them down under.

Herman: "Oh Lily, I don't know what I'd do without you. Believe me Lily, I don't."
Lily: "Do you really mean that, pussycat?"
Herman: "Of course I do, sweetheart. Besides, your name's on all the bath towels."

MUNSTER, GO HOME!

PRODUCER JOE CONNELLY EXPLAINED THAT *THE Munsters*, on the whole, exhausted more funds in their budgets than they had expected, and the concept of a big-screen *Munsters* motion picture was conceptualized to offset the deficit. The decision to film a Technicolor motion picture based on the television series was made during the second half of the second season. The intention was to film a movie for television which is why it was not produced in widescreen. (Later, when it was released theatrically, it was on a double-bill with *The Ghost and Mr. Chicken*, a widescreen motion picture.) Plans were altered, but budgets were not. *Variety* reported in January 1966, that designs were being drawn for the big-screen version, citing that Universal, having pioneered the genre of movies based on TV shows (with relative success of two films based on TV's *McHale's Navy*), was expecting a similarly pleasing turnout. At the time, movies based on TV shows, or spawning television programs, was a growing trend (*The Man from U.N.C.L.E.*, *The Man Called Flintstone*.)

The feature was budgeted at a meager $500,000 with an extremely tight shooting schedule (eighteen to twenty-five days) in order to get the film out for a summer release. At the time, Connelly and Mosher were eager to exploit their creation, but even they did not know this would be Herman's swansong.

Munster, Go Home! was written by George Tibbles, along with Connelly and Mosher, and ultimately directed by Earl Bellamy, who had handled more than a handful of the series' episodes. Connelly and Mosher's original choice for director was Gene Reynolds, who also guided a few standout episodes during the show's second season.

The cast celebrates Debbie Watson's high-school graduation during production of the film *Munster, Go Home!*—complete with a special ice-cream "coffin cake" made by Baskin-Robbins.

Production on the feature was to commence following the wrap of the season, plus a week's hiatus. On March 22, 1966, filming rolled on the Technicolor feature, but after just a few days, Reynolds was suddenly relieved of his duties and replaced with Earl Bellamy. *The Hollywood Reporter* explained the "completely amicable" modification was made due to "a difference in story and character concept."

Reynolds was a former actor who began at the Hal Roach studios in *Our Gang* comedies and later appeared in films such as *Boys Town* and *Love Finds Andy Hardy*. After WWII, he became a supremely competent director who had paid his dues on TV hits like *Leave It to Beaver*, *The Andy Griffith Show*, *Peter Gunn*, *My Three Sons*, and *Hogan's Heroes*. Reynolds became the primary force behind the TV's mega-hit, *M*A*S*H*, as well as a multiple Emmy Award winner, and a highly respected television director and producer. The film and TV veteran explains his truncated Munster experience:

> I did a couple of the Munsters episodes very well. One of them with another monster character with the nasty disposition ("A Visit from Johann") and I had a good time with that and they were impressed with it and that's when I was given the opportunity to do this feature. The opportunity was kind of a question mark. I came into the feature very quickly, and had very little preparation time. And they had a dreadful cameraman on that, a very cranky, difficult guy. He was not easy. I didn't have sufficient preparation time and also I had some other distractions in my life at the time that were severe. Serious invasions of my time. So I just did a few days on the film and they asked me to get off. They said they wanted somebody faster. And so that was that. Yes, I was upset about it. I wish the timing of the opportunity had been a little bit better; I would have loved to have gotten through it. Naturally, I didn't walk away from it. It was to be my first feature. I wished that I had been a little more mature in my career. It was a challenging situation. It was a failure on my part, but there were mitigating circumstances. It was a bump in the road, a defeat not a victory.

The film was disappointing for many reasons, even beyond Reynolds's situation. Another departure that came along with the feature was the replacement of Pat Priest with a Universal contract player, eighteen-year-old ingénue Debbie Watson. Connelly and Mosher felt they wanted someone younger and more perky for the movie Marilyn, who would finally end up embraced in romance in this chapter. Just before the film began, the announce-

Spoiled British relation Freddie Munster (Terry-Thomas) smashes a plate with an ancient halberd as his mother, Lady Effigie Munster (Hermione Gingold), is not amused.

Herman is leery of trusting Grandpa's ideas in *Munster, Go Home!*

Some rare wardrobe test photos in preparation for *Munster, Go Home!* Top to bottom: John Carradine, Yvonne DeCarlo, and Hermione Gingold.

ment was made that the series was being cancelled. It was a relief for some, and a blow to others.

Because the film was being shot in Technicolor, some accommodating alterations had to be made. Costumes were brightened (like Eddie's eye-popping purple pantsuit), the sets took on a little more flavor, and the makeup for all of them was tweaked just a tad. The movie's plot would not pivot around the Munster house on Mockingbird Lane as the series did. This time, the family would be packing their coffins and sailing abroad to Europe. The film was completed on April 22, 1966, and released to theaters two months later.

The big-screen adventure makes no effort to establish the characters, the setting, or the unique concept of *The Munsters*, and rather proceeds on the premise that audiences know the characters already. Like an episode of the TV show, the feature moves directly into setting up the plot: The film opens with an especially joyous event—the reading of a will. Herman's rich Uncle Cavanaugh, the Fourth Earl of Shroudshire, has died in England and bequeathed him the title of Lord Munster along with the stately mansion, Munster Hall. The family sails to England to collect their inheritance and stumble into a counterfeiting right operating at the Hall, run by Munster relatives. The homicidal British cousins attempt to scare the American side of the family out of their ancestral home, but the Munsters are only delighted by sliding panels, chattering corpses and the haunt. A romance is sparked between Marilyn and a longtime Munster nemesis. Herman engages in a drag race to uphold the Munster honor, and all ends happily as the family exits Britain to return home.

Released in June 1966 (in some markets offered as a double feature with Universal's Don Knotts spook-fest, *The Ghost and Mr. Chicken*), the ninety-six-minute Munster movie unveiled for audiences their first glimpse of the characters in dying color, you might say. The absence of a laugh track made for an uneasy silence after the jokes, and the comedy and visual gags remained much the same fare, just transplanted from the small screen to the big screen. In 2001, GoodTimes Home Video released a version for the first time on DVD.

Herman and Grandpa stumble on a counterfeiting operation in *Munster, Go Home!*

Herman is a mess when he boards a ship headed for Britain but can't handle the waves in *Munster, Go Home!*

The Drag-u-la and the Munster Koach were dispatched across America in a promotional tour for the feature, *Munster, Go Home!*

Original reviews for the motion picture were mostly upbeat, but the film never gathered anything beyond kind critical praise. Some appraisal, such as the lashing from *Saturday Review*, failed to understand why there was a need for a big-screen version of *The Munsters* in the first place. Fred Gwynne and Al Lewis toured the country with the Munster Koach and the Drag-u-la in tow, criss-crossing the nation and greeting fans and creating hype for this, the Munster finale. Or was it their encore?

Reviews

"There is far-out novelty to the antics of the family as they go on an adventure to England. Wild, unlikely situations crop up, punctuated by comedy and romance. As such it should delight many patrons. Those seeking depth, subtlety, or sophistication will have to look elsewhere."—*The Film Daily*

". . . more or less a straight transplant from TV to features, and should be a very popular attraction. Writers, producers, and director have not tried anything fancy with the Munsters. The gags are from the most traditional sources, meaning they are as old as Chaplin and Keaton. Judging by the preview audience, they still play with the old impact."—*Hollywood Reporter*

"Producers Joe Connelly and Bob Mosher wisely have transferred the scene of this feature based on the tele-series, *The Munsters*, from the haunted house home base to an opulent English estate. Pic holds up on its own, is well paced, with fine Technicolor lensing. Brisk box office looms for this solid family entertainment."—*Variety*

"Television's wasteland of situation comedies, arid enough on the small screen, now seems to be extending its blight to the large screen . . . What several of the current TV-based movies make glaringly obvious, however, is the need for something more than merely additional footage to expand a successful television half-hour into an equally successful ninety-minute picture. *Munster, Go Home!* might be marked Exhibit Number One in this case. Here the primary difficulty is script. Despite the fact that no less than three writers are credited with the collaboration, they simply have not come up with enough material to sustain the greater length. A feature requires more than an accumulation of incidents and sight gags. There must also be a thickening of texture, and added dimension to the characters that will engage and hold the viewers of the longer period . . . This is one film that literally cries for commercials."—*Saturday Review*

Credits

WRITERS: George Tibbles, Joe Connelly, Bob Mosher

PRODUCERS: Joe Connelly, Bob Mosher

DIRECTOR: Earl Bellamy

ASSOCIATE PRODUCER: Irving Paley

MUSIC: Jack Marshall

DIRECTOR OF PHOTOGRAPHY: Benjamin H. Kline, ASC

CAST: Fred Gwynne (Herman), Yvonne De Carlo (Lily), Al Lewis (Grandpa), Butch Patrick (Eddie), Debbie Watson (Marilyn), Hermione Gingold (Lady Effigie), Terry-Thomas (Freddie), Robert Pine (Roger), John Carradine (Cruikshank), Bernard Fox (Squire Moresby), Richard Dawson (Joey), Jeanne Arnold (Grace), Maria Lennard (Millie), Cliff Norton (Herbert), Diana Chesney (Mrs. Moresby), Arthur Malet (Alfie).

WITH: Ben Wright, Laurie Main, Jack Dodson, Richard Peel, Helen Kleeb, Dennis Turner, Robert Ball, Danny Dee, Henry Hunter, Terence Mitchell, Dick Crockett, Don Knight, John Trayne, Peter James, John Peter Manis, Gary Marsh, Jimmy Garrett, Stacy Morgan, Glenn Randall, David Wendler.

Grandpa returns to human form after being chased up a tree as a wolf, in *Munster, Go Home!*

OVERKILL: THE MUNSTERS' REVENGE

AFTER MANY MOONS, WHEN NO ONE IMAGINED a family reunion of "The Munsters" would or could ever take place, Universal Television gathered up the bodies and dusted them off for a TV movie, *The Munsters' Revenge*. The movie was expected to win a ratings sweep and even possibly spin the web of another prime-time series. Unfortunately, there is no other way to put it: this cheesy TV movie is a frightful attempt at re-creating the original magic of *The Munsters*.

"I couldn't believe it!" Fred Gwynne told writer Jon Johnson a few years later. "I couldn't believe

In *The Munsters' Revenge* original cast members Gwynne, Lewis, and De Carlo reunited for a TV movie seventeen years after they thought they'd buried the characters.

that they were actually, that many years later, going to try to get the old men into those funny costumes again. Then I suddenly thought, well, if they want to, they're gonna pay. So my agent said, 'What should we ask for?' and I named a figure and he said, 'I don't think they're gonna stand for that.' And I said, 'That's the beauty part, I don't care.' There was silence on the other end of the phone and about a minute later he said, 'Oh, I see, yes, that's fine.' And we got it!" he said laughing.

Gwynne admitted he had decided to stick it to the production company since his original agreement on the series left much to be desired. He was no longer getting residuals on the original show, so if he was to undergo

the horrors of the makeup process again after some fifteen years, then someone would have to make it worthwhile. Al Lewis was given a similarly handsome paycheck and the film was on its way.

Most of the cast had been reassembled: Gwynne, Lewis, and De Carlo. Young actor K.C. Martel filled in the shoes—or the fangs—of Butch Patrick, in the role of Eddie, and blonde Jo McDonnell portrayed Marilyn. In an odd juxtaposition, everyone had aged but Eddie and Marilyn.

Fred Gwynne insisted on bringing aboard two of the original makeup men, Karl Silvera and Abe Haberman. Both men were still working in the business, albeit nearing retirement. "Somebody at Universal—one of my colleagues—made a remark that I was too old to handle makeup for Fred on the movie and I think Fred told them either they have me or he doesn't participate. I'll admit, the movie was more work than I had planned for," says Silvera. "If it hadn't been for me, they would have had no show because nobody knew Grandpa's makeup or Fred's

makeup. What they did was they handed me two guys and two hairdressers who were never trained as makeup artists. I had to show people how to do things and a lot of times, tear it apart and redo it because they weren't done right. They'd keep them waiting a couple of hours in the morning. I told them originally I was only gonna do Fred but it didn't work out that way and the producer and I got into some pretty heated arguments."

As TV reunions go, the cast said they felt like filming together again was déjà vu. "By the second day or so, it was like we hadn't left the studio," remembers Yvonne De Carlo. "We had tried to make a go of it for a series, but perhaps the movie wasn't up to par."

There were a few interesting aspects with the TV movie. Composer Vic Mizzy, who scored the original *Addams Family* television show and created its popular snappy theme song, was brought in by producer Ed Montagne to provide a wacky score for this film. Mizzy clearly did not attempt to imitate Jack Marshall's original underscore and contributed his own bizarre blend of

Lily's Cuisine

As the devoted wife and mother that Lily was, she could always be found in the kitchen brewing a Munster delicacy to satisfy her hungry Herman. As she used to tell little Eddie, "Don't just sit there, wolf down your food." Here are some of Lily's most sumptuous meals, handed down from generations.

Top Ten Entrées

1. Chopped lizard livers
2. Cold rhinoceros-tongue sandwiches
3. Fillet of dragon (Chinese food)
4. Eggs, gloomy side up
5. Cream of vulture soup (Herman's favorite soup)
6. Curried lizard casserole
7. Rolled hyena-foot roast
8. Bird's nest stew (Grandpa's favorite)
9. Warm ladyfingers with pickled frog ears
10. Dodo-bird roast

Side Dishes

- Cream of buzzard soup, iguana soup
- Salamander salad with centipede dressing
- Salad with cactus-juice dressing (freshly squeezed)

Beverages

- Bloody Mary
- Piping hot bat milk (in the evening)

Dessert

- Devil's food cake (recipe from a friend of Grandpa's)

R.I.P. (References Involving the Parlor)

As the family breadwinner, Herman proudly labored at the leading funeral parlor in Mockingbird Heights. His actual duties at the parlor were never disclosed, but he brought his modest paycheck home each week. With lunchbox in hand each morning, Herman would set off for Gateman, Goodbury & Graves, where he had worked for twelve years.

According to Grandpa, he started out as a "nail boy." But another episode has Lily commenting on Herman's humble beginnings as a "box boy." Even the parlor's name changed in the series—one episode ("Herman's Driving Test") shows the company as Gateman, Graves & Goodbury on Herman's business card. A shroud of mystery surrounded this odd employee with the funeral parlor. Undeniably, he fit in with the line of work.

It was never clarified whether Herman actually embalmed bodies. Did he arrange flowers? Was he a model for the caskets? Did he drive the hearse as anticipated in one episode? Viewers were *dying* to know. Here are a few of the hints *planted* in the dialogue.

Herman: We were quite busy today. In fact we had quite a turnover.

Grandpa: Down at the parlor, why should you take things lying down?

Mr. Gateman (Herman's boss): Herman's demanded an increase in salary, and down here I'm afraid we're not used to raising people.

Herman: I got into a little argument with a client down at the parlor over money. He thought our carrying charges were too high.

Lily: As it is, you go into the hole three or four times a week.

Herman: Sorry I'm late, but before I left, I had to lay out some work for tomorrow.

Mr. Gateman: You've been quiet as a customer all evening.

Herman: Starting Monday, I'll be driving the hearse. Or as they say in the trade, the Go-Go wagon.

Herman: If any work piles up over the weekend, I'll tell 'em to throw it on ice 'til Monday.

Herman: People are dying to get in here. I think it's because of our layaway plan.

THE MUNSTERS TODAY

SO FAR, *THE MUNSTERS TODAY* AND *THE ODD Couple* remain the only series in television history to be exhumed from the depths of rerun status for a complete overhaul and production of an all-new version. Sure, *Star Trek* returned, but in a different forms, with different characters, taking place in a different era of space travel. Sure, a few oddball shows have returned, like *What's Happening!!*, but the cast returned as well. There have been television-show cast-reunion specials, but it's been a rarity to have a program starring a live cast to return to the airwaves in full-series form with an all-new cast.

Here was the concept: *The Munsters Today* was an updated version of the original series. According to the show's opening sequence (sung by Herman), Grandpa has performed an unsuccessful experiment that accidentally freezes the family for twenty-five years. They awake in the late eighties, singing and dancing to a mild rock version of the theme song. The episodes start in black-and-white and bloom into a muted color.

In *The Munsters Today*, the house has been rearranged, Herman has gained fifty pounds, and Marilyn has regressed to the age of sixteen. Premiering in the fall of 1988 for first-run syndication, the show featured John Schuck as Herman, Lee Meriwether as Lily, Howard Morton as Grandpa, Jason Marsden as Eddie, and Hilary Van Dyke as Marilyn.

"Fortunately, in this show, anybody can become the

cast. It's just a makeup job," said Norman Abbott quite boldly. There are plenty of actors and viewers who would readily disagree. Abbott directed the pilot and several episodes of the original series and perhaps he didn't recognize the genius of Fred Gwynne and company. Abbott returned to the same chore for a handful of the new episodes. "I'd say they are as equally talented as the old cast. John Schuck has brought as good a character to the part as Fred Gwynne initially did."

On the other side of the tombstone, actress Lee Meriwether, a former Miss America now remembered by television fans for her role as Buddy Ebsen's girl Friday on *Barnaby Jones*, played an appropriately straight Lily Munster. Howard Morton's breathy Grandpa added a new dimension which was occasionally funny. Morton knew better than imitate Al Lewis and attempted to mold his own crusty Grandpa, something akin to a Paul Lynde delivery.

Executive-producer Arthur Annecharico (the Arthur Company in collaboration with MCA-TV) attempted to re-create the series as convincingly as possible while updating the humor. "We decided not to use any of the old cast, but our choices for the roles are very good," he says. "Some of the old props such as the front doors, Lily's necklace, and a few pieces of furniture are from the old series." The cuckoo clock from the original series was located in a Los Angeles prop shop and leased for the new production.

Aside from the new cast, additional adjustments were incorporated to effect the Munster mood. The show was shot with a four-camera videotape technique rather than on film like the original series. Twenty percent of the color had been removed utilizing special Beta cameras, which allowed the action to be shot with less detail—thereby producing a softer image. In addition, a number-two fog filter covered the lens to wear off any sharpness left. The outcome was a gloomy, pea-soup effect which made viewers squint or continually rub the foreign matter out of their eyes.

The house had been decorated apropos of the Munsters, with a slightly different floor plan. For an exterior shot of the mansion, an elaborate miniature model had been built for medium and long shots. (On the set, you always knew when you were near the model of the house exterior. The meticulously detailed miniature smelled like a pizzeria because dried and crumbly oregano, doubling for leaves, was spread all over the front and back lawn.)

The show fell short of its predecessor—in humor and in longevity. Occasionally some of the scripts captured some of the old Munster charm and a few interesting guest stars popped in (Paul Williams, Bill Daily, Ruth Buzzi, astronaut Gordon Cooper, Kathleen Freeman, Zsa Zsa Gabor, Billy Barty among them). Jokes such as having Spot fart as he exits the kitchen only went so far with audiences. Despite its shortcomings, the series lasted three seasons (sixty-six episodes), nearly as long as the original. At one time, the plan at Universal/MCA was to colorize the original series and package it for television stations along with *The Munsters Today*. There were no takers.

In time *The Munsters Today* will become one of those odd little burps in the timeline of television history. Wait, it already is. You can smell it.

MUNSTER MOMENT

In the sixties sitcom *Green Acres* episode titled "Jealousy, English Style," Arnold the pig, while preparing for school, has trouble choosing a new lunchbox in Drucker's Hooterville store. Two metal lunchboxes are shown and one of them is clearly the current Munsters lunchbox of the day, altered slightly with dark paint in order to render it nearly unrecognizable. Arnold opts for the more stylized dome metal lunchbox instead.

THE ADDAMS FAMILY

"*The creators have the right approach, the approach that was so completely missing from* The Addams Family. *. . . In never suggesting its premise needs an explanation,* The Munsters *has a head start.*"

—*NEW YORK TIMES*,
September 25, 1964

THE ADDAMS FAMILY DEFINITELY WAS A MONSTER of another breed. There has, for years, been a great debate as to which of the two primetime "monster" sitcoms is funniest. Followers of both *Addams* and *The Munsters* can argue about which is funnier until they're green in the face, but it remains entirely subjective. Today, people tend to take sides. No winners in that argument. Both shows, unique in their approaches, achieved excellence and earned a permanent place in popular-culture history. Both had theme songs which perfectly attuned viewers with their respective show. Both peculiarly twisted viewers' notion of death, and in some respects, evil.

Based on the Charles Addams cartoons which dated back to the late thirties and became popular in the *New Yorker* magazine, The Addams Family of creeps lured

cult allegiances on ABC-TV just like their sister show of monsters on CBS. The characters were christened with a name once they hit television, but the images themselves had already become a popular-culture trademark of sorts with fans all across America. Boris Karloff, who played the grandpappy of all popular monsters on film, the Universal Frankenstein's monster, was an avid fan of Charles Addams's cartoons. In his foreword to the published collection of Addams's artwork titled *Drawn and Quartered*, he wrote: "Perhaps Mr. Addams is happiest in his dealing with the macabre. His preoccupation with hangman's nooses and lethal doses is always innocent and gay. He has the extraordinary faculty of making the normal appear idiotic when confronted by the abnormal, as in his scenes of cannibals, skiers, and skaters." Karloff continued and thanked the artist Addams for immortalizing him in the personage of the butler. If he liked Lurch, it would *really* be interesting to know what Karloff thought about Herman Munster.

The Munsters was already in development by in the fall of 1963 when David Levy, a former NBC programming executive, decided to adapt Charles Addams's drawings/characters for a television sitcom. By February 1964, ABC had finalized a deal with Filmways Television (*The Beverly Hillbillies*, *Mr. Ed*, *Green Acres*) to produce the series with stars John Astin, Carolyn Jones, Jackie Coogan, and Ted Cassidy. ABC-TV was originally interested in *The Munsters*, but for some reason was unable to acquire the property. Obviously, *Addams* became their answer to CBS's upcoming *Munsters*. As fate would direct, both series premiered in the same week in the fall of 1964, and both left the air the same week in 1966.

LIFE magazine dubbed 1964 "The Year of the Ghouls." The magazine warned and assured audiences that the TV monsters "will burst upon us next month like a spray of lightning over Frankenstein's castle . . . strictly from beyond the grave. Let parents have no qualms, it will be played solely for guffaws."

It was, perhaps, survival of the hideous during those years. "There definitely was a rivalry between the shows," admitted Rose Mosher Perry, widow of *Munsters* producer Bob Mosher. "They always tried to top one another. Each worked harder to produce the better show."

Addams producer David Levy told the press in September 1964: "If people are looking for something new, we're as far out as any show following the trend to fantasy. But we're not grotesque. I'd say we're whimsical. [Charles] Addams named the characters and spelled out the descriptions. He saw the set and the pilot film and felt it was in the spirit of what we wanted to do."

Levy further distinguished his show from *The Munsters:* "Ours really isn't a horror show. Our people have red blood. They're, well, bizarre. We aren't giving the Addams' house an excessively cobwebby look. The atmosphere is pleasant. We are reaching for an audience of children and adults."

Without a doubt, Gomez and Morticia Addams were the more provocative, malevolent creatures who relied on much darker (and unapologetically sexier) humor than Herman and Lily Munster; this is primarily the reason *The Addams Family* attracted a more adult and sophisticated audience—then and now. But there were similarities: both the Addams clan and the Munsters brood were peace-loving families, actually good role models for children. Both shows were macabre in flavor, but disarmed the public by their solid nature.

Aesthetically speaking, the Addams' household was just as creepy as the Munsters, but in a kooky manner. While the Munster house had cobwebs and bats, the Addams house was cleaner with bizarre furnishings and a more eclectic décor. The humor of the Addamses was a tad more demented and nonconforming with the characters thriving in a bland, colorless society.

John Astin describes his show by noting, "The Addams family were a cultured people. Art was a theme in this show.

"At the same time, we were satirizing the world of so-called cultured people. I recall someone asking me when we first started the show, 'Do you think that a bread-and-butter network like ABC is going to be successful with a show based on sophisticated *New Yorker* cartoons?' I remember my answer was, 'Well, the adults may miss it, but the kids will pick it up.' Kids pick up sophistication quickly."

Just like the Munsters, the Addamses lived on and were resurrected for TV reunion specials, cartoons, and the like; more successfully, the Addams family jumped the fence and were artfully (and expensively) adapted to the big screen twice by Paramount Pictures in the nineties.

Credits

FIRST PRIMETIME TELECAST: September 18, 1964

FINAL (FIRST-RUN) PRIMETIME TELECAST: September 2, 1966

TIMESLOT: Friday 8:30–9:00 PM, ABC-TV

FILMED EPISODES: 64

LOCATION: Episodes Filmed at General Service Studios, Hollywood

PRODUCTION COMPANY: Filmways Television

CAST: John Astin (Gomez Addams), Carolyn Jones (Morticia Frump Addams), Jackie Coogan (Uncle Fester), Ted Cassidy (Lurch), Blossom Rock (Grandmama Addams), Ken Weatherwax (Pugsley Addams), Lisa Loring (Wednesday Addams), Felix Silla (Cousin Itt), Tony Magro (voice of Cousin Itt), Ted Cassidy (Thing).

MUNSTER MANIA

IN 1966, DURING A BREAK IN FILMING THE FEATURE *Munster, Go Home!*, Fred Gwynne shared this story with a reporter:

> Al Lewis and I went to see the L.A. Blades for the last year. We had season tickets. Every once in a while a young girl or young boy would come up—and I was always hoping they would not ask me because then I would be able to say to Al, 'You see, they don't know me. I've done a series for two years and I kept my anonymity. You thought *your* makeup was drastic! It wasn't at all. They didn't make you look any uglier or older. That's just exactly how you look, Al Lewis!' I wasn't too successful. I'd say one out of six would ask him for an autograph and not me. Gave me quite a chuckle.

That was perhaps the last time Fred Gwynne might have been recognized for anything *but* Herman Munster. From the moment he removed those heavy boots, he was haunted by the shadow of a Munster. It lurked in Gwynne's unmistakable resonant voice, his stature, and his familiarity. Gwynne could not shake Herman Munster and eventually came to grips with it, at least outwardly. "Some days he was tired of being recognized as Herman Munster," said Madyn Gwynne on the A&E *Biography* of her father. "And other days he was fine with him because Herman Munster was a nice guy." Still, he was reticent to grant interviews over the next thirty years. The legacy of *The Munsters* was something not to be ignored, but Gwynne tried.

Al Lewis could never fully grasp his costar's secret battle with the character. "I can only surmise it was hell for him during those years and he didn't want to discuss it," said Al Lewis in recent years. "He was my bucks. The fans' fiercely competitive pursuit continues to keep *The Munsters* a successful franchise for its owner, Universal Studios. The studio has never ceased to introduce more Munster products.

Pop-culture writer and radio-show host Frank DeCaro, forty-three, has prized his own Munsters lunchbox since he was a kid attending grade school. "I only took it to school once because I broke the thermos the first day and I was discouraged, so I have a pristine lunchbox from 1966," he says. "I really grew to love *The Munsters* in reruns the way so many people did. As much as I like the performances on *The Addams Family*, nothing comes close to the genius of Fred Gwynne. His creation of Herman Munster, that sort of ridiculous man-child under all that makeup, is really one of the greatest acting jobs ever done on television.

"The show is really a brilliant mix of real traditional sitcom with tremendous physical humor and a streak of vaudeville in there. Fred Gwynne is this classically trained actor, Lily is this B-movie queen who is exquisite looking but actually a good actress in her own right, and then Al Lewis is this sort of Borscht Belt comedian in Dracula garb. There are so many levels there to sink your, well, fangs into. It holds up beautifully for me and it's something you can watch with little kids and it's funny for them."

DeCaro says he knows the secret of the show's longevity: "It worked because it's a sweet, loving family comedy about people who are anything but traditional, but have tremendous love. And that resonates even today," he adds. "You have this family of total freaks and yet they think the entire world is not nearly as fortunate as they are. That's a very comforting message, particularly today when so many families don't resemble characters on *The Donna Reed Show* . . . and they really *do* resemble the Munsters a lot more."

As a commodity, the Munsters have proven themselves evergreen. Since the television show was never officially released in the VHS format, the long-awaited DVD package (both seasons) released in 2005 sent fans rushing out like angry villagers to hunt down the venerable complete boxed sets which featured re-mastered, uncut episodes plus bonus elements such as the unseen color pilot. In recent years, for instance, it has not been difficult to find Herman and Lily on toy-store shelves in the guise of Barbie doll characters and pose-able figures or stuffed bear versions. The Munster likenesses were also recently licensed to appear on trick-or-treat bags, Illinois State lottery tickets, Las Vegas slot machines, cookie jars— even Munsters sugary Halloween treats made specially by Hostess. Talk about product consumption.

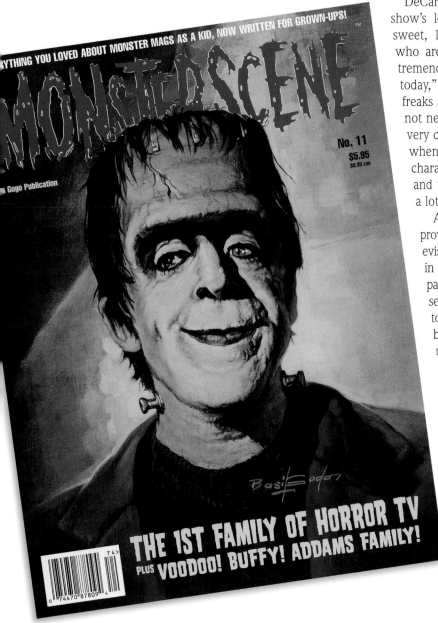

ᴺʸᵀᴴᴵᴺᴳ YOU LOVED ABOUT MONSTER MAGS AS A KID, NOW WRITTEN FOR GROWN-UPS!

MONSTER SCENE

No. 11
$5.95
$8.35 can

Gogo Publication

Basil Gogos

THE 1ST FAMILY OF HORROR TV
PLUS VOODOO! BUFFY! ADDAMS FAMILY!

◄ Don Post himself unveils for Al Lewis the deluxe (complete with hair) Grandpa rubber Halloween mask produced by Don Post Studios in 1965.

▼ The prop "Woof Woof" doll as it appears today. (James Madden, Jr. Collection)

DRAG RACE GAME

More Vintage Munster Memorabilia

- Herman Munster kite (Pressman Toy Co.)

- Munsters dashboard dolls (Remco Industries)

- Munsters souvenir hat (Arlington Hat Co.)

- Munsters pocket flashlight (Bantam-Lite, Inc)

- Munsters Halloween costumes (Ben Cooper, Inc)

- Munsters tie clasps, earrings, bracelets, cufflinks, pens, necklaces (Harry Klitzer Co.)

- Munsters paint-by-number sets, board games, "Rub-Ons" magic-picture transfers (Hasbro, Inc.)

- Munsters bowling set, target game, hand puppets, figures (Ideal Toys)

- Munsters jigsaw puzzle, hardback story books, paper dolls, coloring book, sticker book, magic slate (Whitman)

- Munsters plastic assembly kit (Aurora)

- Munsters metal lunchbox and thermos (King Seeley Thermos)

- Munster Koach and Drag-u-la model kits (AMT)

- Munsters comic books series of sixteen issues (Gold Key)

- Munsters LP record album, *At Home with the Munsters* (A.A. Records/Golden Records)

- Munsters LP record album, *The Munsters* (Decca)

- Munsters 45-record, "Theme from *The Munsters*"/Jack Marshall (Capitol)

- Munsters View-Master reels (Sawyer's Inc.)

- Munsters Stardust: Touch of Velvet Art kit (Hasbro, Inc.)

- Munsters card game (Milton Bradley)

- Munsters latex rubber masks (Don Post Studios)

- Munsters Castex casting set (Emenee)

- Munsters trading cards (Leaf)

- Munsters Kenner Easy Show 8-mm Movie Projector (Kenner)

- Munsters Hypo-Squirt Water Gun (Hasbro, Inc.)

FANG MAIL:

Confessions of a Munsters Collector

I guess it all started on June 18, 1964. It was my ninth birthday and a neighbor of mine gave me my first Aurora Monster model. (This same neighbor's father was a television writer and would later go on to write scripts for *Lost in Space* and *Star Trek*.) The model I received was the Customizing Kit with the "Vulture and Mad Dog"; within the instructions it offered me the opportunity to "Collect Other Aurora Monster Kits!" This was my introduction to the names "Frankenstein," "Dracula," "Wolfman," and others.

During the course of that summer I bought every Aurora monster model I could get my hands on. I went to the library and read every available book on monsters I could find (often settling for the easier to read classics, "Classics Illustrated" versions), and sent my twenty-five cents to Warren Publishing for my introductory issue of *Famous Monsters of Filmland*. It was already the era of the Beatles and James Bond, and now monsters. What a great time to be a kid.

Sometime in August, another friend mentioned there was going to be a television series featuring all the original monsters. It was going to be called *The Munsters* and was being filmed at Universal Studios (the same studio responsible for all those classic films my mother forbid me from watching!). *LIFE* magazine did a story about the new trend toward TV monsters and included a picture of Fred Gwynne in a full-page shot made up as Herman Munster. There were lots of pictures from another new series, *The Addams Family*, but I was unfamiliar with the "*New Yorker* cartoon family" and they seemed like second-generation monsters anyway.

When *The Munsters* debuted in September, I was hooked. What a cool family! (We used expressions like that in those days.) That neat house, all those cobwebs, the makeup and the special effects!

Award-winning filmmaker and documentary producer Kevin Burns is a former head of the film-production program at Boston University. In the early nineties, he relocated to Los Angeles and worked as an executive at 20th Century-Fox's television division, Foxstar. Burns's own production companies, Prometheus Entertainment and Van Ness Films, co-produced television specials about *The Munsters* as well as individual *Biography* documentaries devoted to Fred Gwynne, Al Lewis, and Yvonne De Carlo for the A&E channel. (His *Biography* specials on Boris Karloff, Shirley Temple, *The Planet of the Apes*, and the history of 20th Century-Fox Studios are among the most acclaimed in the network's long-running series.) Unquestionably, Burns has never lost his passion for such television classics as *The Munsters*, *Batman*, and *Lost in Space* and maintains a formidable collections of ephemera from them all. Burns is the proud owner of one of Lily's original bat necklaces and Grandpa's one and only electric chair from the *The Munsters*. He insists he doesn't "collect" . . . he "accumulates."

I started drawing pictures of the various cast members and of a few of the scenes I could remember. At one point, my mother suggested that if I liked the show that much, I should send some of my drawings to series star Fred Gwynne. Never having sent a fan letter in my life, I was reluctant, but I did anyway—just in case.

Just after Christmas, as I was under the tree and playing with my newly acquired Munster dolls (by Remco), the postman surprised me with a postcard, sent all the way from Hollywood, California. On one side was a great black-and-white portrait of

KEVIN —
I like the picture VERY much!
I'm sorry I took so long to answer
but I've been on VACATION.
VERY best Regards
"FRED
HERMAN"
GWYNNE

▲ Mailed with a four-cent stamp, this postcard response from Fred Gwynne was sent to youngster Kevin Burns in Schenectady, New York, in August 1965. It sparked in Burns an infinite passion for the television show.

◄ Munsters collector extraordinaire, Kevin Burns, amongst his "Munsterabilia." Burns, a Los Angeles–based film producer, has amassed probably the most extensive archive and collection on *The Munsters* ever assembled. (Photo by Jon Gawne)

Herman Munster, and on the back, your typical studio-issued message thanking me for my interest in the series. But what was more impressive was that this card came direct from Herman himself, as proven by the handwritten postscript which thanked me personally for the drawings.

For the next year-and-a-half, I continued corresponding with Fred Gwynne and received several more cards and even a few drawings from him. I also became quite obsessive where the show was concerned and made a deliberate effort to collect everything that existed on the show.

Well, nothing lasts forever. The series was cancelled in 1966 (the reality of which I refused to admit for about six months), Fred Gwynne, Al Lewis, Yvonne De Carlo, and the rest of the cast went on to do different things—and so did I. My interest in *The Munsters* has waxed and waned over the years, but I have always credited that show and the modest interest Fred Gwynne took in me for the direction my career has taken.

I have maintained my rather extensive collection of "Munstermobilia" and have been lucky enough to establish a nice relationship with most of the cast members.

—Kevin Burns

CAST BIOGRAPHIES

FRED GWYNNE

In 1964, *TV Guide* said of Fred Gwynne, "The disguise [as Herman Munster] will likely remain his hallmark for many years." For Gwynne, that was an understatement. The shadow of Herman is a hulking one. Although his life was filled with many personal accomplishments, the Munster role haunted him to the day he died—and thereafter—in every obituary printed about the man.

Born on July 10, 1926 in New York City, young Frederick Gwynne traveled around the country because of his father's health. He spent his childhood in South Carolina, Florida, Colorado, and New York—the state he really preferred. After graduating high school, the six-foot-five, lantern-jawed Gwynne enlisted in the Navy to serve as a radio man, third class, on a sub chaser in the Pacific. He begged to be relieved of that particular duty

▲ Fred Gwynne, accomplished actor and artist, in the late eighties in his New York City loft. (Courtesy of Simon and Schuster)

▶ Fred and Jean "Foxy" Gwynne on a night out in 1966.

because the incessant beeping was driving him to his wits' end and aggravating the claustrophobia he suffered out at sea.

Following his discharge, he entered Harvard and joined the Brattle Theatre group while still in college, continuing with the group for a few years following his graduation in 1951. Gwynne drew cartoons for the Harvard Lampoon and became its president; while at Harvard he also acted in the famed Hasty Pudding Club.

Gwynne performed many roles in the group's productions, but it was the successful portrayal of the character of Bottom in *A Midsummer Night's Dream*, which gave him the confidence to tackle the Great White Way. He landed a role in a production of *Mrs. McThing*, which led to additional stage performances and a number of television guest spots such as *The Phil Silvers Show*. His list of credits was growing, but he took on a job as a copywriter with the J. Walter Thompson advertising agency to pay the bills, squeezing in acting when he could. At the J. Walter Thompson, one of the leading agencies in New York City, his natural artistic abilities came into play as he helped create advertising campaigns and slogans.

In the theater, his big break came when he was cast in Broadway's *Irma la Douce*. It was during this successful run that he was spotted by producer Nat Hiken and offered the role of Francis Muldoon in a television sitcom called *Car 54, Where Are You?*

Tragedy struck Gwynne and his family in July 1963 when Fred and Jean's infant son, Dylan, fell into the family swimming pool and drowned. Devastated by the loss, Fred immersed himself in work to cope; however, the sad events led to strain and a separation between he and his wife. Within months of the cancellation of *Car 54*, a new door in television had opened for the actor.

Gwynne rode *Car 54* straight to Mockingbird Lane, when he was cast as Herman Munster by producers Joe Connelly and Bob Mosher. Fred and his wife, Jean "Foxy" Gwynne, reconciled and were raising four children now on the West Coast, where *The Munsters* got underway by the early part of 1964. Following his two-year gig in monster garb, Gwynne's career in television took a sharp turn for the worse. He starred in a pilot for 20th Century-Fox Television titled *Anderson and Company*, but the show did not sell. "Casting directors treated me like I had leprosy," he told one reporter. "So I retreated to things I wanted to get back to, like art."

Gwynne, by this time quite an accomplished painter and sculptor who once studied with noted portrait artist E.S. Merryman at New York's Phoenix School of Design,

▲ Fred Gwynne and Joe E. Ross are Officers Muldoon and Toody in Nat Hiken's NBC sitcom hit, *Car 54, Where Are You?* (1961–63). Gwynne's artistry is displayed in this publicity shot.

▶ Harvard-educated Fred Gwynne was a writer and artist before becoming an arresting figure in television on NBC-TV's *Car 54, Where Are You?*

"But it is Mr. Gwynne who walks off with the show and makes palatable even the extremes of broad slapstick to which the program is not immune. His gift for underplaying adds enormously to the hilarious image of the heart of gold beneath the forbidding facial exterior."

—*NEW YORK TIMES,*
September 25, 1964

relocated to the East Coast. He landed roles in television occasionally, but theater came calling again and soon he became involved in Shakespearean theater and musicals performing some meaty roles including the role of Big Daddy in the 1974 Broadway revival of *Cat on a Hot Tin Roof*. Gwynne won rave reviews as the stage manager in *Our Town* at the American Shakespeare Festival in Stratford, Connecticut in 1975 and as the colonel in Preston Jones's *Texas Trilogy* on Broadway the following year. Fred won an Obie award for best actor in the off-Broadway play *Grand Magic* in 1979.

Fred and "Foxy" divorced after twenty-eight years of marriage in the late seventies and he remarried in 1988 to Debbie Loveless. The couple lived in New York City until they purchased a home in rural Maryland where Gwynne built an art studio for himself.

In the eighties and nineties, Simon and Schuster published a collection of his artwork as children's books utilizing a theme of homonyms, a theme inspired by his daughter, Madyn. His fancifully illustrated books, such as *The King Who Rained*, *A Chocolate Moose For Dinner*, and *A Little Pigeon Toad* became popular with kids and teachers alike, as he continued to draw and paint in his New York loft.

Gwynne knew the curse of Herman Munster had been lifted as casting directors did an about-face with the

actor, placing him in prominent roles in such motion pictures as *The Cotton Club* (as Frenchy), *Ironweed*, *Fatal Attraction*, and *Pet Sematary*. In *My Cousin Vinny*, his final film role, Gwynne played a stern Southern judge presiding over a murder trial. Gwynne's smooth, resonant voice lent perfectly for voiceover work as he became the commercial spokesman for leading ad campaigns like Hyundai, Dreyer's ice cream, Hardees, Colgate, and Maytag.

While his acting career jetted in diverse directions during the last years of his life, Gwynne rarely looked back fondly with regard to *The Munsters*. Said his ex-wife, Foxy Gwynne, in 1988: "I still get mail here for Fred. I give it to him and he just throws it away. He just wants to be left alone to paint and do other things. He wants to forget *The Munsters*." The show represented a period of his life that he did not wish to reflect on, and the death of his son might have weighed heavily in that.

In May 1993, tabloids broke the news that Gwynne had been diagnosed with pancreatic cancer with just months to live. The actor bravely faced the inevitable with strength and courage and lived out his days peacefully in Maryland with friends and relatives at his side. Fred Gwynne died on July 2, 1993, just days before his sixty-seventh birthday.

In his dressing room, Fred and his daughter, Gaynor Gwynne, clown around with the chimp that appeared in the episode "Come Back, Little Googie." (February 3, 1965)

Monster Garb

Fred Gwynne was a tall, lanky, six-footer when he took on the role of Herman. He weighed about 180 pounds, but his weight gradually dropped after he started filming the series. That was not something he had bargained for when he took on the show.

In a daily routine during the filming, Gwynne pulled on a pair of trousers lined with foam-rubber padding to create the Herman Munster bulk. He wore a heavy, padded shirt beneath his undersized jacket which was swollen with more layers of padding in the sleeves, and shoulders. More than the weight it applied, it also forced Gwynne to constrict his movement and make it part of the character. "I looked at the first shows," said Gwynne during the series, "and I discovered that I had to keep my neck stiff for the monster effect. When I bend, I bend my whole body. It's a mental thing, keeping it stiff."

No one told him it would be easy, but within the first ten episodes, Gwynne had Herman's movement down pretty well, finally growing accustomed to gracefully mastering all of that padding and suffering through the layers of greasepaint. Gwynne even painfully learned to handle his ten-pound leather boots with finesse.

"For the first three weeks," Gwynne told *TV Guide*, "my back, everything hurt. My body was not used to the costume, and the high-heeled boots stretched my tendons. I could hardly walk at the end of the day."

The foam rubber inserted in the costume caused Gwynne to suffocate under the wraps, and he lost nearly ten pounds. "I ate salt tablets for a while because I was sweating so much," Gwynne said at the time. "Maybe they helped me over the first week or two. When I'm really sweating, I get so dry that I drink about a gallon of water. Water isn't that enjoyable, and I can't drink vodka on the set, so I settled on lemonade without sugar."

Fred Gwynne puts his feet up during rehearsal. The stress of starring in a network show, handling a busy schedule, extensive makeup sessions, and weighty wardrobe all took a toll on Gwynne during production. The exhausted actor commented to writer Erskine Johnson in 1965, "I'm really curious to see if I'll make it to the end of the first season."

For further comfort in between scenes, Gwynne sought the relief provided by a portable compressed-air tank. When he became a little overheated, a stagehand would poke its nozzle inside the neck of Gwynne's costume and release cool air. "I was fighting for breath," said Gwynne. Following filming days, Gwynne also indulged in the healing magic of a masseur regularly, which rejuvenated the actor for the next week's torture.

Gwynne's makeup and costume were the most demanding of all the cast. Yvonne De Carlo's makeup didn't involve any foam latex, and her costume was light and airy. De Carlo's lengthy wig was constraining at times, but she handled it aptly. Al Lewis's tuxedo could get hot under the studio lights, but he cheated by wearing a sleeveless white shirt with a backless vest.

"The show was very physically demanding on Fred," Lewis said "More than anyone else. He perspired unbelievably, the foam was so thick. Obviously from his attitude about the show, maybe his summation is that it was hell."

Gwynne forever suffered some physical side effects from portraying Herman. Because of the makeup on his head and the heavy costume, it was difficult for Gwynne to move fluidly—or at all. "He couldn't bend or move his neck," Lewis said "I remember him going to the doctor and getting cortisone shots in his neck, it was so painful."

YVONNE DE CARLO

When Peggy Yvonne Middleton stepped foot onto the Universal soundstage decked in her shroud-like gown and flowing silver streak in her hair, she was no newcomer to the business. Better known to movie audiences as Yvonne De Carlo, the curvaceous actress was a full-fledged B-movie queen, but weekly television was rather a fresh area in her repertoire and privately, the actress was nervous. Twenty years earlier, she was signed by Universal Studios for her first motion-picture starring role in *Salome, Where She Danced*. This debut launched a career of leading roles in more than forty films, with supporting appearances in forty more. Of the *Munsters* cast, De Carlo was the most prolific in cinema.

Born on September 1, 1922, in Vancouver, British Columbia, Canada, the aspiring young entertainer trained at the Vancouver School of Dance and came to Hollywood at age seventeen with her mother. She enrolled in the Franchon and Marco Dancing School and performed professionally at the Florentine Gardens and the Earl Carroll Theatre in Hollywood before deciding to make movies. Her initial break in motion pictures, she has noted, came when she was cast for a small role in *This Gun for Hire* (1942) and for the next three years she accepted lesser roles such as secretaries, chorus girls, hatcheck girls, and harem dancers—until the *Salome* opportunity appeared.

According to her memoirs, De Carlo was a "first" with respect to many aspects of her career. She was the first Hollywood actress to star abroad in a for-

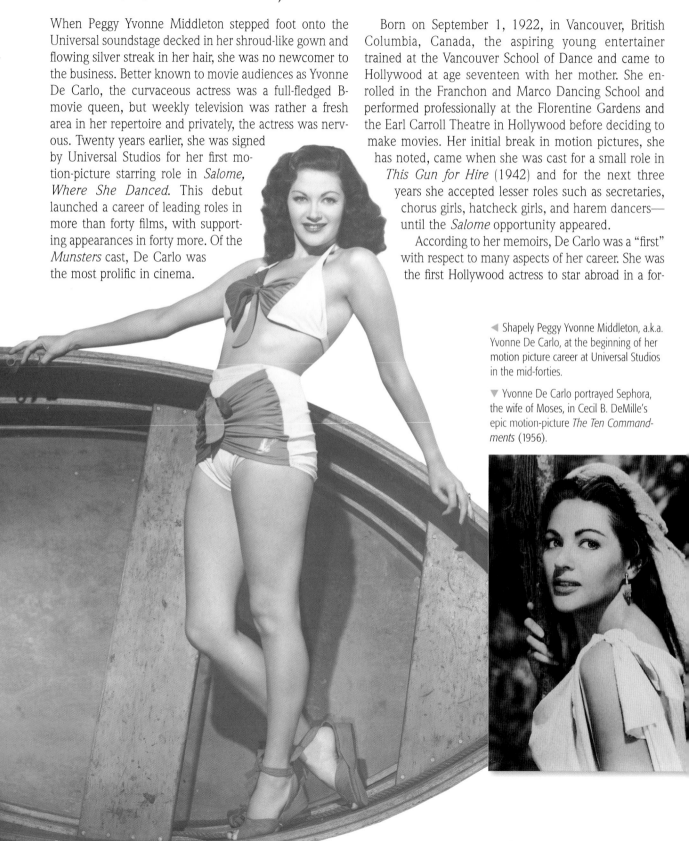

◀ Shapely Peggy Yvonne Middleton, a.k.a. Yvonne De Carlo, at the beginning of her motion picture career at Universal Studios in the mid-forties.

▼ Yvonne De Carlo portrayed Sephora, the wife of Moses, in Cecil B. DeMille's epic motion-picture *The Ten Commandments* (1956).

eign-language film, the French-made *Castiglione*. She appeared in the first hour-long live-television show in the United States, Robert Sherwood's *Backbone of America*.

As one of motion picture's true glamour girls, De Carlo found herself romanced by many of Hollywood's leading men, prominent world figures, "and a few truck drivers in between," she has joked. Her 1987 autobiography *Yvonne* candidly describes her flings with Sterling Hayden, Howard Hughes, Ray Milland, Rudy Vallee, Prince Aly Kahn, Jock Mahoney, Burt Lancaster, and others.

While filming her role of Sephora, the wife of Moses, in Cecil B. DeMille's *The Ten Commandments*, she met stuntman Bob Morgan and not long after the couple were married in 1955 in Reno, Nevada; the couple eventually had two sons, Bruce and Michael. In 1962, De Carlo continued to act in motion pictures such as *The Captain's Paradise*, *McLintock!* with John Wayne, *Law of the Lawless* with Dale Robertson, and *A Global Affair* with Bob Hope. In 1962, Bob Morgan escaped death, but was severely injured while working in the film *How the West Was Won*, and the stuntman lost one of his legs. Afterward, Yvonne dropped her career plans to care for her husband and nurse him back to health. Eventually, she says, the money began to run short and she started grabbing every acting role offered—including that of Lily Munster.

After her two-year run as the Munster matriarch, De Carlo continued to act in films and guest-starred in several television shows. She toured with a nightclub act and went on to star in such productions as *Hello, Dolly!*, which toured the country and originated the role of Carlotta in Stephen Sondheim's *Follies* on Broadway, belting out the familiar song "I'm Still Here."

In 1974, she and Bob Morgan divorced. Yvonne continued to immerse herself in work until the eighties when she decided to retire with only sporadic television and film appearances. Yvonne escaped life in Hollywood and moved north of Santa Barbara up near wine country where she could tend to a simpler life. Outside of rare television appearances (such as *The Vickie Lawrence Show* and *Tales from the Crypt*) in the early nineties, she has remained retired making just a few personal appearances. In 2000, the actress was the subject of an A&E *Biography* which explored her lengthy career well beyond *The Munsters*. Proudly sporting her original Lily Munster bat-necklace, De Carlo was featured in a rare on-camera interview in the 2003 A&E *Biography* series special about *The Munsters* produced by Kevin Burns.

The Munsters play host to visitors Phyllis Newman, Judy Carne, and Bob Morgan (Yvonne De Carlo's husband).

Following the series, Yvonne De Carlo was relieved to shed the ghoulish makeup and refocus her career with an emphasis on the theater.

Yvonne De Carlo and Rod Steiger starred in the cheesy horror flick *American Gothic* in 1987.

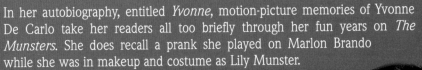

Brando Branded

In her autobiography, entitled *Yvonne*, motion-picture memories of Yvonne De Carlo take her readers all too briefly through her fun years on *The Munsters*. She does recall a prank she played on Marlon Brando while she was in makeup and costume as Lily Munster.

De Carlo had previously met Brando on the set of *The Appaloosa*, a movie he was shooting on the Universal lot. She writes, "When I returned a few days later, I was cornered by some of the crew, who asked me if I was game to play a prank on Brando. I agreed. They took me into a confessional booth of a church set, where Brando was about to make a confession to a priest. When his speech started, I was instructed to open the curtain and let him see me. I did it at the appointed time, and Marlon's reaction was priceless. He fell off the stool and pretended to walk off the soundstage. But he loved it."

AL LEWIS

Albert Meister (a.k.a. Al Lewis) was born on April 30, 1923, in upstate Wolcott, New York, to parents of Polish and German descent. (His father's actual last name was Maister and the family later changed it to Meister.) Young Albert grew up in Brooklyn and attended Thomas Jefferson High School.

He dabbled in a wildly diverse number of occupations including waiter, salesman, and a hot-dog vendor at Ebbets Field before he enlisted in the Merchant Marines during WWII. Later, changing his name to Al Lewis, he joined Paul Mann's acting studio and began to develop his rubber-faced comic style. Lewis met and married his wife, Marge, in the mid-fifties, and began a family. The couple had three boys: David, Ted, and Paul.

Lewis made his stage debut in the Circle in the Square production of *The Iceman Cometh*. Lewis eventually landed a number of appearances on television in New York including *The United States Steel Hour*, *Studio One*, and *The Armstrong Circle Theater*. An appearance on Phil Silvers's show led to his costarring role of loud-mouth Leo Schnauzer on Nat Hiken's sitcom *Car 54, Where Are You?*

From *Car 54*, the actor was spotted by a Hollywood casting agent who suggested him for the role of cantankerous Grandpa in *The Munsters*. He was finishing a run on Broadway in the musical *Do Re Mi* when the actor flew to Los Angeles and tested for *The Munsters*; he was quickly cast and moved out to Hollywood, staying at the

Al Lewis was in his early forties when he created the role of Grandpa, and played the ol' coot with just the right amount of selective, animated energy.

New York actors Al Lewis and Paul Reed in a scene from TV's *Car 54, Where Are You?* A few years later, Reed and Lewis worked together again when Reed portrayed Transylvania descendant, Henry J. Fregosi in the memorable episode, "The Fregosi Emerald."

Coming Unglued

When it aired originally, *The Munsters* received relatively good ratings. The public loved the show and critics gave the program moderate to good reviews, but nothing spectacular. The top-rated shows at the time were *Bonanza, Gomer Pyle, Bewitched, Batman, The Andy Griffith Show,* and *The Fugitive.*

Probably the sharpest criticism, however, came from within the network, and it infuriated Al Lewis in particular—the words not regarding performance or ratings, but a personal jab: ethnicity. The words came from Hunt Stromberg, Jr., an executive at CBS at the time.

"He was left over from nepotism," says Al Lewis, the target of Stromberg's criticism. "So much so that after he lost his job his next job was owning a pet shop. That's what he went to. He sought his own level."

According to Lewis, network executive Stromberg strongly and openly objected to his being on the show "because he didn't want a 'dime-store Fagin.'" Additional remarks about Lewis and the original nose extension on Grandpa appearing "too Jewish" made their way back to the actor. The nose was not the only thing coming unglued.

"I went to CBS headquarters on a day off," Lewis says, "went past his numerous secretaries directly to his office and slightly tightened his tie until he reached a shade of light purple. I said to him in the appropriate language, that if I ever hear him make that remark again, he will be like the song, 'Deep Purple.'"

That seemed to clear things up, according to Lewis.

Al Lewis's Greenwich Village eatery featured Fred Gwynne's caricature logo.

Montecito Hotel until his wife and kids joined him on the West Coast where they eventually purchased a house. For a time, Lewis—who never drove a car in his life—was chauffeured to and from the studio until he eventually learned to drive and obtained his own license.

Said his ex-wife, Marge Lewis, in 1989: "Al loves his boys. He spent more time with the kids than most fathers who are actors do. There's a little bit of hero worship in there. I think they worshipped him and they were afraid of him because he was very demanding at times, in terms of school and grades and commitments.

"The kids loved reading the scripts with Al at home and giving him his cues," she added. "He was always a well-prepared actor."

By the age of forty-two, Al Lewis had locked in the aged character he would be known for the rest of his life. The next years professionally were difficult as he became typecast as Grandpa, but accepted guest-starring roles in television wherever he could. He became a political ac-tivist and had a keen eye for basketball, scouting for several professional teams. Lewis continued to work in dinner theater and appeared in motion pictures such as *They Shoot Horses, Don't They?* in 1969.

In 1977, Al and his wife divorced. It wasn't long thereafter when he pulled up stakes and moved back to New York. There, he met actress Karen Ingenthron while working in the play *California Suite*, and the two were married in the mid-eighties. Lewis was shrewd enough to capitalize on his cult-hero status and opened an Italian restaurant in Greenwich Village; appropriately called "Grampa's," it became a popular eatery which fans flocked to for food and the opportunity to meet the famous proprietor. The restaurant flourished until Lewis closed its doors in the mid-nineties.

In a surprising career move, Lewis ran as the Green Party candidate in the New York gubernatorial race in 1998 against George Pataki. The outspoken Lewis campaigned against draconian drug laws and the death penalty. Although he was defeated, the actor received more than 52,000 votes in his home state and kept the political party alive.

In 2003, Al entered Manhattan's Mount Sinai Hospital for a routine angioplasty heart procedure which turned nearly fatal as complications set in and an immediate bypass was performed; surgeons also ended up having to amputate his right leg just below the knee and all five toes from his left foot. Lewis finally emerged from a month-long coma, and his life was never the same. Following several years of failing health, Al Lewis died on February 3, 2006. While most obituaries listed the actor as having reached the ripe age of ninety-five, everyone's favorite Grandpa was actually eighty-two years old.

▲ The cast surprised Al Lewis on the set with a "floating" birthday cake.

▶ Al Lewis's kids made him an honest Grandpa. Al is here mugging in this 2003 snapshot with his granddaughter Julia, and sons David and Ted.

Up in Smoke

To pass time on the set, Fred Gwynne and Al Lewis smoked. Cigarettes for Gwynne and cigars for you-know-who. When they took a break, they could not lie down because of their makeup, so they smoked some more. Because they had so much to do in each scene, they couldn't get involved with anything else on the set except memorizing lines while waiting to be called—so they lit up. After lunch, they smoked even more. This was at a time when smoking was allowed anywhere. Remember then?

The set was enveloped in a cloud of smoke, say some of the cast. "The two of them were fun, but it got to be hard to take, being around both of them smoking," says Yvonne De Carlo. "At least in a confined area."

Naturally, Al Lewis conveniently added the cigar to his characterization of Grandpa; thus Lewis was able to smoke not only off the stage, but a stogie was lit in his scenes, too. Undoubtedly, the image of Grandpa with a cigar lodged between two fingers was an appropriate touch, as Lewis used it more as a personal prop for himself than a fix.

"Al and his cigars," Beverley Owen says, referring to his favored Denobli brand. "They were the worst-smelling Italian things I have ever come across."

Al Lewis gladly incorporated his indulgence of cigars into the character.

BUTCH PATRICK

A ring he wears features a large, diamond-studded PL shining boldly. Given to him by his stepfather when Butch had a kidney removed when he was in his early twenties, it signifies his real name: Patrick Lilly.

"Butch" was born on August 2, 1953, in Los Angeles. He made his acting debut in 1961, at the age of eight, opposite Eddie Albert and Nancy Kulp in the film *The Two Bears*. While he wasn't an aspiring, driven child actor, he went out for roles because it was something to do at that age and he found that he was rather good at the "acting" thing.

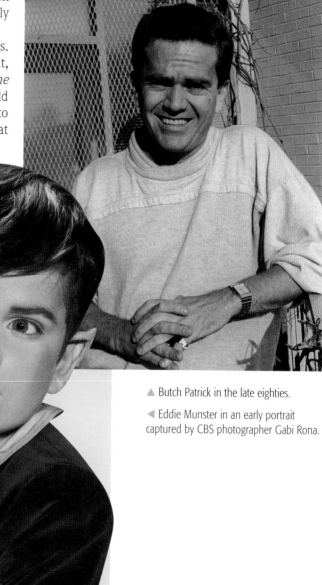

▲ Butch Patrick in the late eighties.

◀ Eddie Munster in an early portrait captured by CBS photographer Gabi Rona.

Butch Patrick presents his TV dad a monster-sized box of candy for a Father's Day publicity photo in 1965.

While living in the Midwest with his grandmother for a summer, Butch was flown back to Los Angeles to test for the role of Eddie Munster at CBS Studios. "I went in and an hour later I came out with the job," he recalls. Although a cute little kid, he could play the brat parts effortlessly. Aside from acting, an underlying interest has always been baseball. (His stepfather was the late Ken Hunt, a former professional ballplayer who rallied for the Yankees and the Washington Senators briefly, among other teams in a lengthy career.)

Butch's schooling was rather unconventional. As required by law, he spent four hours a day with a tutor (even during hiatus, when the rest of the cast was gone) and another four hours he was made available for working. He remembers more recreation than schooling during those years. "Universal Studios was my playground back then and I loved to explore the soundstages and the makeup department. I was like a kid in a candy store," he says. "I was the studio mascot, you know. I was the little kid in the Eddie Munster costume. I could wander anywhere."

Besides his two-year stint as a wolf-boy with pointed ears, he had recurring roles on TV's *The Real McCoys*, *General Hospital*, and *My Three Sons*; and hit the drama series with guest shots on *Ben Casey*, *Death Valley Days*, and *Marcus Welby, M.D.* In between, he appeared in numerous commercials and guest spots on some of the most popular situation comedies throughout the sixties (*I Dream of Jeannie*, *My Favorite Martian*, *Mister Ed*, *The Monkees*, and *Family Affair* among them.)

In seventh grade Butch became a regular student, as awkward as it was for him, and he struggled to get through it and entered high school. During his sophomore year he left the country to film the movie *Sandpit Generals* in Brazil, which he says was never released in the U.S. "I was supposed to be studying school at the same time, but I hardly did any of that. I spent six months in a hotel suite in Brazil, running around this country, living with pockets full of money. It was like my 'Summer of '42.' I came back a new person. I met a few other American kids over there and that's where I met Pelé and he taught me how to play soccer. I have a signed team ball that Santos gave me."

In 1971, at the age of eighteen, Butch grew his hair long and became a teen idol starring in the psycho-trip Saturday morning series, *Lidsville*, opposite Charles Nelson Reilly. The popular Sid & Marty Krofft series, which featured bizarre hat people and a gender-bending genie named "Weenie the Genie" (Billie Hayes), lasted two years and thrust Patrick into a teen-idol phase of his career with his face splashed on the covers of countless teen magazines in the early seventies.

Following *Lidsville*, little was heard from Butch Patrick. He quit show business "to grow up," he says "because my first twenty years were spent working in an adult world. I made up for it by being a hell raiser for the next ten years." The money that was socked away soon ran out and Patrick was working odd jobs and traveling around the country. He formed his own rock band and put out a single "Whatever Happened to Eddie?" with some mild success. The next two decades have been

During a teen-idol phase in his career, Butch Patrick starred in Sid & Marty Krofft's popular psychedelic Saturday morning kids' show, *Lidsville*.

years of chasing and conquering his own demons such as drug abuse and run-ins with the law—all detailed in the tabloids, of course. All in all, Patrick considers himself luckier than most former child stars and is one of the "survivors" from the era, he says.

At one time, Patrick was bothered—and rather haunted—by the role of Eddie Munster, but not any-more. He celebrates his past and appears at car shows and nostalgia shows around the country and takes on roles whenever offered. He even lent his own voice as himself on an episode of *The Simpsons*. Halloween is definitely his season. Today, Butch is working on his au-tobiography and resides between New York and Los Angeles. He has remained single, "but looking" he adds.

Original cast members Pat Priest, Al Lewis, Butch Patrick, and Yvonne De Carlo make a cameo appearance in the 1995 TV-movie *Here Come the Munsters,* starring Edward Hermann as Herman.

PAT PRIEST

Born on August 15, 1936, beautiful blue-eyed Patricia Ann Priest was very young when her family moved from Salt Lake City, Utah, to the small picturesque town of Bountiful, in the same state. There she grew up and became involved in entertainment through her mother, Ivy Baker Priest.

Ivy Baker Priest was a prominent politician, well known as the United States Treasurer from 1953 to 1961 (the Eisenhower Administration) and a two-term California state treasurer; although politically minded, her mother was always interested in show business—writing, directing, and producing road shows for the Mormon church. Pat's mother had become increasingly active in politics and soon became a figure of national prominence as treasurer, her signature apparent right on the dollar bill. Pat was in her junior year at Davis High School excelling in speech and drama when her mother was named treasurer, and Pat suddenly left the tranquility of a small town and was thrust into the glitter of the nation's capital and the society scene.

Pat was known as one of the prettiest girls on the Washington scene. Chosen as the queen of the President's Cup Regatta, a major annual capital social event, she later was crowned queen of the Winchester, Virginia Apple Blossom Festival, and the first queen of the Azalea Festival in Norfolk, Virginia. (Lady Bird Johnson and Peggy Goldwater were later crowned Azalea Festival queens.)

Munsters star Pat Priest and director Earl Bellamy attend an Academy of Television Arts & Sciences Emmy Ball in May 1965.

Pat Priest provides a tour of the set for her mother, Ivy Baker Priest, the former United States Treasurer.

Despite her mother's political prominence, Pat was still stage-struck, she says, and made her first professional television with Art Lamb in Washington. Soon after, she trekked to the West Coast where she gained solid dramatic experience working in community theater with the Alameda Little Theatre company, the London Circle Players in Oakland, and the Players of the Golden Hind in Berkeley.

Pat was married at age nineteen to Pierce Jensen, Jr., who was a naval aide at the White House. When her husband transferred to Point Mugu, fifty miles north of Los Angeles, Pat acquired an agent and began some modeling work as well as auditioning for television roles. (It's little known, but Pat Priest was one of many young curvaceous girls who tested at CBS for the role of Mary Ann on *Gilligan's Island*.)

Before she landed the role of Marilyn on *The Munsters*, replacing actress Beverley Owen mid-season, she worked in a few television shows and films. She made her film debut as a student in the motion picture *East of Eden* in 1955. One film she is constantly quizzed about is *Easy Come, Easy Go*, in which she costarred opposite Elvis Presley in 1967. She recalls:

Pat Priest costarred with Elvis Presley in the film *Easy Come, Easy Go* (1967).

"Elvis was wonderful to work with. He never argued with anybody, and was not temperamental. He treated me beautifully. Quite a religious person and kind of shy.

"Incidentally, I bought his car from him. It was a black Cadillac Eldorado and I bought it for $4,000. He wanted to sell it at the time and I wanted to buy it. Do you know what that would be worth today if I still had it? I remember the keys had a keychain that said EP. The keychain alone would be worth a fortune today."

Pat was raising two sons, Pierce and Lance, during *The Munsters*. She appeared in episodic television (including several guest shots on *Bewitched*) and occasional movie roles and even dubbed some of Jane Fonda's lines in *Barefoot in the Park*. Fans of *The Mary Tyler Moore Show* remember her as the sister of Sue Anne Nivens (Betty White) on the hit sitcom.

Today, Pat and her second husband, Fred Hansing, a retired dentist, live in Utah and Pat occasionally makes personal appearances around the country regarding her most famous role on *The Munsters*. Pat has dabbled in varied interests over the years, including skiing, but she more recently abandoned that following an accident on the slopes which nearly killed her. At one time, she owned a llama-breeding ranch, but gave up that endeavor and now enjoys more mainstream hobbies like gardening and traveling.

Pat Priest, Al Lewis, and Butch Patrick reunited in 1988 for a comedy sketch at the Shrine Circus in Evansville, Indiana. Here, the actors go over lines during rehearsal.

BEVERLEY OWEN

After just thirteen episodes, twenty-five-year-old Beverley Owen was replaced as the original Marilyn on *The Munsters* so she could move back to New York to get married to Jon Stone (one of the creators of *Sesame Street*).

Born in Ottumwa, Iowa, Beverley Ogg ("We went through every Ogg joke on the set," snapped Al Lewis with a laugh) early on had aspirations to become an actress. During WWII, Beverley lived in Tucson, Arizona and San Diego, California, where her father was stationed with the Navy. After the war, the family lived briefly in Chicago before settling in Ames, Iowa, where her father was a professor of agricultural economics at Iowa State University. Throughout high school and college (both Ohio Wesleyan University and the University of Michigan), Beverley was active in theater, radio, and television projects. After graduation from the University of Michigan, she moved to New York City to pursue a career in television production.

She laughs now about the few years she worked as a frustrated secretary at a CBS casting office and

Beverley Owen: "Al Lewis may contradict this, but my recollection is that none of us could imagine that the show would be successful."

how she was fired for her lack of typing skills. Soon after, Ed Sullivan fired her from his staff for lack of shorthand skills. She took classes to improve her secretarial skills and eventually became the senior typist working on *The Captain Kangaroo Show.*

"But by then, I was so miserable, I started taking acting classes," she says. Her first professional role in January 1962 was on the CBS religious/inspirational drama, *Lamp Unto My Feet* (Larry Hagman was her costar), followed by appearances on the daytime drama *As the World Turns.* Under contract to Universal Studios, Beverley landed roles on *Wagon Train*, *Kraft Mystery Theatre*, and *The Virginian*, traveling between coasts. But being cast in *The Munsters* meant a relocation to Los Angeles and separation from the man she loved. "The person I'd love to see again sometime, just because I

liked him so much as a little kid, is Butch Patrick," says Owen. "I remember I took him to see *Mary Poppins* at Grauman's Chinese Theatre as a sort of a date, and he was so cute.

"But the best thing that came out of doing *The Munsters* was my friendship with Fred Gwynne," says Owen today. "Fred was a very special person to me, like a brother. We stayed in close touch. He was an incredible human being and talent." When Owen turned fifty, Gwynne drew her a special birthday card. "I have it framed. It's a picture of me with Herman, Lily, and Grandpa, and a cobweb over all of them. The card reads: *Beverley Owen is not feeling nifty . . . Marilyn Munster has just turned fifty. Imagine how others in Munsterland feel, their eon-old bodies have begun to congeal.*"

Beverley was rarely recognized from *The Munsters* because of her long, naturally brown hair. Since then she continued to act in soaps and commercials and in 1989 she returned to the classrooms and earned a master's degree in history from New York University. Of late, Beverley has done the thespian thing again, this time in regional theater in upstate New York tackling some choice roles such as Aunt Penniman in *The Heiress*, Gertrude in *Hamlet*, and Eleanor of Aquitaine in *The Lion in Winter*. She divides her time between New York and Vermont and is proud to be a new grandma.

▲ Twenty-five years after they met on *The Munsters*, Al Lewis and Beverley Owen reminisced about the series. This photo was taken outside Lewis's popular Greenwich Village Italian eatery, "Grampa's Bella Gente," in 1989.

◄ Beverley Owen in the film *Bullet for a Badman* (1964).

The Ultimate Munsterrific Trivia Challenge

1. What is the name of the boarder to whom the Munsters rent their spare bedroom?

2. What is the Munsters' version of goose bumps?

3. Which Munster relative was the Creature from the Black Lagoon?

4. What is the name of the female bat for whom Igor fell?

5. What happened to the original blueprints for the construction of Herman's body?

6. Who fronted the down payment on the Munster house?

7. What secret code led Herman and Grandpa to Morgan's treasure?

8. What did Grandpa give Marilyn on her birthday?

Answers appear on page 205.

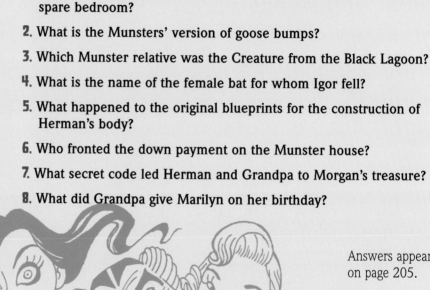

WACH
STETER

172

9. What is the Munsters' address?

10. What book does Grandpa refer to for his potions and magic?

11. What does Uncle Charlie (Herman's brother) give to Eddie as a gift?

12. Where did Herman and Lily want to take a cruise?

13. What publication chose the Munster family by computer to represent the "average American family"?

14. When Herman thinks Lily is having an affair, what does he do first?

15. What nickname do Eddie's classmates pin on him?

16. Why didn't Herman's job as night watchman in the city morgue work out?

17. When Lily gets bored at home, she finds a job doing what?

18. What does Grandpa's license plate from the Old Country have on it?

19. Eddie missed doing what to have his tonsils removed?

20. Herman is a charter member of what fan club?

21. What small town does Herman find to take his driving test?

22. What newspaper does Grandpa read? What magazine?

23. What is Herman's ham-radio handle?

24. What does Grandpa say about Herman's singing?

25. Herman and Lily were married in what year?

26. Where did the Munsters send Boris, Grandpa's playmate for Eddie?

27. Where did Grandpa get his electric chair?

28. Who lives next door to the Munsters?

29. Where did Herman and Lily go on their honeymoon?

30. When Herman becomes a part-time investigator, what does he call himself?

31. How many wives did Grandpa have?

32. What is at the top of the stairway in the Munster house?

33. Which star from TV's *Hogan's Heroes* appears in the movie *Munster, Go Home!*?

34. Where is the Munster telephone located in the house?

35. What trick can Eddie perform with his pointed ears?

36. Who was "a mouse that joined the Transylvanian Air Corps"?

37. What is the Munsters' favorite old fun song to sing around the organ?

38. What former child star makes appearances in two episodes?

39. What did Eddie bring in a jar to the school science fair?

40. What does Marilyn sculpt for her art class?

THE MUNSTERS: AN EPISODE GUIDE

Series Credits

FIRST PRIMETIME TELECAST: September 24, 1964

LAST PRIMETIME TELECAST: September 1, 1966

TIMESLOT: Thursday 7:30–8:00 PM, CBS-TV

PRODUCERS: Joe Connelly, Bob Mosher

DEVELOPED BY: Norman Liebmann, Ed Hass

FROM A FORMAT BY: Al Burns, Chris Hayward

MUSIC: Jack Marshall

LOCATION: Episodes Filmed at Universal Studios, Hollywood

PRODUCTION COMPANY: Kayro-Vue

CAST: Fred Gwynne (Herman Munster), Yvonne De Carlo (Lily Munster), Al Lewis (Grandpa, a.k.a. Sam Dracula), Beverley Owen (Marilyn, 1964), Pat Priest (Marilyn, 1964–66), Butch Patrick (Edward "Eddie" Wolfgang Munster), Mel Blanc, Bob Hastings (voice of The Raven).

Br: Broadcast Date

GC: Guest Cast

FIRST SEASON

1. "Munster Masquerade"

Written by Joe Connelly and Bob Mosher. Directed by Lawrence Dobkin.

Marilyn's new boyfriend invites the Munsters to a Halloween costume party. Herman attends as King Arthur, Lily is Little Bo Peep, and Grandpa dresses as Napoleon. Herman wins the prize for best costume—for wearing one mask under another—and the family exit the party insulted.

Br: 9-24-64. **GC:** Mabel Albertson, Frank Wilcox, Linden Chiles, Lurene Tuttle, Walter Woolf King, Nina Roman, Paul Bradley, Berniece Dalton, Roy Darmour. (Notes: Mabel Albertson portrayed Darrin Stephens's mother in TV's *Bewitched*. Frank Wilcox portrayed Mr. Brewster, the man who purchased Jed Clampett's oil-rich swamp, on TV's hit show *The Beverly Hillbillies*. Oddly, the first bit of dialogue from the Raven in the clock does not feature the voice talents of Mel Blanc; the second exchange, involving the black cat, *is* the voice of Blanc.)

◀ The Munsters wish audiences Merry Christmas in 1965.

▶ Herman and Lily make a splash at the Halloween party in "Munster Masquerade," the first episode to air on television, September 24, 1964.

2. "My Fair Munster"

Written by Norm Liebmann and Ed Hass. Directed by David Alexander.

Grandpa concocts a love potion to stimulate Marilyn's sagging love life. Instead, the potion imparts a romantic aura to the wrong Munsters. The potion is slipped into the breakfast oatmeal, but when Marilyn skips the meal, it is inadvertently consumed by the rest of the family. The neighbor lady becomes enthralled by Herman and the mailman falls madly in love with Lily. Grandpa wonders if everyone has gone berserk.

Br: 10-1-64. **GC:** Claire Carleton, John Fiedler, Edward Mallory. (Notes: This is the first episode filmed but the second to be broadcast. This episode incorporates footage from one of the early pilot presentations. The scene where Eddie is chased down the street by a group of screaming little girls is the only time in the series where he is seen without his famous widow's peak. Actor John Fiedler, who portrayed the mailman, went on to be a semi-regular as Mr. Peterson on TV's *The Bob Newhart Show* and for years supplied the voice of Piglet in Walt Disney's many *Winnie the Pooh* productions.)

Herman shakes the entire foundation at the closing of the first episode, "My Fair Munster," filmed April 30, 1964.

3. "A Walk on the Mild Side"

Written by Norm Liebmann and Ed Hass. Directed by Norman Abbott.

Afflicted with insomnia, Herman takes late-evening strolls in Mid-City Park. The city becomes paralyzed with hysteria due to reports of a fiend roaming the city's parks. With the police on alert, they mistake Herman for the infamous "maniacal marauder of Mid-City Park."

Br: 10-8-64. **GC:** Cliff Norton, Roy Roberts, Barry Kelley, Larry Blake, Harrison Lewis, Kate Murtagh, Almira Sessions, Mike Gordon, Jim Gruzel, Paul Baxley. (Notes: This is the first of several episodes directed by Emmy Award–winner Norman Abbott, who got his start in show business at Universal Studios from his famous uncle, comedian Bud Abbott—of the legendary comedy team Abbott & Costello.)

4. "Rock-A-Bye Munster"

Written by Joe Connelly and Bob Mosher. Directed by Norman Abbott.

When Herman and Grandpa eavesdrop on Lily and Marilyn in the kitchen, they overhear the two discussing the fact that Eddie is going to have a new little playmate soon. Overjoyed, Herman assumes Lily is going to have a baby, but just hasn't found the right time to break the news. The new playmate is actually Dr. Dudley's young son who will be staying with the Munster family for a week. Meantime, Lily's actual big surprise for Herman is a new customized family car for his birthday.

Br: 10-15-64. **GC:** Paul Lynde, Marilynn Lovell, Sid Melton, Peter Robbins. (Notes: The Munster Koach, designed and built by George Barris, is introduced in this episode. This is the first of three episodes in which Paul Lynde portrayed myopic Dr. Dudley. Character-actor Sid Melton, who portrays the car salesman, is most known

Lily purchases cars from Diamond Jim (Sid Melton) in "Rock-A-Bye Munster."

as Uncle Charlie on TV's *The Danny Thomas Show* and Alf the carpenter on *Green Acres*. Young Peter Robbins, who portrayed Elmer, the cute little tyke visiting the family, was the voice of Charlie Brown in the classic animated holiday special, *A Charlie Brown Christmas*.)

In the episode "Rock-A-Bye-Munster" Herman suspects Lily is pregnant and naturally assumes the "new playmate for Eddie" is going to be his own offspring. The prop used in this episode was an actual battery-operated, remote-control "Frankenstein monster" tin toy manufactured by Marx. Today, this vintage toy in mint condition with its original box can fetch up to $4,000. (Courtesy of Bob Morris)

Peter Robbins on The Munsters

Round-faced Peter Robbins was a child actor in the sixties, who appeared on *The Munsters* in a memorable episode, "Rock-A-Bye-Munster." This show, where Herman assumes Lily is expecting "a new playmate for Eddie," was the fourth produced. Robbins possessed a pleasingly husky voice when he was a youngster, and he went on to perform the original voice of Charlie Brown in several classic TV specials such as *A Charlie Brown Christmas* and *It's the Great Pumpkin, Charlie Brown*. Robbins shares his memories of visiting the Munsters:

"What strikes me was how big Fred Gwynne was. He was a huge man. He was quite an imposing character, but funny. He was like playing with a big doll.

"The show was shot in black-and-white and the set was in a lot of gray tones, very dark and I remembered they had this machine that actually spun cobwebs. I had never seen anything like that. It was like a metal gun with a thing that would rotate and the prop guys would spin up cobwebs in the corners and make it all look very creepy.

"I really liked that remote-controlled Frankenstein monster robot. I thought, 'What a neat toy.' I got along with Butch just fine. I was only on the show for a few days and there [were] no child rivalries or anything like that under those circumstances. I'd seen Butch before, going on interviews because we were about the same age.

"I was lucky, I got to be in three shows that were like my favorites, *The Munsters*, and *F-Troop*, and then *Get Smart*."

5. "Pike's Pique"

Written by Norm Liebmann and Ed Hass. Directed by Seymour Berns.

When the City Gas Company attempts to lay an underground pipeline under the Munster house, they accidentally crash through the dungeon. Gas Company official Borden T. Pike is incredulous when company workers hysterically inform him of the Munster family and their creepy house. Pike decides to visit the Munsters and investigate things himself in an effort to convince the family to accept a settlement offer.

Br: 10-22-64. **GC:** Richard Deacon, Jane Withers, Pat Harrington, Jr., Henry Hunter, Joe Brooks. (Notes: Balding actor Richard Deacon played fussy Mel Cooley on *The Dick Van Dyke Show*. This is the first of two episodes with former child-actress Jane Withers. Pat Harrington, a regular on Steve Allen's variety show in the fifties, went on to play Schneider the cool superintendent on the sitcom *One Day at a Time*. Joe Brooks was a regular on TV's *F-Troop* as trooper Vanderbilt.)

6. "Lo-Cal Munster"

Written by Norm Liebmann and Ed Hass. Directed by Norman Abbott.

Herman embarks on a crash diet when he is invited to a reunion of his old Army unit and discovers he cannot squeeze into his old uniform. Determined to drop some pounds, Herman has Grandpa strap him onto a slab in the dungeon, but Herman just can't resist feasting on a Thanksgiving dinner.

Br: 10-29-64. **GC:** Paul Lynde, Dick Winslow, Monty Margetts, Elsie Baker, Diane Cortney, Scott McCarter, Caryl Rowe, Ronnie R. Rondell, Michael Jackson.

7. "Tin Can Man"

Written by Norm Liebmann and Ed Hass. Story by Robert Lewin. Directed by Earl Bellamy.

Eddie has been getting notes sent home regarding his failing science grades, but is ashamed and hides them

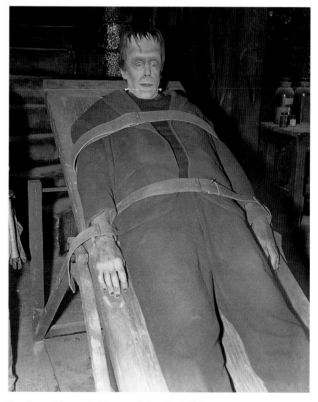

It's Munsters versus the gas company in "Pike's Pique", with guest-star Richard Deacon.

No diet could restrain Herman during the holidays.

from Herman and Lily. When Herman finds out, he is furious and demands Eddie work harder on his science project. With the help of Grandpa, Eddie builds a robot as a science project for school. Before Eddie can exhibit the robot, a school official sabotages it and the family performs surgery in an attempt to repair the tin-can man.

Br: 11-5-64. **GC:** Arch Johnson, Richard Simmons, Kathleen O'Malley, Rand Brooks, Dee Carroll, Murray Alper. (Notes: This is the first of many episodes directed by Earl Bellamy, who also worked on the feature film *Munster, Go Home!* Bellamy began directing television in 1949 with *The Lone Ranger* and became one of the medium's most prolific, having steered more than 1,500 episodes, directing regularly on more than forty different series throughout his career.)

8. "Herman the Great"

Written by Joe Connelly and Bob Mosher. Directed by Earl Bellamy.

One of Eddie's friends witnesses Herman tie a steel rod into a knot and relates this fantastic feat to his father, a fight promoter. Eventually, Herman is offered a job as a professional wrestler. In order to earn extra money to fund Eddie's college education, Herman moonlights as a wrestler, the Masked Marvel. Gullible Herman finds his own sympathetic nature a great drawback in the ring and throws the matches.

Br: 11-12-64. **GC:** John Hubbard, Johnny Silver, Joe Mell, Teddy Eccles, Jimmy Lennon. (Notes: This episode also includes real-life professional wrestlers: Tiger Joe Marsh, Count Billy Varga, Gene Le Bell, Jay York, The Great John L., and Matt Murphy.)

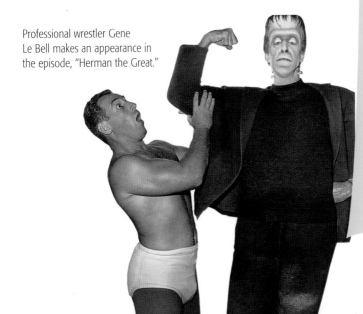

Professional wrestler Gene Le Bell makes an appearance in the episode, "Herman the Great."

9. "Knock Wood, Here Comes Charlie"

Written by Norm Liebmann and Ed Hass. Directed by Lawrence Dobkin.

Herman is apprehensive when he learns his conniving twin brother, Charlie, is coming to visit the family. Charlie, a flamboyant playboy type, claims to have invented a device which extracts uranium from seawater. Grandpa, thinking he has broken Charlie's apparatus, refurbishes it to perfection.

Br: 11-19-64. **GC:** Mike Mazurki, Jean Willes. (Notes: Fred Gwynne plays a dual role in this episode as Herman and his brother.)

Herman's flamboyant brother Charlie comes for a visit and attempts to sell the family his new invention: a machine designed to extract uranium from seaweed.

10. "Autumn Croakus"

Written by James Allardice and Tom Adair. Directed by Lawrence Dobkin.

Grandpa decides to find a wife through an advertisement and Herman sulks in disapproval. Grandpa's mail-order bride, Lydia Gardner, is actually the notorious Black Widow, who marries, then murders her husbands for their money.

Br: 11-26-64. **GC:** Neil Hamilton, Linda Watkins, Richard Reeves, Jerry Mann. (Notes: Neil Hamilton is

recognizable as Commissioner Gordon from TV's *Batman*. Grab the remote for a rewind, here's a blooper: In the opening scene near the staircase, an unidentified studio worker in a white T-shirt can be spotted walking in the background.)

11. "The Midnight Ride of Herman Munster"

Written by Joe Connelly and Bob Mosher. Directed by Ezra Stone.

An exhausted Herman falls asleep in the back of the family car. A gang of bank robbers steal the car and when Herman awakens, he finds himself the unwilling accomplice in a bank heist. The thieves mistake Herman for an accomplice known as "Big Louie" and appointed him the driver. Herman intentionally crashes the car so the gang will be captured. Of course, the police think Herman has been horribly disfigured in the accident.

Br: 12-3-64. **GC:** Lennie Weinrib, Maxie Rosenbloom, Lee Krieger, Joe Devlin, Val Avery, Joel Donte, Pat McCaffrie, Vince Williams, Mike Ross. (Notes: The 1938 Cadillac V-12 limousine in which Herman falls asleep was actually a vintage car owned by producer Bob Mosher, an avid classic-car buff. Stocky character-actor Lennie Weinrib, one of the robbers, went on to voice the wacky Sid & Marty Krofft TV character "H.R. Pufnstuf." This episode marks the first of several directed by former radio-actor Ezra Stone, famous for his character Henry Aldrich. Stone later appeared in the TV reunion movie *The Munsters' Revenge*.)

Val Avery, Fred Gwynne, and Lennie Weinrib in the episode, "The Midnight Ride of Herman Munster."

Lennie Weinrib on *The Munsters*

Character-actor Lennie Weinrib played a crook in the episode "The Midnight Ride of Herman Munster." Weinrib, a master voice talent and impressionist, provided the voice of H.R. Pufnstuf, among many other Sid & Marty Krofft creations, and cartoon characters. Weinrib recalls his *Munsters* scenes with Fred Gwynne:

I remember the fear of being in George Barris's car, and we didn't have stunt people. We were in that old car speeding around corners, going over trash cans, careening off walls. We did a bank robbery or something. I think it may have been a stuntman wearing Fred's costume who was driving. Us, we were expendable.

I loved Fred Gwynne. I thought Fred was one of the more amazing people I ever had the pleasure of meeting or working with. We went to lunch a couple of times and I was amazed at how he had to wear that stuff. He told me he had headaches all the time from the headpiece clamped on his head and the makeup. But what impressed me was his brilliance, and when you talked to him, you realized his IQ was through the roof and that he was an absolute master at everything. And with all the discomforts he was having on the set, he was always sweet, nice, a gentle man who was courteous. He made that set a very happy place to be. It was a quiet set because of him. He really brought a stability to the whole production that made the set happy.

12. "Sleeping Cutie"

Written by James Allardice and Tom Adair. Directed by Norman Abbott.

A frustrated Marilyn is dead on her feet, wandering around the house like a zombie. Grandpa gets his formulas mixed up and inadvertently puts Marilyn into a semi-permanent sleep when he attempts to cure her insomnia. It takes the kiss of a "prince" to wake Marilyn. When a fellow by the name of Dick Prince visits the Munster home, the family thinks help has finally arrived.

Br: 12-10-64. **GC:** Grant Williams, Walter Woolf King, Gavin MacLeod, John Hoyt. (Notes: Gavin MacLeod wears a ridiculous mop of hair in this episode. The balding actor was a regular on TV's *McHale's Navy*, and later costarred as writer Murray Slaughter on the long-running hit *The Mary Tyler Moore Show*. In the seventies, MacLeod sailed into sitcom history as Captain Merrill Stubing on *The Love Boat*.)

13. "Family Portrait"

Written by James Allardice and Tom Adair. Directed by Lawrence Dobkin.

Event magazine, a national publication, makes a ghastly choice when its research computers select the Munsters as the average American family from a host of subscribers. Grandpa, annoyed with being labeled "average," doesn't want to cooperate with the magazine's plans to run a spread on the family. The photo opportunity, as well as the accompanying prize money, is now in jeopardy. A reporter and photographer are dispatched to spend the weekend with the Munster family and obtain the story, but the two men are horrified by what they find.

Br: 12-17-64. **GC:** Harvey Korman, Roy Roberts, Fred Beir, Bill Daniels. (Notes: This is the final episode featuring Beverley Owen as Marilyn. This is the first of three episodes to feature guest-star Harvey Korman; the comedian would later become a regular on *The Carol Burnett Show*.)

Herman's stand on water-gun control: "From my cold, dead hands . . ."

14. "Grandpa Leaves Home"

Written by Richard Conway and Roland MacLane. Directed by Norman Abbott.

Grandpa feels the family no longer loves him or wants him around and he and threatens to leave. The family calls his bluff, but when Lily can't find Grandpa she becomes overly worried. Grandpa has flown the coop and taken a job in a shabby nightclub performing his rusty magic act. Herman and Lily visit Grandpa's mediocre performance and try to coax him to return home.

Br: 12-24-64. **GC:** Robert Strauss, Iris Adrian, Sarah Jane Ross, Bill Duncan, Bill Couch, Nicky Blair. (Notes: Pat Priest makes her debut in this episode as Marilyn, and of course, the show's opening has been re-shot to accommodate the change in cast. The show's new opening is

similar to the original, but now features Fred Gwynne's credit first as he descends the staircase, and the rest of the cast follow. Robert Strauss, the gravelly voiced actor who portrayed the nightclub owner, is known to movie fans for his role as a slovenly prisoner-of-war in the Billy Wilder classic *Stalag 17*.)

Grandpa feels unloved and neglected by the family and declares he's going to split in "Grandpa Leaves Home."

15. "Herman's Rival"

Written by Richard Conway and Roland MacLane. Directed by Joseph Pevney.

Herman has privately lent Lily's brother, Lester (Grandpa's son) $5,000—the entire family savings. Grandpa is concerned Herman may not get the money back because Lester "is a bum." Lily, thinking the family

Fred feeds lines off-camera to Al while filming a scene where Grandpa and Herman are spying on Lily at work in "Herman's Rival." (December 3, 1964)

is broke, secretly takes a job reading palms in a quaint tearoom called "The Golden Earrings." Her mysterious absences from home provoke Grandpa and Herman to spy on her and investigate her activities. They conclude she is having an affair with Ramon, the handsome owner of the tearoom.

Br: 12-31-64. **GC:** Lee Bergere, Karen Glynn, Chet Stratton, Tommy Farrell, Irwin Charone (Lester, the werewolf). (Notes: This is the first of many episodes directed by Joseph Pevney, who went on to direct many of the best original *Star Trek* episodes including "The Trouble with Tribbles.")

16. "Grandpa's Call of the Wild"

Written by Joe Connelly and Bob Mosher. Directed by Earl Bellamy.

The Munsters nearly lose Grandpa permanently on a camping trip at Shadow Pine Park. Yearning for the Old Country, Grandpa turns himself into a Transylvanian wolf and goes out at night carousing. Grandpa is captured by park rangers and a worried Lily drives to the ranger station to claim him. Unfortunately, Grandpa has forgotten how to turn himself back. It's up to Herman to rescue poor Grandpa from captivity.

Br: 1-7-65. **GC:** Ed Peck, Mike Ragan, Bing Russell, Don Haggerty, Curt Barrett. (Notes: Ed Peck, the park ranger with the deep resonant voice, later portrayed the hard-nosed Officer Kirk on TV's *Happy Days* in the late seventies and early eighties." Peck also portrayed an FBI agent in the beginning of the cult-classic film, *Willy Wonka & the Chocolate Factory.* Bing Russell, who portrayed the second Ranger, was the father of actor Kurt Russell.)

17. "All-Star Munster"

Written by Joe Connelly and Bob Mosher. Directed by Earl Bellamy.

While trying to straighten out Marilyn's tuition problems at Westbury College with the dean, Herman is mistaken for basketball recruit Moose Mallory and inadvertently gets signed up to play. Meanwhile, the real basketball-recruit Moose Mallory and his hick father show up and pay an angry visit to the Munster home. The hillbillies confront Herman about slickerin' Moose out of his scholarship. "We come here to marinate yer gizzard in sheep

dip." In the interest of fair play—and Herman's gizzard—the confusion is straightened out.

Br: 1-14-65. **GC:** Pat Buttram, Robert Easton, Frank Maxwell, Gene Blakely. (Notes: Walleyed Pat Buttram is most known to Western fans as Gene Autry's whiskery sidekick with the creaking voice. Later he became the hilarious con man Mr. Haney on *Green Acres.* Robert Easton was no stranger to hick roles in the movies and on television; eventually Easton became one of Hollywood's leading dialect coaches tutoring Robert DeNiro, Tom Cruise, and Robin Williams to name just a few of his clients.)

Herman's hook shot was something to behold in the episode "All Star Munster."

Robert Easton on *The Munsters*

In "All-Star Munster," the seventeenth episode, lanky actor Robert Easton played half-witted hayseed Moose Mallory, recipient of a basketball scholarship at Marilyn's college. Hand in hand with Pat Buttram (known for his role of Mr. Haney on *Green Acres*), the pair played a couple of backwoods bumpkins suspicious of gettin' slickered by the big-city folk. Today, Easton is one of Hollywood's most respected dialect coaches and here he recalls a few memories of his guest appearance:

Having come back from England, people were finding out about me and I started breaking out of the old typecasting. Every once in a while, a good part would come up and I would resurrect my old country characters. *The Munsters* gave me a good chance to do that. I think my favorite line in the whole show was when I said to Pat Priest, "Ma'am, you're just as perty as a bucket fulla hog livers."

Pat Buttram I knew for a lot of years because I used to work for Gene Autry on those old el-cheapo Westerns he did like *Annie Oakley.* Pat Buttram had that quaver in his voice, which was just a television persona. When he was the emcee at many, many Pacific Pioneer Broadcasters luncheons, he was still country, but he used very sophisticated material. A lot of ideas on the *Munster* episode were Buttram's. There's the scene where we get off the bus and we're gonna cross the street and he says, "Take my hand, son."

Remember the scene where we're sitting next to the fireplace and my feet re-angled toward the fire? My shoe catches fire. I knew that it would play funnier if I reacted very slowly to the foot on fire. They had large-sized clodhopper boots on me, and inside they had wrapped my foot in asbestos and a thick sock and another thick sock and the boot. To get the timing on it, I really let the thing run on a little long and my foot was getting uncomfortably hot. The director loved it, but it got to the point of getting burned. But in those days, I'd do nearly anything for a laugh.

I had always admired Fred Gwynne and Al Lewis and I had seen them on *Car 54.* Gwynne had a great ear for dialects. Years later I saw him in *Pet Sematary* and he did an excellent New England; and in *My Cousin Vinny* he was again excellent as the Southern judge.

Robert Easton was no stranger to playing hillbilly types on television in the fifties and sixties. Eventually, Easton became one of Hollywood's premiere dialect instructors.

18. "If a Martian Answers, Hang Up"

Written by Joe Connelly and Bob Mosher. Directed by Norman Abbott.

While messing around with a ham radio in Grandpa's laboratory, Herman (using the handle/ham-radio license number "W6XR-L4") thinks he has contacted Martians who are planning to invade earth in flying-saucer X-14. Herman has unknowingly accessed a frequency used by youngsters playing with walkie-talkies. Thinking they've actually made contact with aliens, Grandpa and Herman use a transistorized divining rod at night to track the Martians.

Br: 1-21-65. **GC:** Ray Montgomery, Larry Thor, Ronnie Dapo, Pat Rosson, Dort Clark, Herbert Rudley. (Notes: In the show's opening, Herman receives a radio transmission from Milan, Italy. The voice is that of veteran character-actor Vito Scotti. Sitcom fans may remember Scotti in memorable guest-starring roles as both the mad Dr. Balinkov and the wacky Japanese soldier on *Gilligan's Island*. Herbert Rudley, who portrays Captain Halbert, was a regular on the sitcom *The Mothers-in-Law* as Eve Arden's husband.)

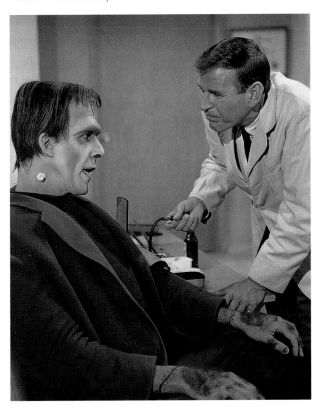

19. "Eddie's Nickname"

Written by Richard Baer. Directed by Joseph Pevney.

Eddie comes home from school depressed because his classmates bully him and call him "shorty." Eddie doesn't want to return to school, but Herman and Lily insist. Grandpa puts on the boxing gloves and attempts to teach Eddie self defense, but Herman objects to any kind of brutality. Grandpa then gets the formulas mixed up when he tries to concoct for Eddie a special "magic milkshake" to induce a six-inch growth spurt overnight. Instead, Eddie develops a full-grown beard. Herman takes his freakish son (with a bag over his head) to Dr. Dudley who can do nothing for the young bearded boy except prescribe for him a new nickname: Fuzzy. At dinner, Lily's soup ends up being the accidental antidote.

Br: 1-28-65. **GC:** Paul Lynde, Alice Backes.

20. "Bats of a Feather"

Written by James Allardice and Tom Adair. Directed by Jerry Paris.

Grandpa finds it necessary to substitute himself for Igor the bat so Eddie has something to take to the school pet fair. Not knowing it's Grandpa, Eddie trades the bat for his pal Timmy Brubaker's pet squirrel; in turn, young Timmy sells the bat to his father who works in a rocket laboratory in Washington D.C. Grandpa nearly becomes an unwilling candidate for space travel. Frantically, the family flies to Washington to retrieve Grandpa who is being held in a laboratory cage.

Br: 2-4-65. **GC:** Barbara Babcock, Tom McBride, Ronnie Dapo, Jimmy Mathers, Alvy Moore, Gilbert Green, Sally Mills, Frank Gardner, Alan Hunt. (Notes: Alvy Moore, who portrays one of the laboratory scientists, is best known as the confused county agent, Hank Kimball, on TV's *Green Acres*. One of the boys in this classroom, Jimmy Mathers, is the younger brother of actor Jerry Mathers—a.k.a. "the Beaver" on TV's *Leave It to Beaver*. Jimmy Mathers, who looked much like his brother Jerry, had a short-lived television career, appearing in a handful of shows such as *Bewitched*, *My Three Sons*, and *Adam-12*. This episode was the first of several directed by actor Jerry Paris, known to viewers as neighbor Jerry Helper on *The Dick Van Dyke Show*. Paris later directed much of TV's *Happy Days*.)

25. "Come Back, Little Googie"

Written by Leo Rifkin, Joe Connelly, and Bob Mosher. Directed by Joseph Pevney.

Grandpa thinks he's used his magic to turn Eddie's obnoxious little pal Googie Miller into a monkey, but the calculating youngster is really hiding out to fool the Munsters. A frantic Herman and Grandpa don't know what else to do but sheepishly return the "boy" to his father late at night in hopes that Mr. Miller won't notice he's a chimp.

Br: 3-11-65. **GC:** Billy Mumy, Russ Conway. (Notes: Veteran child-actor Billy Mumy, best known for his role of Will Robinson on TV's *Lost in Space*, was originally considered for the role of Eddie Munster. Young Mumy, who was a natural redhead, would have had to undergo repeated hair-coloring in addition to the extensive makeup the role would entail, so his parents persuaded him to decline.)

26. "Far-Out Munsters"

Written by Richard Conway, Joe Connelly, and Bob Mosher. Directed by Joseph Pevney.

The family moves to a hotel after renting their home for a weekend to a popular rock 'n' roll group seeking refuge from their fans. The family dislikes their clean, fresh luxury hotel and abruptly returns to tranquil 1313 Mockingbird Lane only to discover a wild party in progress. Instead of objecting to the party, they swing with the crowd of hipsters. The music sends Grandpa out of this world. ("I've been there before," he tells Eddie.) Herman joins the groove and recites some extraneous bohemian-style poetry. Next, Lily plays the harp and performs a variation of an old hillbilly folksong (sung more like a Negro spiritual) called "Over Yandro." The Standells perform a number called "Everybody Ringo" and also cover the Beatles' hit, "I Want to Hold Your Hand."

▲ In "Far-Out Munsters," the beatnik groove hits Mockingbird Heights.

◄ Herman thinks Grandpa has turned Eddie's little friend into a chimp in "Come Back, Little Googie."

Br: 3-18-65. **GC:** The Standells, Alex Gerry, Zalman King, Kelton Garwood, Sue Winton, Tom Curtis, Frank Killmond. (Notes: The Standells appear as themselves: Larry Tamblyn, Gary Lane, Tony Valentino, and Dick Dodd. In the opening of the episode, Eddie samples the Standells' song "Just a Little Bit" on the family record player. Zalman King, seen as the hipster with a full beard, went on to become a hugely successful film writer, director, and producer with such titles as *9 1/2 Weeks*, *Wild Orchid*, and *Red Shoe Diaries* to his credit.)

27. "Munsters on the Move"

Written by George Tibbles, Joe Connelly, and Bob Mosher. Directed by Joseph Pevney.

The family sells their beloved mansion when Herman decides he wants to accept a lucrative job promotion and move to everyone to Buffalo. The Munsters hold open house and after a series of interested parties are driven off out of fear, the house finally sells. Unfortunately, Eddie is not happy about being uprooted because he's recently been made the captain of the school baseball team. The family is completely unsettled and the plans are finally changed, but the house's buyer wants to hold the Munsters to their contract in order to demolish the old mansion. The family feels they have no choice but to fight to keep their beloved abode.

Br: 3-25-65. **GC:** Bert Freed, Eddie Hanley, Lenore Shanewice, Alma Murphy, Jan Arvan, Bella Bruck, Charles Seel, Joey Scott, Nydia Westman.

28. "Movie Star Munster"

Written by Joe Connelly and Bob Mosher. Story by James Allardice and Tom Adair. Directed by Jerry Paris.

Herman is signed to a contract to "star" in a bogus movie documentary being produced by a pair of con artists who pose as movie producers, stage deliberate accidents, and then defraud insurance companies. Naturally, Herman's contract includes a double indemnity clause. The entire showbiz façade goes to Herman's head and he is consumed with visions of movie stardom and fame—all the while innocently ruining the con artists' repeated attempts to exterminate him.

Br: 4-1-65. **GC:** Jesse White, Walter Burke. (Notes: Character-actor Jesse White was for many years the sad Maytag Man in television commercials.)

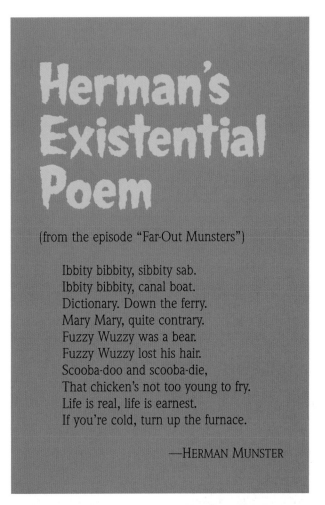

Herman's Existential Poem

(from the episode "Far-Out Munsters")

Ibbity bibbity, sibbity sab.
Ibbity bibbity, canal boat.
Dictionary. Down the ferry.
Mary Mary, quite contrary.
Fuzzy Wuzzy was a bear.
Fuzzy Wuzzy lost his hair.
Scooba-doo and scooba-die,
That chicken's not too young to fry.
Life is real, life is earnest.
If you're cold, turn up the furnace.

—HERMAN MUNSTER

A rare candid of Al Lewis and director Jerry Paris on the set during filming of the episode "Movie Star Munster." Paris was an outstanding television director and actor, recognizable as neighbor Jerry Helper from *The Dick Van Dyke Show.*

29. "Herman the Rookie"

Written by Joe Connelly and Bob Mosher. Directed by Jerry Paris.

After his mighty line-drive sails out of the local ballpark and beans Leo Durocher on the head eight blocks away, Herman is given a Major League tryout by the Los Angeles Dodgers' coach. Will Herman become the greatest long-ball hitter in the history of baseball?

Br: 4-8-65. **GC:** Leo Durocher, Elroy Hirsch, Gene Darfler, Ken Hunt. (Notes: Famed baseball player, coach, commentator, and manager Leo Durocher was a hugely popular sports figure for several decades. Durocher appeared on many television shows as himself, including *The Jack Benny Show*, *The Beverly Hillbillies*, *Mister Ed*, and *What's My Line?* Also in the cast is former L.A. Rams football-star Elroy "Crazylegs" Hirsch. Ken Hunt, who portrayed the catcher fearful of Herman, was the stepfather of cast member Butch Patrick. Hunt, who played for several major league teams, shouts the line: "I quit . . . I'm going back to the minors!")

Famed L.A. Dodgers manager Leo Durocher gives Herman a major-league tryout.

30. "Country Club Munster"

Written by Douglas Tibbles. Directed by Joseph Pevney.

Herman wins for the entire family a membership to the exclusive Mockingbird Heights Country Club. Lily wants to make an elegant first impression in her new Transylvanian original—the one with the lovely shroud. Grandpa and Lily visit, but decide the club is "depressingly cheerful" and its members are just too snooty for their tastes. Herman "Arnie" Munster, however, wants to join the club to continue his golfing.

Br: 4-15-65. **GC:** Woodrow Parfrey, J. Edward McKinley, Dan Tobin, Janet Dey, Sally Ross, Al Checco, Johnny Jacobs (TV announcer).

31. "Love Comes to Mockingbird Heights"

Written by Joe Connelly and Bob Mosher. Directed by Joseph Pevney.

Uncle Gilbert sends the Munsters a crate filled with $180,000 in rare gold coins to deposit in the bank for him. The bank sends an armored car to haul the loot off the premises. The young assistant manager of the bank becomes intrigued with Marilyn—but even more interested in the fortune he thinks belongs to her. Grandpa is suspicious of his motives and is eventually proven correct. Uncle Gilbert shows up at the end to collect the money.

Br: 4-22-65. **GC:** Charles Robinson, Duncan McLeod, and Richard Hale as Uncle Gilbert, the Creature from the Black Lagoon.

32. "Mummy Munster"

Written by Joe Connelly and Bob Mosher. Directed by Ezra Stone.

Grandpa has developed a new "alarm-clock pill" which can be set to make Herman sleep for just a specified period of time. Under the influence of the pill, Herman is mistaken for an ancient mummy when he is discovered slumbering inside an Egyptian sarcophagus at the history museum.

Br: 4-29-65. **GC:** Pat Harrington, Jr., Philip Ober, Diana Frothingham, Dennis Cross, Pat McCaffrie, Ralph

Smiley. (Notes: Balding actor Philip Ober was married to actress Vivian Vance, and portrayed General Stone in the first season of *I Dream of Jeannie*.)

33. "Lily Munster, Girl Model"

Written by Joe Connelly and Bob Mosher. Story by Dick Conway. Directed by Earl Bellamy.

Lily decides she is no longer useful around the house. After repeated attempts to find gainful employment, she is hired by famous couturier Laszlo Brastoff to be a fashion model. Herman becomes insanely jealous at the notion that Lily might be lusted after by strange men. With Grandpa's help he disguises himself as a wealthy "Texas Playboy" so he can make Lily jealous. To top it off, Grandpa turns himself into a beautiful blonde to be Herman's escort.

Br: 5-6-65. **GC:** Roger C. Carmel, Lois Roberts, Sally E. Morris, Sondra Matesky, Nina Shipman, Susan Wedell, Tracy Butler, Kimberly Beck, John Alvin, and Teke. (Notes: Mustachioed Roger C. Carmel, a veteran character actor on television in the fifties through the seventies, was a regular on the sitcom *The Mothers-In-Law*.)

Herman and his escort (Grandpa turned into a woman) attempt to make Lily jealous in "Lily Munster, Girl Model."

34. "Munster the Magnificent"

Written by Dick Conway. Directed by Joseph Pevney.

Eddie volunteers his pop to entertain at the school talent show claiming he is a great magician. Grandpa is offended because he is a real magician, but he still comes to the rescue and secretly assists Herman with the fancy prestidigitation.

Br: 5-13-65. **GC:** Dave Ketchum, Eddie Ryder, Stuart Nisbet. (Notes: The Raven in the clock pokes his beak out and exclaims, "Rahhh, What's up, doc?" It's especially humorous considering the bird's vocals are supplied by none other than Mel Blanc, the voice of Bugs Bunny. In this episode the Raven finally reveals its own name: Charlie. Actor Dave Ketchum portrayed recurring mysterious character Agent 13, usually hidden away in file cabinets and mailboxes, in the sitcom *Get Smart*.)

35. "Herman's Happy Valley"

Written by Dick Conway. Directed by Ezra Stone.

Herman is sucked in by a magazine advertisement and invests in ten acres of wasteland through the mail. Intending to make it a vacation spot, Herman packs up the family and treks to Happy Valley. When the con artists discover there is gold in the old ghost town, they scramble to buy it back from a reluctant Herman and attempt to scare the Munsters into vacating. Rather delighted with the haunted hideaway, the Munsters refuse to be driven off of their paradise.

Guess what the mailman just dropped and ran?

Br: 5-20-65. GC: John Hoyt, Richard Reeves, Bartlett Robinson. (Notes: Character-actor John Hoyt later portrayed wisecracking Grandpa Stanley on the sitcom *Gimme a Break!*)

36. "Hot Rod Herman"

Written by Joe Connelly and Bob Mosher. Directed by Norman Abbott.

When Herman hops up the family vehicle and enters it in a drag race, he loses both the race and the car. Disgusted, Grandpa modifies a casket and creates a powerful roadster to race again and win back the family Koach.

Br: 5-27-65. GC: Henry Beckman, Brian Corcoran, Eddie Donno. (Notes: Un-credited cast include Ray Montgomery as a father and Murray MacLeod as his teenage son. The famous Drag-u-la, designed and built by George Barris, is introduced in this episode. Stunt driver Jerry Summers steered the Drag-u-la in the racing scenes. George Barris receives credit as Technical Advisor in this episode, with racing cars courtesy of Barris Kustom Cars.)

37. "Herman's Raise"

Written by Joe Connelly, Bob Mosher, and Douglas Tibbles. Story by Douglas Tibbles. Directed by Ezra Stone.

Herman is fired from his job at the funeral parlor when Lily prods him to demand an increase in his salary. Afraid of Lily's reaction, Herman pretends to go to his regular job when in fact he seeks employment elsewhere, including a Chinese laundry. Herman proceeds to ruin the laundry establishment. Lily finds out about Herman's job loss and goes directly to Mr. Gateman to privately plead for his reinstatement.

Br: 6-3-65. GC: John Carradine, Benny Rubin. (Notes: Celebrated horror film star John Carradine makes the first of two appearances as Herman's employer, Mr. Gateman. The respected actor also appeared as the creaky family butler, Cruikshank, in the feature film *Munster, Go Home!* Benny Rubin, a longtime comedian and dialectician who portrayed Fong the Laundromat owner, was a semi-regular on TV's *The Jack Benny Show*.)

38. "Yes, Galen, There is a Herman"

Written by Joe Connelly and Bob Mosher. Directed by Norman Abbott.

Herman heroically rescues a little boy he finds trapped between an iron fence and strikes up a friendship with the lad. Both Herman's and the boy's family accuse them of fabricating the story. In order to prove Galen exists, Herman invites his little friend over to watch home movies with the Munster family. Galen's parents have a child psychologist accompany the boy to the Munster house to squelch his stories of a cob-webbed mansion, a fire-breathing pet, and of course, Herman himself.

Br: 6-10-65. GC: Brian Nash, Walter Brooke, Marge Redmond, Harvey Korman. (Notes: Harvey Korman was supplying the voice of the little green alien, "The Great Gazoo" on TV's *The Flintstones* in 1965. Brian Nash played middle-brother Joel on the short-lived sitcom, *Please Don't Eat the Daisies*. Actress Marge Redmond gained fame in television portraying Sister Jacqueline on TV's *The Flying Nun*.)

▶ Brian Nash plays Herman's friend, Galen. Nash says today of the episode: "It's funny the things you remember. When you're a kid, you're around kids. But then when you're a kid and you're around a lot of adults, well, I just remember lots of bad breath."

◀ Lily lobbies Mr. Gateman (John Carradine) to restore Herman's job at the parlor: "Pussycat looks up to you the way Richard Chamberlain looks up to Raymond Massey."

SECOND SEASON

39. "Herman's Child Psychology"

Written by Joe Connelly and Bob Mosher. Directed by Ezra Stone.

Herman applies subtle parental psychology and coyly gives his approval when Eddie announces that he is running away from home. Herman's reverse psychology worries Lily who promptly dispatches Herman to locate their son. Herman accidentally retrieves a sleeping bear cub in a cave. When he returns the cub to its mother, Herman makes friends with the giant grizzly living in a cave.

Br: 9-16-65. **GC:** Michael Petit, Bill Quinn, Gene Blakely, Lee Henry. (Notes: Diminutive actor Janos Prohaska, known for playing gorillas many times in his career in television and films, portrays Olga the dancing bear. Balding character-actor Bill Quinn later portrayed Mary Richards's father in *The Mary Tyler Moore Show*. A few years later, Quinn portrayed blind Mr. Van R., Archie Bunker's bar chum on *All in the Family*. This second-season premiere features a new opening-credits sequence.)

40. "Herman the Master Spy"

Written by Douglas Tibbles. Directed by Ezra Stone.

The family goes on an outing at the beaches of Paradise Cove and all Grandpa wants to do is get buried in the sand. Clumsy, misdirected scuba diver Herman is scooped up in the nets of a Russian fishing trawler whose startled crew thinks they have found a sea monster . . . or the missing link. Moscow suspects he might be a spy.

Br: 9-23-65. **GC:** Leonard Yorr, John Lawrence, Bella Bruck, John Zaremba, Robert Millar, Howard Wendell, Val Avery, John Silo, Edward Mallory, Henry Hunter, and Ed Reimers (as the announcer).

41. "Bronco Bustin' Munster"

Written by Joe Connelly and Bob Mosher. Story by Dick Conway. Directed by Ezra Stone.

A frightened Herman begs Grandpa to concoct an instant bravery potion to steady his nerves after Eddie entered him in a rodeo bronco-riding contest. The Rodeo plans to put Herman atop their wildest horse named "Volcano." Grandpa turns himself into a horse to help Herman, but the pill wears off before the event.

Br: 9-30-65. **GC:** Don "Red" Barry, William Phipps, Leonard P. Greer, and Dick Lane (the announcer). (Notes: Don "Red" Barry was Red Ryder in the Republic Pictures' *Adventures of Red Ryder* serials in the forties. Barry appeared in a long list of Western movies and in episodic television; in 1980 he committed suicide by shooting himself.)

"I'm a rootin'-tootin', fancy-bootin', two-gun shootin', pistol-packin' papa from Possum Prairie."

42. "Herman Munster, Shutterbug"

Written by Dick Conway. Directed by Earl Bellamy.

Herman takes up photography and annoys the family with his new hobby. He eventually finds himself in a jam when he inadvertently takes pictures of a bank robbery and becomes wanted by both the police and the crooks. Herman unwittingly possesses the evidence to incriminate the desperate criminals. The bank robbers locate Herman and hold him and the family up in their home.

Br: 10-7-65. **GC:** Herbie Faye, Joe DeSantis, Alma Murphy, Jesse Kirkpatrick, Robert Morgan. (Notes: Yvonne De Carlo's husband, Bob Morgan, makes a cameo appearance as a police officer. Bill Foster—who went by the professional name Jefferson County—plays the Daniel Boone statue frightened by Herman. Foster was Fred Gwynne's stand-in and stunt-double throughout the series.)

43. "Herman, Coach of the Year"

Written by James Allardice and Tom Adair. Directed by Norman Abbott.

Eddie is depressed because the guys at school have nicknamed him "Lead Foot" due to his inabilities in track and field. Herman becomes Eddie's self-appointed track coach and trainer—with disastrous results. Grandpa whips up some "go-go pills" to induce superior athletic abilities, but Eddie doesn't like the taste of the "vitamins" and succeeds on his own when he runs the hundred-yard dash in record time.

Herman's attempt at the shot-put ends up demolishing an automobile in the episode, "Herman, Coach of the Year."

Br: 10-14-65. **GC:** Emmaline Henry, Henry Beckman. (Notes: Emmaline Henry portrayed nosy Amanda Bellows, the wife of psychiatrist Dr. Bellows, on the supernatural sitcom *I Dream of Jeannie.*)

44. "Happy 100th Anniversary"

Written by Douglas Tibbles. Directed by Ezra Stone.

Both Herman and Lily simultaneously withdraw $1,000 from their bank account in order to buy each other a handsome anniversary gift. Both checks bounce when they draw on the same joint bank account. Individually, both Herman and Lily secretly acquire part-time jobs welding at the Crosby Shipyards at night and end up working side by side. Since both are wearing welding masks, they do not recognize each other and after some flirting with each other, they embarrassingly realize they were falling in love with each other all over again. At least that's how Marilyn and Grandpa classify the alleged affair in the end and salvage the marriage.

Br: 10-21-65. **GC:** Vinton Hayworth, William O'Connell, Robert Cornthwaite, Jack Grinnage, Noam Pitlik, Foster Brooks. (Notes: Blooper Time. In the first scene, notice the bank manager holding two checks—one signed by "Herman Munster" and another signed by "Lily Dracula Munster." After the bank has returned the checks due to insufficient funds, Lily's signature magically reads "Mrs. Herman Munster." Actor Vinton Hayworth portrayed stuffy General Schaeffer on TV's *I Dream of Jeannie.* Noam Pitlik appeared in many sitcoms in the sixties and seventies, but might be most known as Mr. Gianelli on *The Bob Newhart Show.* Pitlik went on to a successful career directing sitcoms such as *Barney Miller, Taxi,* and *Wings.* And yes, also appearing in this episode is comedian Foster Brooks, most known for his hilarious drunk act.)

45. "Operation Herman"

Written by Joe Connelly and Bob Mosher. Story by Dick Conway. Directed by Norman Abbott.

Eddie is nervous and seriously reluctant about having his tonsils removed, and Herman becomes faint at the very idea of an impending surgery. Grandpa, who certainly is no stranger to the sight of blood, wants to perform the procedure. Instead Lily opts for google-eyed Dr. Willoughby. When Herman and Grandpa slip into the

Herman and Lily's wedding portrait, circa 1865. This rare image was seen only briefly, pasted in Herman and Lily's old family photo album, in the episode "Happy 100th Anniversary." (That's Yvonne De Carlo's stand-in, Maria, on the right.)

Mockingbird Heights Hospital for an after-hours visit with Eddie, Herman is mistaken for a near-dead patient in grave need of medical attention.

Br: 10-28-65. **GC:** Dayton Allen, Marge Redmond, Don Keefer, Bill Quinn, Justin Smith. (Notes: Comedian Dayton Allen, who portrays the wacky Dr. Willoughby, was a regular on *The Steve Allen Show*. Allen was also the voice for cartoon characters Deputy Dawg and those silly magpies Heckle & Jeckle.)

46. "Lily's Star Boarder"

Written by Douglas Tibbles. Directed by Ezra Stone.

The Munster family ignores Herman's vehement objections to renting their spare room to a stranger. Most of the people answering their newspaper ad are scared off at the door, but Lily finally gets accepts smooth-talking, handsome young man named Chester Skinner as their new boarder. Herman is crazed when Lily attempts to make Chester at home by plying him with delicacies such as owls' eggs and vulture livers. Herman even

prank calls Lily at home to check up on her. Skinner acts "sneaky" which infuriates Herman in the process and makes him suspicious. After Grandpa and Herman search Chester's room and find a handgun, Herman is convinced he's a dangerous gangster.

Br: 11-4-65. **GC:** Charles Bateman, Buddy Lewis, Chet Stratton.

MUNSTER MOMENT

Don't Blink: In the John Hughes hit sci-fi-comedy movie *Weird Science*, watch closely for clips of *The Munsters* playing on the television at peak moments.

47. "John Doe Munster"

Written by Richard Baer. Directed by Earl Bellamy.

Herman develops amnesia when he is struck on the head by a falling 300-pound safe. The Police take the confused Herman into protective custody until he can be claimed. Lily goes to court and legally adopts her husband so she can bring him home and somehow jolt his memory back. In a strange ruse, Grandpa dresses as a Rudolph Valentino–lover type and tries to put the moves on Lily in order to make Herman jealous and trigger memories of his married life.

Br: 11-11-65. **GC:** Frank Maxwell, Joe Quinn, Willis Bouchey, Olan Soulé, Vince Williams, Michael Blake, Monica Rush, Barry O'Hara, Peter Dawson. (Notes: Character-actor Willis Bouchey was one of the more frequent judges on the bench in TV's *Perry Mason*. Spindly, bespectacled actor Olan Soulé, who portrayed the bailiff, is recognizable to fans of *The Andy Griffith Show* for his recurring role as the choir director. Soulé was a busy character actor with many credits, including recurring roles on *Perry Mason* and *Dragnet*, to name but a few.)

Masquerading as a Rudolph Valentino–type, Grandpa pretends to be Lily's lover in an attempt to coax Herman out of his amnesia in the episode "John Doe Munster."

48. "A Man for Marilyn"

Written by James Allardice and Tom Adair. Directed by Ezra Stone.

Grandpa decides to produce a husband for Marilyn in his laboratory after her boyfriends disappear at top speed when she brings them home to meet the family. Grandpa experiments in order to produce a prince from a near-sighted frog. That way, when the frog is transformed, he won't notice Marilyn's bad looks. Grandpa changes the potion to a fly and allows the frog to eat the fly. Eventually, a passerby is mistaken for the prince Grandpa hoped to produce.

Br: 11-18-65. **GC:** Roger Perry, Don Edmonds, Dick Wilson, Dave Willock, Jan Barthel, Jackie Coogan, Jr. (Notes: Roger Perry is a recognizable character actor who was married to comedienne Jo Anne Worley for many years. Dick Wilson starred for more than twenty-five years as "Mr. Whipple" in Charmin toilet paper commercials . . . "Please don't squeeze the Charmin." Child-actor Jackie Coogan, Jr. was the young son of motion pictures' first child star, Jackie Coogan—famous for his role in the silent classic *The Kid* with Charlie Chaplin. Interestingly, Coogan, Jr. appeared here on *The Munsters* while his old man was starring as kooky Uncle Fester on *The Addams Family* on the rival network ABC-TV.)

49. "Herman's Driving Test"

Written by Dick Conway. Directed by Ezra Stone.

Herman must renew his driver's license in order to accept a promotion as driver of the hearse with the funeral parlor. Grandpa helps Herman study up on the rules of the road, but he flunks the test. Grandpa then suggests he try again in some remote town where the testing might be simpler. In the sleepy town of Groverville, the near-sighted old public attendant, Charlie Wiggins, assumes Herman and Grandpa wish to obtain a license to be married.

Br: 11-25-65. **GC:** Charlie Ruggles, Francis DeSales, Irwin Charone, Will J. White. (Notes: Charlie Ruggles went way back. The actor started in motion pictures during the silent era, with his debut in 1915; he continued his extensive career in film and television until the late sixties. Charlie Ruggles starred in one of television's first series, called *The Ruggles* in 1949 on ABC-TV.)

Charlie Ruggles portrays the inept license-bureau chief in "Herman's Driving Test."

From beautiful downtown Mockingbird Heights . . . broadcaster Gary Owens appears in the episode, "Will Success Spoil Herman Munster?"

50. "Will Success Spoil Herman Munster?"

Written by Lou Shaw, Joe Connelly, and Bob Mosher. Story by Lou Shaw. Directed by Ezra Stone.

Herman gets his hands on an audiotape recorder which belongs to Eddie's playmate. When Eddie returns the recorder to his pal, the tape lands in the hands of a radio disc jockey who loves the song Herman has anonymously recorded. The DJ assumes it is an audition tape and airs the weird tune on a radio show. Herman's rendition of "Dry Bones" becomes a smash hit which Eddie plays on the radio for the family. Grandpa laughs and thinks the song sounds like "a werewolf with laryngitis." Herman, however, emerges as the sensational mystery folksinger with delusions of superstardom. Naturally, Lily wants to put a stop to the egomaniac, so Grandpa helps out by whipping up a batch of Nuthin' Muffins to ruin his golden throat.

Br: 12-2-65. **GC:** Gary Owens, Penny Kunard, Frank Evans, Don Dillaway, Nolan Leary, Debbie Butler, Sandra Ferra, Gail Ganley. (Notes: Jack Marshall and Bob Mosher composed and adapted the version of "Dry Bones" sung by Herman in this episode. Marshall and Mosher titled it "That's How Herman Was Born" and actually copyrighted the song. Although Fred Gwynne was himself a guitarist, the show's soundtrack actually features Jack Marshall on guitar accompanying Gwynne's vocals. If you watch closely, notice Gwynne's guitar strumming does not synch with the music, and he deliberately bends over, with his hands and guitar out of camera shot, for the elaborate ending. Also of note in the cast is real-life broadcaster and DJ Gary Owens, who became famous to television audiences on TV's *Laugh-In*. Owens was also the voice of Hanna-Barbera's animated cartoon superheroes Space Ghost and the Blue Falcon. Bob Hastings provides the voice of the Raven in this episode.)

51. "Underground Munster"

Written by Joe Connelly and Bob Mosher. Directed by Don Richardson.

Herman causes a major crisis when he chastises Spot for tracking mud into the house and the sensitive, fire-breathing family pet runs away from home. Spot hides in the sewer system causing panic in the city when he is sighted by citizens of Mockingbird Heights. Lily and Grandpa race to stop the mayor from bombing the sewer system.

Br: 12-16-65. **GC:** J. Edward McKinley, Warren Parker, Jimmy Joyce, Hoke Howell, Bob Harvey, David Azar, John Mitchum, Buck Kartalian, Helen Kleeb, Elsie Baker. (Notes: Veteran character-actress Helen Kleeb is recognizable to TV fans as one of the Baldwin sisters on the long-running series, *The Waltons*. Hoke Howell was a longtime bit actor in television; he is known to Andy Griffith fans as hillbilly "Dud Wash" in several episodes of *The Andy Griffith Show*.)

52. "The Treasure of Mockingbird Heights"

Written by George Tibbles. Directed by Charles Rondeau.

While searching for the fuse box, Herman and Grandpa discover a secret dungeon with a mysterious clue on the wall. The handwritten clue indicates how to locate a treasure map leading them to pirate Henry Morgan's hidden fortune, riches from the Spanish Main. The clue: MORGAN'S TREASURE IN THIS VALLEY/LOOK BEHIND THE NOBLE SALLY. (Sally being a carved image of a salamander in the stone wall.) The two decode the clue, dig in the backyard as directed and discover the whereabouts of Morgan's Treasure buried near an old oak-tree stump. When a locked chest full of treasures is found, Herman and Grandpa turn greedy and suspicious of one another, closely guarding the treasure—from each other—twenty-four hours a day.

Br: 12-23-65. (Notes: The voice of the Raven in this episode was supplied by Bob Hastings.)

53. "Herman's Peace Offensive"

Written by Douglas Tibbles. Directed by Ezra Stone.

Eddie returns home from school angry because the school bully has been picking on him. Eddie just wants to stomp the bully. "Did I overhear my sweet little off-shoot contemplating homicide? . . . Now, now, Eddie—sensitive intelligent creatures such as we do not stomp one another." Peace-loving Herman urges his son to turn the other cheek and ignore the troublemaker. Meanwhile, Herman is having troubles of his own with a fellow worker, Clyde Thornton, who persists with practical jokes aimed at embarrassing him. Herman is forced to practice what he preaches, but when both he and Eddie come home with black eyes, he decides to reevaluate his own philosophy and retaliate.

Br: 12-30-65. **GC:** Jackie Minty, Chet Stratton, Bryan O'Byrne. (Notes: Whoops! At work Herman is clearly socked in his right eye, but returns home later in the day with his *left* eye blackened.)

Fred Gwynne had the clown-like ability to beautifully transcend layers of makeup and induce laughter with simple, but well-calculated eye and facial movements, as demonstrated by this series from "Underground Munster."

54. "Herman Picks a Winner"

Written by Dick Conway. Directed by Ezra Stone.

Herman tries to teach Eddie a lesson on the futility of gambling by contacting a bookie and deliberately betting on the worst horses at the track. Herman ends up winning big because of the tremendous odds, and the bookies use some unconventional tactics in order to force Herman to pick more winners.

Br: 1-6-66. **GC:** Charlie Callas, Barton MacLane, Joyce Jameson, Sammy Shore, Joe Hernandez (race announcer). (Notes: Barton MacLane, who portrays "Daddy," may be recognizable as General Peterson from TV's *I Dream of Jeannie*. Sammy Shore is the father of comedian Pauly Shore. Charlie Callas was a frequent guest on *The Dean Martin Show*.)

An estrogen-enhanced Herman—the result of an experiment gone awry—in the episode, "Just Another Pretty Face."

55. "Just Another Pretty Face"

Written by Richard Baer. Directed by Gene Reynolds.

Herman is zapped by a bolt of artificial lightning from one of Grandpa's laboratory mechanisms and is "disfigured." Horrified, Herman begs Dr. Dudley to perform plastic surgery and restore his old appearance. The family finds it difficult adjusting to Herman's appearance.

Br: 1-13-66. **GC:** Dom DeLuise, Joan Swift, Jackie Joseph, Lenore Kingston. (Notes: For this episode only, Dom DeLuise assumes the role of Dr. Dudley, a role created by Paul Lynde. Universal pulled from retirement special effects designer Kenneth Strickfadden for this episode. Strickfadden designed the lightning wizardry for the original Frankenstein features at Universal in the thirties. The director of this episode, Gene Reynolds, began his career as a child actor working in Hal Roach's *Our Gang* comedies. Reynolds later directed episodic television, steering such shows as *The Andy Griffith Show*, *Leave It to Beaver*, and *Hogan's Heroes* before winning Emmy Awards as a director and producer of *M*A*S*H* for many years.)

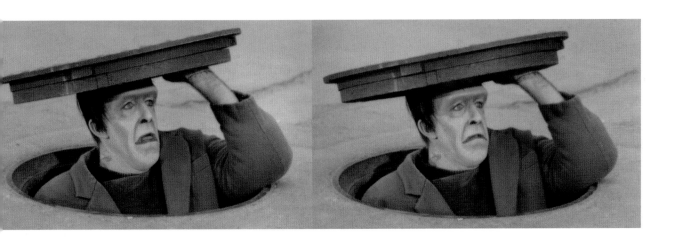

Herman is struck by a bolt of electricity in Grandpa's laboratory and hideously "disfigured" in the extraordinary episode "Just Another Pretty Face"—the only episode to unmask one of the characters.

56. "Big Heap Herman"

Written by Joe Connelly and Bob Mosher. Directed by Ezra Stone.

The Munster family is vacation-bound to Buffalo Valley. Herman is accidentally left behind at a desert train station at Indian Flats and blunders into a remote Indian village where he is hailed as the long-awaited Mighty Spirit Wanitoba.

Br: 1-20-66. **GC:** Ned Romero, Len Lesser, Felix Locher, Sally Frei, Richard Jury. (Notes: Len Lesser, who plays the money-driven Indian, Manikoo, may be recognizable to *Seinfeld* fans as odd "Uncle Leo." During the Indian wedding ceremony, watch the nervous young Indian boy who keeps "spiking the lens"—or looking directly into the camera's eye—spoiling the shot.)

57. "The Most Beautiful Ghoul in the World"

Written by Ted Bergman. Directed by Ezra Stone.

Cousin Wolverine from Transylvania has died—again—and has left the Munsters a $10,000 fortune. The family decides to pool the funds and invest in separate schemes. Grandpa and Herman spend their half on the completion of Grandpa's newest invention—a device which trans-mits electrical power through the air; Lily and Marilyn invest their share by opening a beauty parlor, Madame Lily's. Both endeavors fail miserably.

Br: 1-27-66. **GC:** Elvia Allman, Mary Mitchell, Charles Lane, Adele Claire. (Notes: Bob Hastings supplies the voice of the Raven in this episode. Hatchet-faced character-actress Elvia Allman is recognizable to *I Love Lucy* fans for her classic scene as the boss in the chocolate-candy factory ordering: "Speed it up!" Allman frequently appeared on *The Beverly Hillbillies* and *Petticoat Junction*. Prolific character-actor Charles Lane, who lived past the age of 100, has been seen in countless motion pictures and television shows in his lengthy career. Usually portraying bespectacled curmudgeons, lawyers, and landlords, Lane was a regular as "Homer Bedloe" on TV's *Petticoat Junction*. Lane was a founding member of the Screen Actors Guild.)

58. "Grandpa's Lost Wife"

Written by Douglas Tibbles. Directed by Ezra Stone.

In the magazine *Startling Detective Stories*, Herman spots an ad with a monetary reward for information leading to the whereabouts of Grandpa. The ad has been placed by Pamela Thornton, of Sioux City, Iowa, who seeks to claims Grandpa as her long-lost husband. Lily is aghast when Herman wants to turn Grandpa in and collect the reward. The whole twisted plot ends up being a scam and Grandpa must come crawling back to Herman and Lily.

Br: 2-3-66. **GC:** Jane Withers, Douglas Evans. (Notes: Jane Withers went on to star as "Josephine the Plumber" in a long-running series of Comet Cleanser commercials.)

59. "The Fregosi Emerald"

Written by Richard Baer. Directed by Ezra Stone.

Great misfortune descends on the Munster family during Marilyn's birthday party when Eddie gives her a ring he found in the attic. The ring is a feared piece of ancient jewelry known as the Fregosi Emerald which Grandpa claims carries a powerful Transylvanian curse. In order to vanquish the hex, Grandpa tracks down the sole Fregosi descendant in Detroit, Michigan—Henry J. Fregosi, chairman of the board of Amalgamated Motors. The Munsters immediately fly to Detroit and present the cursed ring to Fregosi, forcing him to expose his past and break the spell.

Br: 2-10-66. **GC:** Paul Reed, Louise Glenn, Joan Swift, Marilyn Bell. (Notes: Paul Reed played cranky Captain Block in TV's *Car 54, Where Are You?* with Fred Gwynne and Al Lewis.)

60. "Zombo"

Written by Dennis Whitcomb. Directed by Ezra Stone.

Herman becomes insanely jealous when his son Eddie is entranced by a new hero—the "monster" host of a children's horror program. Eddie is excited when he wins a trip to the TV studio to meet Zombo in person, but ends up disenchanted with the host when he realizes his appearance is merely makeup, wigs, and fake teeth.

Br: 2-17-66. **GC:** Louis Nye, Digby Wolfe, Mike Barton, Jimmy Stiles, Jackie Minty. (Notes: The voice of the station announcer is broadcaster Gary Owens. Butch Patrick says he sometimes writes "You Kill Me" on autographs today, reminiscent of a phrase printed on the life-sized Zombo cutout in this episode. Notice, TO EDDY is imprinted on one cardboard Zombo cutout and another life-sized cutout of Zombo spells it to EDDIE. Comedian Louis Nye was a regular on *The Steve Allen Show* and later created the hilariously prissy character, Sonny Drysdale, on *The Beverly Hillbillies*.)

"Grandpa, you've done it . . . I'm adorable." Herman tries to out-Zombo Eddie's TV kiddy-show hero.

Louis Nye on The Munsters

The late comedian Louis Nye played Zombo, the creepy kiddy-show host who shakes Eddie's spirit. In a 2000 interview, Nye shared a brief recollection about the episode:

Ezra Stone directed me and in one of the scenes where I talked to the little boy; he said, "Just do it your own way. You don't need any direction from me." We just did it cold and with no rehearsal and it worked. It was a great show to work on. What more can I say about a one-shot deal? The makeup took a little while, it was a strange makeup as Zombo, you know, but that's okay, I just wanted to look . . . stunning. I'm simply amazed at how many people remember this single show from my career. That and the handful of *Beverly Hillbillies* I did as Sonny Drysdale. Somehow those characters resonate with fans, and I must say, I'm honored by this . . . after all, I *was* Zombo the magnificent!

61. "Cyrano de Munster"

Written by Douglas Tibbles. Directed by Joseph Pevney.

Herman ghostwrites love letters for a shy coworker, Clyde Thornton. When Lily discovers the love poetry, she assumes Herman is having an affair.

Br: 2-24-66. **GC:** Chet Stratton, Joan Staley, Eileen O'Neill. (Notes: Actress Joan Staley was a *Playboy* model turned actress. Staley costarred with Don Knotts in the cult-classic film, *The Ghost and Mr. Chicken*, and was a regular on the short-lived sitcom, *Broadside*.)

62. "The Musician"

Written by Richard Baer. Directed by Ezra Stone.

Grandpa whips up a potion to provide instant talent for Eddie when he tone-deaf youngster has made the school orchestra and assigned the trumpet. Herman couldn't be more excited about his son taking music lessons. Herman invites his boss, Mr. Gateman, home to witness the young musical prodigy.

Br: 3-3-66. **GC:** John Carradine. (Notes: The trumpet solos were performed by famous jazz-trumpeter Jack Sheldon who worked closely with musician Jack Marshall on the show's scoring sessions. Sheldon was the bandleader for Merv Griffin on his daytime-television talk show. Additionally, Sheldon sang in many of the popular animated *Schoolhouse Rock* segments for Saturday morning television in the seventies.)

63. "Prehistoric Munster"

Written by Douglas Tibbles. Directed by Joseph Pevney.

Herman mistakenly assumes that a summons to appear at the state university indicates that he is the winner of the Father of the Year contest. The request actually came from the anthropology department. Scientists at the university think they have found the missing link after seeing a lifelike bust of Herman which Marilyn sculpted for her art class.

Br: 3-10-66. **GC:** Harvey Korman, George Petrie, Richard Poston. (Notes: Character-actor George Petrie, who played Professor Hansen, may be recognizable for his multiple guest appearances on TV's *The Honeymooners*. The unique prop bust of Herman used in the episode was later painted and displayed under glass in the seventies and eighties in the Universal Studios mini-museum with additional film and television artifacts.)

A trio of anthropologists examine Herman in the episode "Prehistoric Munster." George Petrie, Richard Poston, and Harvey Korman portray the scientists.

64. "A Visit from Johann"

Written by Joe Connelly and Bob Mosher. Directed by Gene Reynolds.

Dr. Victor Frankenstein IV arrives in town with Herman's primitive cousin, Johann (one of Frankenstein's original rejects, pre-Herman). Johann ends up being a near look alike of Herman. Reluctantly, Herman has agreed to secretly hide his unpolished cousin in the dungeon laboratory and "smooth out the rough edges" with lessons in manners and culture. Lily mistakenly takes Johann on their planned romantic weekend getaway at the Happy Valley Lodge.

Br: 3-17-66. **GC:** John Abbott, Forrest Lewis, Helen Kleeb, Jefferson County. (Notes: Fred Gwynne plays a dual role as Herman and Johann.)

65. "Eddie's Brother"

Written by Dick Conway. Directed by Ezra Stone.

Eddie has put Herman on the spot by announcing that he wants a little brother. Grandpa tries to ease the situation and creates a small robot he names Boris, as a playmate for Eddie. Boris becomes a favorite of the family and Eddie ends up feeling resentful toward the helpful robot. Eddie thinks Herman loves Boris better and runs away.

Br: 3-24-66. **GC:** Wendy Kottler, Rory Stevens as the Robot. (Notes: The voice of the broadcaster heard on Grandpa's old radio is that of prolific character-actor Vito Scotti. Bob Hastings supplies the voice of the Raven in this episode.)

66. "Herman the Tire Kicker"

Written by James Allardice and Tom Adair. Directed by Ezra Stone.

Herman decides to buy a car for Marilyn and falls easy victim to the familiar pitch of a fast-talking salesman, Fair Deal Dan. The old convertible he has purchased turns out to be a lemon and falls apart. Herman reluctantly attempts to return the car, but the auto lot has vanished. Herman is stopped and arrested by the police because it ends up the car had been stolen.

Br: 3-31-66. **GC:** Frank Gorshin, Johnny Silver, Pat McCaffrie, Jimmy Cross, Jack Perkins, Rian Garrick,

Guest-star Frank Gorshin clowns around with Pat Priest on the set. Gorshin (best known as "The Riddler" on TV's *Batman*) portrayed shyster Fair Deal Dan in the episode "Herman, the Tire Kicker."

Dennis Cross, Saul Gorse, Fred Carson, Jack Wilson. (Notes: Comedian/impressionist Frank Gorshin was most known for his role as the green-clad villain, the Riddler, on TV's campy hit show *Batman*.)

67. "A House Divided"

Written by Dick Conway. Directed by Ezra Stone.

Under top-secret conditions, Herman and Grandpa have been spending many hours creating a birthday present for Eddie. During a test spin, Herman accidentally wrecks the motorized go-cart that he and Grandpa built. Grandpa becomes furious, fears Eddie's birthday is ruined, and orders Herman to leave the house. Herman takes Grandpa literally when the elder vampire insists that he is half owner of the house; Herman divides the house into two parts—with a painted white line marking the territories (even down the center of the bathtub . . . "and Grandpa can't get hot water on his side"). The two bicker endlessly until Lily puts a stop to the nonsense and makes them get back into the garage and build a new birthday gift for Eddie.

Br: 4-7-66.

68. "Herman's Sorority Caper"

Written by Douglas Tibbles. Directed by Ezra Stone.

Herman—placed in a frozen trance by Grandpa to rid him of hiccups—is mistaken for a mannequin by two fraternity inductees who enter the creepy Munster house at night as part of their initiation. As a prank, they haul Herman off and plant him in a college sorority house where he awakens the next day in a girl's closet. Desperate to get out of the sorority house filled with young women, Herman makes his way to a payphone and begs Lily for help. Grandpa takes a bat pill and flies to the rescue.

Br: 4-14-66. **GC:** David Macklin, Bonnie Franklin, Ken Osmond, Michael Blodgett, Frank Gardner, Vicki Draves, Vicki Fee, Hedy Scott, William Fawcett, Mike Ross. (Notes: Bonnie Franklin, who portrays one of the students in the dorm, went on to play Ann Romano on TV's *One Day at a Time*. Later, Franklin directed episodes of the revival series *The Munsters Today*. Ken Osmond is recognizable to TV fans as the obnoxious "Eddie Haskell" on the sitcom *Leave It to Beaver*. Bob Hastings supplies the voice of the Raven in this episode.)

69. "Herman's Lawsuit"

Written by Douglas Tibbles, Joe Connelly, and Bob Mosher. Directed by Ezra Stone.

While walking to work one day, Herman is struck by a car in the middle of the street. The driver of the car assumes she is liable for disfiguring Herman and eagerly wants to settle out of court. Unharmed but feeling guilty, Herman misunderstands an attorney's letter and assumes he must pay $10,000 to the woman driver whose car was demolished in the collision. When the driver's attorney is dispatched to the Munster house to discuss a settlement offer, he is convinced the family is poor and seeks a greater settlement figure. Distraught at the notion of having to fork over such a sum, Herman runs away.

Br: 4-21-66. **GC:** Simon Scott, Dorothy Green, Jerome Cowan, Fabian Dean, Eddie Marr, Bob Harvey, Than Wyenn, Monroe Arnold. (Notes: Bob Hastings supplies the voice of the Raven in this episode.)

70. "A Visit from the Teacher"

Written by Joe Connelly and Bob Mosher. Directed by Ezra Stone.

Concerned school officials check on Eddie's home life when the youngster composes a wild essay, handwritten in blood, describing his "normal" American family. It doesn't take long for the visiting principal to realize Eddie was not exaggerating.

Br: 5-12-66. **GC:** Pat Woodell, Willis Bouchey. (Notes: Pat Woodell, who portrays Eddie's teacher, Miss Thompson, spent two years in Hooterville as "Bobbie Jo Bradley" on TV's *Petticoat Junction*.)

The Ultimate Munsterrific Trivia Challenge Answers

1. Chester Skinner

2. Vulture bumps

3. Uncle Gilbert

4. Cleo

5. Dr. Frankenstein autographed them and gave them to Grandpa

6. Grandpa (That meant he owned exactly half of the house, according to the agreement)

7. "Morgan's treasure in this valley; look behind the noble Sally."

8. An imported tarantula-skin wallet

9. 1313 Mockingbird Lane, Mockingbird Heights

10. *The Encyclopedia of Voodoo*

11. A bat in the box

12. On the Dead Sea

13. *Event* magazine

14. Writes to Dear Abby

15. Shorty

16. Every time he took a short nap, someone put him in the icebox

17. Modeling clothes

18. Dragula Born 1367–Died?

19. Playing the wolf in the school production of *Little Red Riding Hood* ("and I practiced my howl all week.")

20. The Pat Boone Fan Club

21. Groverville

22. The *Vault Street Journal. Tomb & Garden*

23. W6XR-L4

24. ". . . sounds like a werewolf with laryngitis."

25. 1865

26. To Death Valley to live with Uncle Garrett and Aunt Mina

27. The prison surplus store

28. Mrs. Cartwright, an eccentric widow

29. Devil's Island

30. Secret Agent 702

31. 167 (according to the "Munster Masquerade" episode)

32. A suit of armor

33. Richard Dawson

34. Inside the casket standing upright in the hallway (concealed until the pull-cord is yanked)

35. Open tin cans

36. Igor the bat

37. "Bury Me Not on the Lone Prairie"

38. Jane Withers ("Pike's Pique" and "The Most Beautiful Ghoul in the World")

39. A black widow spider

40. A life-size bust of Herman

WACH STETER

EPITAPH

AFTERWORD BY BUTCH PATRICK

Fans of vintage television, and especially the sixties pop-culture era, will embrace this book. Steve Cox has definitely captured the essence of the 1964–1966 show *The Munsters*. I should know, because I was there. For two incredible years of my life I was the luckiest kid on the block—the block known as planet earth. Our show was out of this world, and that's why people loved it. It was an era we can't relive or touch again. Back then, no one could foresee the impact and staying power of what we did. Black-and-white television featuring these colorful monsters in suburbia . . . who would have thought? It was television at its best, and to prove that, all you have to do is give it the test of time. *The Munsters* have survived like no other. I continue to see it in the eyes of fans I meet, fans from all corners of the world.

Non-reality shows were the ticket during the sixties, and although I worked with a genie, a talking horse, and even a Martian, nothing prepared me to be a Munster. TV was fresh and so were the sitcoms back in the day, so if you're a nostalgia fan—a fan of comedy or just a plain ol' TV fan—you'll find that this book seizes all aspects of *The Munsters* and the time and place. For me, this book is a little keepsake and a reminder of those two amazing years that literally altered my life for good.

I'm amazed that here we are forty years later, and cable television, satellite TV, VHS, DVD, and all other media forms continue to broadcast and lovingly exploit *The Munsters*. Even *The Simpsons* parodied our show, so you know you're a part of popular culture when that happens.

Sadly, Al Lewis is now gone. Fred Gwynne left us over a decade ago. What a team these guys were. They were friends, partners in comedy on film and in life itself. Al taught me how to laugh and what was truly funny. Fred helped me with my acting as well as teaching me how to keep my balance between work and play. And now being the last male cast member standing, I feel even more privileged to have worked with them and to be able to carry the torch. We were truly a TV family and to me, that's why generations of viewers still find *The Munsters* a superior product, some of the most wholesome entertainment ever produced for television. I'd go out on a limb and call it a work of art.

Butch Patrick

March 2006

ABOUT THE AUTHOR

A lifelong TV buff, Stephen Cox grew up in St. Louis and began corresponding with actor Al Lewis while in grade school. Cox, now forty, graduated with a B.A. in communication arts and journalism from Park University in Kansas City, Missouri in 1988. As a freelance writer, he has contributed to *TV Guide* and the *L.A. Times*, and has written more than a dozen books on film and television. He resides in southern California.

In 1980, at age fifteen, the author meets his first Munster.

JACK O' LANTERN COSTUME PARTY

Materials Needed

fondant
(orange, black, purple, white, green & light gray)

raw spaghetti

Cutters Needed

1¼-inch circle cutter

round tips
#3, #7, #10 & #12

mini crescent cutter

small teardrop cutter

Tools Needed

rolling pin with
⅛-inch guide rings

precision knife

knife tool

modeling tool

rolling pastry cutter

small ball tool

Sweet Tips

SIMPLIFY
Create a pumpkin candy basket by following the tutorial for the Jack O' Lantern, but use a large ball tool to hollow the top out a bit more. Cut a strip of black fondant to glue as the basket handle and add little balls in different colors for candy.

ACCENTUATE
Cut out a white circle with the 1½-inch circle cutter and layer it over the jack o' lantern to create an easy ghost!

PERSONALIZE
Punch initials or ages out of fondant and glue them to the front of pumpkins instead of the jack o' lantern faces.

EXPAND
Follow the tutorial from the Sweet Tooth collection (p. 41) to create Halloween candies by simply changing the colors to match.

DECORATE & DISPLAY
Use a spider web embossing mat to imprint the pattern onto fondant to cover the domes of cupcakes. Use Halloween cupcake liners and wrappers. Use decorative spider webs, Halloween decor, and candy corn to accent your presentation.

Jack O' Lantern

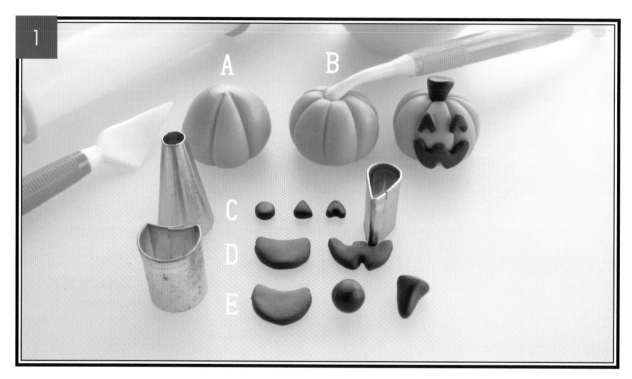

How to:

1. Roll orange fondant into a ball (approximately 1 inch). With the knife tool, start at the bottom of the ball and indent a line into the fondant all the way to the top **(A)**. Continue all around the ball with equal spacing and use the small ball tool to indent the very top **(B)**. With the rolling pin, roll out black fondant ⅛ inch thick. Use round tip #12 to cut out 2 circles for the eyes. Shape them into triangles and use the narrow tip of the teardrop cutter to cut out a portion of the bottom of the eyes **(C)**. Cut 2 crescent shapes out of the black fondant with the cutter. (If you do not have a crescent cutter, use the bottom of the round tip to cut out a circle and then trim a bit off the top.) Use the narrow end of the teardrop cutter to cut 2 sections out of the top of 1 crescent shape and another section out of the bottom to make the jack o' lantern's mouth **(D)**. Roll the second black crescent shape into a ball, shape it into a cone, and flatten the top to make the stem **(E)**. Glue all pieces to the pumpkin. Allow to dry thoroughly. If adding Halloween costumes, please read ahead to each costume since you might need to wait before gluing all the necessary pieces together.

Female Jack O' Lantern Costumes

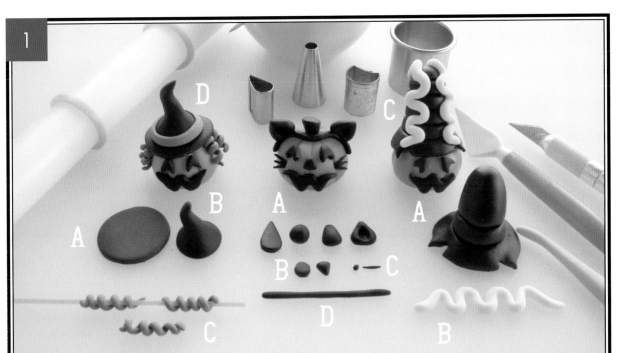

How to:

Witch: (**Please note**: A stem is not necessary for the witch.) With the rolling pin, roll out black fondant ⅛ inch thick and cut out 2 circles with the 1¼-inch cutter. Set a circle aside for the hat brim (**A**). Roll the other into a ball, shape it into a cone, and then zigzag it a bit and make the end pointed (**B**). Roll purple fondant thin onto your work surface and cut 4 strips for the witch's hair. Coil the strips around the raw spaghetti and allow to dry a bit to keep its shape (**C**). Once dry enough, glue the hair to the jack o' lantern and then assemble and glue the witch's hat. With the rolling pin, roll out purple fondant ⅛-inch thick and use the rolling pastry cutter to cut a strip to shape around the hat. Trim it and glue it in place (**D**).

Black Cat: With the rolling pin, roll out black fondant ⅛ inch thick and cut 2 teardrops with the cutter. Roll them into balls and shape them into cones. Use the modeling tool to indent the center of the cones for the ears (**A**). Cut 1 circle out of the black fondant with round tip #10 and shape it into a triangle for the cat's nose (**B**). Cut out 6 circles with round tip #3, ball them up, and roll them out onto your work surface to shape the whiskers (**C**). (You can also draw on the whiskers with edible-ink markers.) Cut out another teardrop shape, roll it into a ball, and roll it onto your work surface to create the headband (**D**). Glue all pieces to the jack o' lantern.

(continued on next page)

(continued):

Frankenstein Bride: (**Please note**: A stem is not necessary for the bride.) Roll black fondant into a ball (approximately 1 inch) and shape it into a cone for the hair. Round out the top. Begin to pull the bottom of the cone outward with your fingers, all the way around, to shape over the jack o' lantern. Use the precision knife to cut out sections on each side and straighten the bangs by pushing the middle section inward. Use the knife tool to make indentations around the hair, all the way to the top (**A**). Roll out white fondant thick with your fingers onto your work surface to make a spaghetti shape and mold it into a wave pattern (**B**) and glue it to the side of the hair. Make another wave pattern and glue it to the opposite side and glue all pieces together (**C**).

Male Jack O' Lantern Costumes

How to:

Vampire: (**Please note**: Add the stem last in this tutorial). With the rolling pin, roll black fondant ⅛ inch thick and use the rolling pastry cutter to cut out a strip (approximately ½ inch wide) and shape around the jack o' lantern for the cape collar. Trim the ends diagonally with the precision knife (**A**). Cut out a circle with the 1¼-inch cutter from the rolled black fondant. Use the same cutter to trim 2 sections off the front to shape the vampire's hair (**B**). With the rolling pin, roll white fondant ⅛ inch thick. Cut out 2 circles with round tip #10 and shape them into triangles. Use the knife tool to indent creases on the 2 triangle tips (**C**) and glue the tips together to create a bow tie. Cut 2 more circles out of white fondant with round tip #7 and shape them into vampire fangs (**D**). Glue all pieces onto the jack o' lantern. Use the small ball tool to indent the hair at the top and insert and glue the stem (**E**).

(continued on next page)

(continued):

Frankentstein's Monster: (**Please note:** Add the facial features and stem last in this tutorial.) Roll green fondant with the rolling pin ⅛ inch thick and cut out a circle with the 1¼-inch cutter for the face (**A**). Glue to the front of the jack o' lantern. With the rolling pin, roll black fondant ⅛ inch thick, cut out a circle with the 1¼-inch cutter, and use the rolling pastry cutter to cut off a small section for the front of the hair (**B**). Use the knife tool to indent the straight side to form the bangs. Glue the hair to the top of the jack o' lantern, indent the middle with the small ball tool, and glue the stem into the center. With the rolling pin, roll out light gray fondant ⅛ inch thick and cut out 2 teardrops with the cutter. Roll them into balls and shape them into screws for the sides of the head. Use round tip #3 to indent the center of each screw (**C**). Glue them to the sides of the head. With the rolling pin, roll out black fondant ⅛ inch thick and cut out a circle with round tip #7. Roll it into a ball and then roll it out long onto your work surface. Using the knife tool and your fingers, shape it into a lightning bolt (**D**) and glue it to the side of the face. Glue the rest of the facial features to the jack o' lantern (**E**).

Mummy: (**Please note:** Add the facial features last in this tutorial.) With the rolling pin, roll out white fondant ⅛ inch thick and cut out several strips (approximately ¼ inch wide) (**A**). Add glue to the back of the strips and begin to wrap them around the jack o' lantern to create the mummy. You want the strips to be uneven and show a bit of the orange pumpkin. Glue the rest of the facial features to the jack o' lantern (**B**).

GOBBLE 'TIL YOU WOBBLE

Materials Needed

fondant
(brown, light brown, maroon, orange, light green, yellow & black)

raw spaghetti

toothpick

black edible-ink marker

tylose powder

Cutters Needed

1¼-inch circle cutter

small & medium teardrop cutters

round tips
#3, #10 & #12

large daisy cutter

Tools Needed

rolling pin with
⅛-inch guide rings

2 wooden dowels

knife tool

precision knife

large ball tool

large veiner tool

thin foam mat

rolling pastry cutter

wood-grain embossing mat

Sweet Tips

SIMPLIFY	Omit the pilgrim hat and accessories from the turkey.
ACCENTUATE	Make additional signs and write different Thanksgiving wishes.
PERSONALIZE	Add fondant initials or ages to the front of fondant pumpkins.
EXPAND	Follow the tutorial to make pumpkins from the Jack O' Lantern Costume Party collection (p. 192), using brown to make the stems and adding coiled light green fondant to further accentuate the pumpkins.
DECORATE & DISPLAY	Utilize fall and Thanksgiving-themed liners and wrappers. Embellish your presentation with rustic elements, such as burlap, hay, corn, and pumpkins.

Pilgrim Turkey

How to:

1. Knead tylose powder into brown fondant and roll it into a 1-inch ball and a 1¼-inch ball. Insert a piece of raw spaghetti into the 1-inch ball, protruding enough to hold the turkey head **(A)**. Shape the larger ball into an egg shape for the head. Make a hole in the head with the spaghetti to later fit over the body. Roll orange fondant thick with the rolling pin and wooden dowels. Cut out 2 medium teardrops with the cutter and 1 circle with round tip #12. Round out the orange teardrops and use the knife tool to make 2 indentations at the wider end for the feet. Flatten the tip a bit and then glue them together and to the turkey's body. Roll the orange circle into a ball and then into a cone to form the beak. Glue it to the turkey's face **(B)**. Roll maroon fondant thick with the rolling pin and wooden dowels. Cut out 2 circles with round tip #10. With your fingers, shape them into teardrops and glue them to each other with the narrow tips facing upward. Then use the bottom of the circle cutter to trim off the top **(C)** and glue the bottom underneath the turkey's beak. With the rolling pin, roll out black fondant ⅛ inch thick and cut out 2 circles with round tip #3 for the turkey's eyes **(D)** and glue them in place. Roll out brown fondant thick with the rolling pin and wooden dowels. Cut out 2 small teardrops with the cutter. Round them out with your fingers and use the knife tool to make indentations for the wings **(E)**. Glue them to the sides of the turkey's body.

2. Roll out black fondant thick with the rolling pin and wooden dowels. Cut out a 1¼-inch circle with the cutter. Roll it into a ball and shape the top into a cylinder by rolling it between your fingers. Then pull out the bottom with your fingers all the way around to form the hat brim. Use the large ball tool to indent the inside center of the hat to fit over the turkey's head **(A)**. With the rolling pin, roll out light green fondant ⅛ inch thick and use the rolling cutter to trim a long strip **(B)**. Fit it

(continued on next page)

around the hat, trim it, and glue it in place. With the precision knife, cut a small rectangle out of the light green fondant and trim it into a bow tie. Make a couple of indentations at the center of each bow **(C)**. With the rolling pin, roll out yellow fondant $\frac{1}{8}$ inch thick and use the precision knife to trim a small rectangle **(D)**. Glue it to the front of the hat over the light green trim. With the rolling pin, roll out white fondant $\frac{1}{8}$ inch thick and use the rolling pastry cutter to trim a strip (approximately $\frac{1}{3}$ inch wide). Fit it around the turkey's neck and then trim the sides diagonally with the precision knife to form a collar and use the 1¼-inch circle cutter to trim the center of the strip **(E)**. Glue the collar at the top of the turkey's body and then add the bow tie. When the body is dry enough to hold the weight of the head and hat, glue them in place. If the body is not firm enough, it can begin to crack, so waiting overnight is recommended.

3. With the rolling pin, roll out orange and maroon fondant $\frac{1}{8}$ inch thick. Cut a large flower with the daisy cutter out of each color **(A)**. Sprinkle powdered sugar over the thin foam mat and place the orange flower on it. Cut off 2 petals with the precision knife and use the large veiner tool to indent each remaining petal **(B)**. Repeat the process with the maroon flower and allow them both to dry a bit. Once firm enough, form them around the back of the turkey to create the tail feathers and glue them in place **(C)**. With the rolling pin, roll out light brown fondant $\frac{1}{8}$ inch thick and spread a bit of shortening over the fondant. Place the wood-grain embossing mat over the fondant and use the rolling pin to impress the pattern onto it **(D)**. Use the rolling pastry cutter to cut a long strip (approximately ½ inch wide) and slowly insert a toothpick through the center. You might need to use the embossing mat once again after you insert the toothpick. Trim another rectangular shape with the rolling pastry cutter and use the precision knife to cut pieces out of the sides to form the sign **(E)**. When dry enough, glue the sign to the piece with the toothpick. When completely dry, write "Eat Beef" with the black edible-ink marker on the sign and insert the toothpick in the cupcake when decorating. Allow to dry thoroughly.

DREIDEL, DREIDEL, DREIDEL

Materials Needed

fondant
(blue, light blue & white)

raw spaghetti

Cutters Needed

⅞-inch & 1½-inch
circle cutters

2¼-inch scalloped
circle cutter

round tips
#1 & #12

small circle cutter

small hexagram cutter

Tools Needed

rolling pin with
⅛-inch guide rings

2 wooden dowels

rolling pastry cutter

Sweet Tips

SIMPLIFY	Make one dreidel without the spaghetti and lay it flat on the bottom topper.
ACCENTUATE	Make additional dreidels to decorate more cupcakes. Make 9 small cylinders with the blue fondant, insert raw spaghetti through them, and add small yellow flames to the top (shaped from a ball and then into a teardrop) to make candles. Insert them in different cupcakes to create a cupcake menorah.
PERSONALIZE	Use fondant initials or age instead of the hexagram on the front of the dreidel.
EXPAND	Follow the tutorial for the Snowball Penguin (p. 149) and replace the snowballs with dreidels to add a playful element.
DECORATE & DISPLAY	Enhance your presentation with shades of blue and traditional Hanukkah decorations.

Dreidel

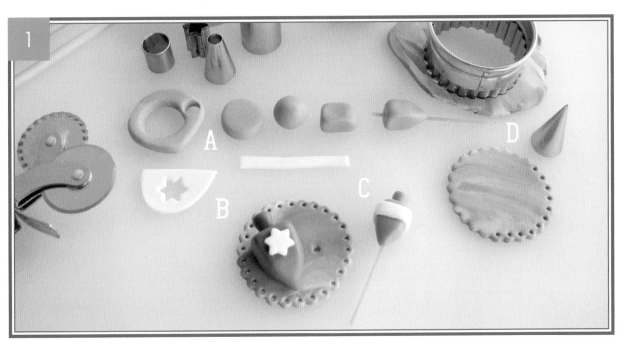

How to:

1. Roll light blue fondant out thick with the rolling pin and wooden dowels. Cut out a circle with the 7/8-inch cutter and a circle with round tip #12. Roll the larger circle into a ball and then into an oval. Square off one end of the oval to create the top of the dreidel. At the other end, smooth out all 4 sides diagonally, meeting in the center to create a pyramid. Insert a raw spaghetti through the center, leaving a tiny bit for the top at the square end and protruding quite a bit from the pointed end **(A)**. Roll the smaller circle into a ball and then into a cone. Apply glue to the tip and insert it in the small piece of spaghetti coming out of the top of the dreidel. Repeat these steps to make a larger dreidel with the blue fondant by using the 1½-inch circle cutter for the dreidel and the small circle cutter for the handle (the latter cut out of ⅛ inch thick fondant), but only insert a small piece of raw spaghetti into the top to hold it together. With the rolling pin, roll out white fondant ⅛ inch thick. Punch out a small hexagram with the cutter. (If you do not have this cutter, you can cut out 2 small triangles, turn 1 upside down, and glue 1 on top of the other.) Glue the hexagram to the larger dreidel **(B)**. Cut a strip out of the white fondant with the rolling pastry cutter, shape it around the small dreidel, and glue it in place **(C)**. Take blue and white fondant and begin to roll them together (as if you were mixing fondant), but do not blend them all the way—rather, make a marbled effect. With the rolling pin, roll it out ⅛ inch thick and cut out a 2¼-inch scalloped circle with the cutter. Use round tip #1 to cut out circles around the perimeter of the scalloped circle **(D)**. Glue the large dreidel to the bottom topper and punch a hole with the raw spaghetti to later insert the small dreidel when decorating your cupcake to make it stand up. Allow to dry thoroughly.

SANTA

Materials Needed

fondant
*(white, ivory, pink,
red & black)*

Cutters Needed

1½-inch & 1⅞-inch
circle cutters

round tip #10

large leaf cutter

medium teardrop
cutter

Tools Needed

rolling pin with
⅛-inch guide rings

2 wooden dowels

knife tool

Sweet Tips

SIMPLIFY	Make hat and beard features more flat.
ACCENTUATE	With the rolling pin and wooden dowels, roll out various colored fondant thick and cut out presents in different shapes and sizes. Make similar faces with different features and accessories to make Mrs. Claus or elves.
PERSONALIZE	Cut rectangles out of fondant and punch a small circle out of one end to create a gift tag. Write names or messages with an edible-ink marker.
EXPAND	Follow the treasure map tutorial from the "X" Marks the Spot collection (p. 87), but instead write naughty and nice names with an edible-ink marker.
DECORATE & DISPLAY	Use festive holiday cupcake liners and decorations to present your cupcakes, such as ornaments and Christmas lights.

Santa Claus

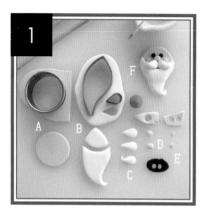

How to:

1. With the rolling pin, roll out ivory fondant ⅛ inch thick and cut out a circle with the 1½-inch cutter for Santa's face (**A**). Roll out white fondant thick with the rolling pin and wooden dowels. Cut out 1 large leaf shape and 2 medium teardrops with the respective cutters. Use the 1½-inch circle cutter to trim off the wider end of the large leaf-shaped fondant and curl the tip (**B**). Smooth out the sides of the beard with your finger dipped in shortening and form it around Santa's face. Round out the sides of the 2 teardrops and curl up the sides to form Santa's mustache (**C**). Roll out ivory fondant thick with the rolling pin and wooden dowels. Cut out a circle with round tip #10. Round it out and shape it into an oval for Santa's nose (**D**). With the rolling pin, roll out black and pink fondant ⅛ inch thick and cut out 2 circles of each color with round tip #10 for the eyes and cheeks (**E**). Glue all the features to Santa's face (**F**).

2. Roll out red fondant thick with the rolling pin and wooden dowels. Cut out a large leaf shape with the cutter. Dip your fingers in shortening and round out the sides. Turn the red leaf on its side and use the 1½-inch circle cutter to trim a section off the bottom to fit over Santa's head (**A**). Glue the hat to the head. Curl the tip under to form Santa's cap. Roll out white fondant thick with the rolling pin and wooden dowels. Cut out a 1⅞-inch circle with the cutter. Use the 1½-inch circle cutter to cut out the bottom section of the circle. Use the top section to shape the trim for Santa's hat. Make indentations across the top and bottom of the trim with the knife tool (**B**). Shape it and glue it to Santa's head. Use round tip #10 to cut a circle out of the excess thick white fondant, roll it into a ball, and flatten it a bit. Use the knife tool to indent it all the way around. Glue the pom-pom to the end of Santa's cap (**C**). Allow to dry thoroughly.

MERRY & BRIGHT REINDEER

Materials Needed

fondant
(light brown, dark brown, ivory, black, white, green, red, blue & yellow)

tylose powder

raw spaghetti

Cutters Needed

round tips
#7, #10 & #12

small, medium & large teardrop cutters

Tools Needed

rolling pin with ⅛-inch guide rings

2 wooden dowels

knife tool

modeling tool

Sweet Tips

SIMPLIFY	Omit the Christmas lights from the reindeer.
ACCENTUATE	Create large Christmas lightbulbs out of fondant to decorate additional cupcakes.
PERSONALIZE	Cut out initials, ages, or words—such as "Noel"—with letter cutters with different colored fondant and add them to a fondant cord to resemble hanging lights.
EXPAND	Add a penguin to the winter scene following the tutorial from the Snowball Penguin collection (p. 149), changing the colors to match.
DECORATE & DISPLAY	Decorate your cupcakes with white frosting to resemble snow and embellish your presentation with Christmas motifs or actual large-bulbed Christmas lights.

Tangled in Christmas Lights

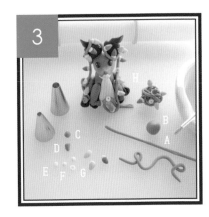

How to:

1. Knead tylose powder into light brown fondant and roll it into balls as follows: body, 1-inch (A); 2 hind legs, ½-inch (B); and 2 front limbs, ¼-inch (C). Roll the body into a cylinder and insert a raw spaghetti to later hold up the head. Shape the hind legs by rolling out the fondant on your work surface, leaving one end thick and flattening it out a bit for the thighs (D). Bend the narrow end underneath the thigh (E). Roll out the smaller balls onto your work surface to shape the front limbs (F). Roll black fondant thick with the rolling pin and wooden dowels. Cut out 4 circles with round tip #10. Flatten them out a bit with your finger and use the knife tool to indent the tops of the circles to create hooves (G). Glue the hooves to the ends of the legs.

2. With the rolling pin, roll out ivory fondant ⅛ inch thick and cut out a large teardrop with the cutter (A). Glue it to the front of the reindeer's body with the narrow tip on top and then glue on the legs. Roll light brown fondant into a ball (approximately ¾ inch thick) and then shape the reindeer's head by rolling a tip into a snout with your fingers (B). Insert the raw spaghetti into the bottom so the head can fit over the body. With the rolling pin, roll out ivory fondant ⅛ inch thick and cut out a small teardrop with the cutter (C). Glue it to the bottom of the reindeer's snout, with the smaller tip of the teardrop at the tip of the snout. Use the larger, rounded end of the teardrop cutter to indent a smile (D). With the rolling pin, roll out black and red fondant ⅛ inch thick and use round tip #7 to cut out 2 black circles and 1 red (E). Shape the black circles into ovals and glue the eyes to the reindeer's face. Roll the red into the nose and glue it to the tip of the snout. Roll out dark brown and light brown fondant thick with the rolling pin and wooden dowels. Cut 2 medium teardrop shapes out of the dark brown with the cutter. Use the tip of the cutter to remove sections from

(continued on next page)

both sides to create the antlers **(F)**. Insert small pieces of raw spaghetti into the wider ends of the antlers and insert into the reindeer's head. Cut 3 circles out of the light brown fondant with round tip #12. Shape 2 of them into teardrops and indent them in the center with the modeling tool **(G)**. Shape them to the reindeer's head, underneath the antlers, and glue them on. Shape the last light brown circle into a teardrop and twist the end a bit to shape the reindeer tail **(H)**. Glue it to the back.

3. Roll a long piece of green fondant onto your work surface for the strand of Christmas lights **(A)**. Drape and glue it over the reindeer, allowing some slack at one end. Roll green fondant into a ball (approximately ½ inch) **(B)**. Roll another long piece of green fondant onto your work surface, then wrap and glue the strand around the ball to create the tangled mess. To make the bulbs, with the rolling pin roll out the red, blue, green, and yellow fondant ⅛ inch thick. Cut out circles with round tip #10 and roll them into balls **(C)**. Shape the balls into cones **(D)**. With a rolling pin, roll out white fondant ⅛ inch thick and cut out circles with round tip #7 **(E)**. Roll them into balls and flatten them a bit **(F)**. Glue them to the wider end of the colored bulbs or, if making the missing bulbs, simply use a raw spaghetti to make a hole in the center of the white circle **(G)**. Glue the bulbs (and missing ones) onto the strand of lights on the reindeer, as well as onto the tangled ball **(H)**. Allow to dry thoroughly.

SANTA ON VACATION

Materials Needed

fondant
(ivory, red, green, black, white & sand)

pink shimmer
dust & brush

Cutters Needed

⅞-inch scalloped
circle cutter

2½-inch circle cutter

round tips
#3, #7 & #10

small oval cutter

Tools Needed

rolling pin with
⅛-inch guide rings

knife tool

precision knife

rolling pastry cutter

large ball tool

Sweet Tips

SIMPLIFY	Instead of a fondant bottom, make the sand angel indentations directly onto the cupcake frosting.
ACCENTUATE	Make additional sand toppers with pieces of Santa's clothes or an empty gift sack leading up to the sand angel Santa. Make sandmen (snowmen out of sand) or melting snowmen on the beach.
PERSONALIZE	Add Santa's list on a separate cupcake with the desired name crossed out.
EXPAND	Add beach details from the Surf's Up collection (p. 109) to additional cupcakes in the red and green color palette.
DECORATE & DISPLAY	Coat your cupcakes with crushed graham crackers to resemble sand and present it on a plate, stand, or tray filled with edible sand and paper drink umbrellas.

Sand Angel Santa

LEVEL OF DIFFICULTY

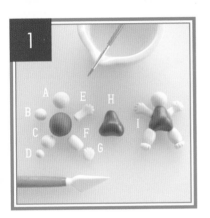

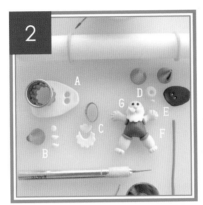

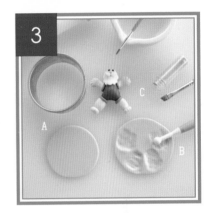

How to:

1. Roll ivory fondant into balls as follows: head, ⅝-inch (**A**); 2 arms, ⅜-inch (**B**); 2 legs ½-inch (**C**); and 2 feet, ¼-inch (**D**). Roll the arms out, leaving a thicker end to form the hands. Flatten the hand and use the knife tool to make 4 indentations to form the fingers (**E**). Roll the legs into a cylinder, narrowing at both the top and bottom (**F**). Form the feet into teardrops, then flatten the thin end and use the knife tool to make 4 indentations to form the toes (**G**). Roll red fondant into a ball (approximately 1 inch) and, with your finger dipped in shortening, form the body by creating a triangle, but ensure you keep a bit of a belly on the bottom half. Narrow and flatten out the top for the neck and indent the center at the bottom, which will naturally create the two thighs. Round out the sides with your fingers (**H**). Glue all the pieces together (**I**).

2. With the rolling pin, roll out white fondant ⅛ inch thick. Cut out 1 scalloped circle with the ⅞-inch cutter and 2 small circles with round tip #10 (**A**). Form the small circles into teardrops and then curl up the pointed ends to create the mustache (**B**). Use the small oval cutter to cut a piece out of the scalloped circle to form the beard (**C**). With the rolling pin, roll out ivory fondant ⅛ inch thick and cut out a circle with round tip #7. Roll it into a ball and then form it into an oval (**D**). With the rolling pin, roll out black fondant ⅛ inch thick and cut out 2 circles with round tip #3 for the eyes (**E**). With the rolling pin, roll out green fondant ⅛ inch thick and use the rolling pastry cutter to cut narrow strips. Wrap them around the limbs bordering the bathing suit and then trim with the precision knife and glue (**F**). Glue the facial features onto Santa's head (**G**).

3. With the rolling pin, roll out the sand fondant just a tad bit thicker than ⅛ inch and cut out a circle with the 2½-inch cutter (**A**). Spread a little shortening over the fondant. Using the large ball tool, make generous indentations where the limbs lie, as well as above and below to make the sand angel pattern (**B**). Brush very little pink shimmer dust with a moist brush on Santa's arms, legs, and head for a little bit of a sunburn (**C**). Glue Santa to the sand angel topper and allow to dry thoroughly.

BABY NEW YEAR

Materials Needed

fondant
(desired skin color, white, black & light gray)

raw spaghetti

silver shimmer
dust & brush

Cutters Needed

⅞-inch & 1¼-inch
circle cutters

2¼-inch scalloped
circle cutter

round tips
#3, #7, #10 & #12

small circle cutter

number cutters
of new year

Tools Needed

rolling pin with ⅛-inch
& 1/16-inch guide rings

2 wooden dowels

knife tool

precision knife

rolling pastry cutter

small modeling stick

Sweet Tips

SIMPLIFY	Omit one or more of the elements of the topper, such as the baby or clock.
ACCENTUATE	Make larger party blowers to enhance additional cupcakes.
PERSONALIZE	Utilize the new year and/or initials to decorate more banners.
EXPAND	Follow the tutorial for party confetti from the Piece of Cake collection (p. 21) in matching colors to decorate extra cupcakes. Add fireworks from the tutorial in the Red, White & Boom collection (p. 188) in matching colors.
DECORATE & DISPLAY	Add sparkle to your presentation with shiny cupcake liners, real party horns and blowers, confetti, and miniature disco balls to ring in the new year.

Baby New Year

How to:

1. Roll out skin-colored fondant thick with the rolling pin and wooden dowels. Cut out 1 circle with the $\frac{7}{8}$-inch cutter and 1 circle with the 1¼-inch cutter. Roll the larger circle into an oval shape for the baby's body and insert a piece of raw spaghetti through the center by carefully twisting it in from the top, leaving enough protruding to hold the head (**A**). Use the small modeling stick to insert a belly button in the front. With the rolling pin, roll out white fondant $\frac{1}{16}$ inch thick and cut out a 1¼-inch circle with the cutter (**B**). Glue it to the bottom of the baby's body, folding it up at the front and back and pinching the sides together to form the diaper. Trim off the sides with the precision knife. Roll the second skin-colored circle into a ball for the baby's head and make a hole in the center with the raw spaghetti to later insert over the body. With the rolling pin, roll out both skin-colored and black fondant ⅛ inch thick and cut out the eyes and nose with round tip #3 (**C**). Glue them to the baby's face and indent a smile with round tip #10 at a 45-degree angle. Roll out additional skin-colored fondant thick with the rolling pin and wooden dowels. Cut out 3 circles with the small cutter. Roll 2 of the circles into balls. Elongate each ball while pushing up one end for the feet. Use the knife tool to make 4 indentations for the toes (**D**) and shape the legs around the baby's diaper, gluing them in place. Cut the third circle in half, roll the pieces into balls, and repeat the same step as the legs, but this time forming the ends into hands by flattening them slightly and indenting fingers with the knife tool (**E**). Bend the arms a bit and form them around the baby's sides, gluing them in place. When the body is firm enough, insert the head over the raw spaghetti and glue it on.

2. With the rolling pin, roll out light gray fondant ⅛ inch thick and cut out 2 strips with the rolling pastry cutter (approximately 3 inches long). With one of the strips, fold the center into 2 loops to create a bow and glue the bottom of the loops in place. Trim the ends by cutting them diagonally (**A**). Roll the second strip into itself and pinch the very end together for the party blower (**B**). Brush silver shimmer dust on the bow and party blower.

Glue the bow over the baby's head. With the rolling pin, roll white fondant ⅛ inch thick and cut out a small circle with round tip #12. Shape it into a cone **(C)** and glue it to the pinched end of the party blower. With the rolling pin, roll out black fondant ⅛ inch thick and cut out a ⅞-inch circle with the cutter and 2 small circles with round tip #7. Use the bottom of the round tip to cut out the center of the larger circle for the clock trim. With the rolling pin, roll out white fondant ⅛ inch thick and use the bottom of the round tip to cut out a circle. Make clock indentations inside the white circle **(D)** with the knife tool and glue it inside the black clock frame. Roll 1 of the small black circles out thin to make the long clock hand and cut the other in half and roll it out to form the small clock hand. Glue the hands to the clock, nearing midnight. With the rolling pin, roll out light gray fondant ⅛ inch thick and cut out a small circle with round tip #7. Brush it with silver shimmer dust and glue it to the center of the clock. With the rolling pin, roll out white fondant ⅛ inch thick and cut a strip with the rolling pastry cutter (approximately ½ inch wide). Form it into a scroll shape and trim both ends in a "V" shape with the precision knife **(E)**. With the rolling pin, roll out light gray fondant ⅛ inch thick and cut out the new year date with the number cutters **(F)**. Brush the numbers with the silver shimmer dust and glue them to the white scroll. With the rolling pin, roll out black fondant ⅛ inch thick and cut out a 2¼-inch scalloped circle with the cutter. Glue the baby, clock, party blower, and year to the bottom topper. Allow to dry thoroughly.

BEARY SWEET BABY

Materials Needed

fondant
(tan & brown)

Cutters Needed

⅞-inch & 1½-inch circle cutters

round tips #1, #3, #5, #7 & #10

small circle cutter

large square cutter

large teardrop cutter

Tools Needed

rolling pin with ⅛-inch guide rings

knife tool

precision knife

rolling pastry cutter

small modeling stick

Sweet Tips

SIMPLIFY	Remove the bear embellishment from the baby pants.
ACCENTUATE	Follow the Onesie tutorial from the Ooh La La collection (p. 225) and replace the poodle with a bear face to decorate extra cupcakes.
PERSONALIZE	Make a separate bib or Onesie with the baby's or mom's initials.
EXPAND	Follow the tutorial from the Binky Baby collection (p. 227) to make pacifiers to accentuate additional cupcakes. Make a three-dimensional baby from the Baby New Year collection (p. 216) and add a little bear hat to his head.
DECORATE & DISPLAY	Add string or baker's twine to your presentation with clothespins so the cupcakes resemble a clothesline.

Bear Bib or Cap

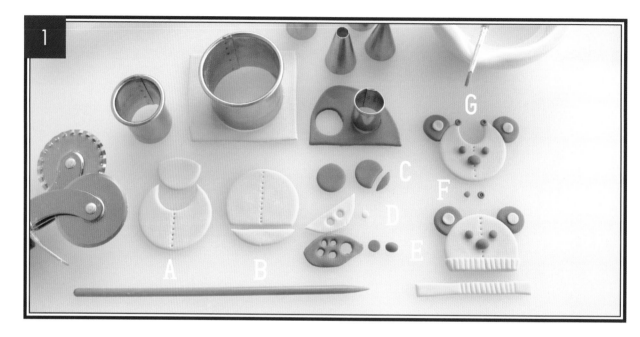

How to:

1. With the rolling pin, roll out tan fondant ⅛ inch thick and cut out a 1½-inch circle. If you're making the bib, use the ⅞-inch circle cutter to trim off the top and push the 2 ends closer together for the bib **(A)**. For the cap, use the rolling pastry cutter to trim off the bottom in a straight line **(B)**. Use the small modeling stick to make little dot indentations across the center vertically. With the rolling pin, roll out brown fondant ⅛ inch thick and cut 2 circles with the small circle cutter. Use the 1½-inch circle cutter to trim off a bit for the bear's ears **(C)**. Fit them on each side of the bear's head and glue them in place. With the rolling pin, roll out tan fondant ⅛ inch thick and cut out 2 small circles with round tip #7 **(D)**. Flatten them out slightly and glue them to the center of the ears. With the rolling pin, roll out brown fondant ⅛ inch thick and cut out 1 large circle with round tip #10 and 2 small circles with round tip #5. Form the larger circle into an oval nose **(E)** and glue it to the bear's face. Glue the smaller circles as the bear's eyes **(F)**. If you're making the bib, cut out 2 more small circles in the brown fondant with round tip #3, roll them into balls and flatten them out slightly. Use round tip #1 to indent the centers and glue them as the snaps of the bib at the tips **(G)**. If you're making the cap, with the rolling pin roll out tan fondant ⅛ inch thick and cut out a strip with the rolling pastry cutter. Use the knife tool to indent vertical lines along the strip. Fit it over the bottom of the cap, trim it to size with the precision knife, and glue it in place. Allow to dry thoroughly.

Bear Bum

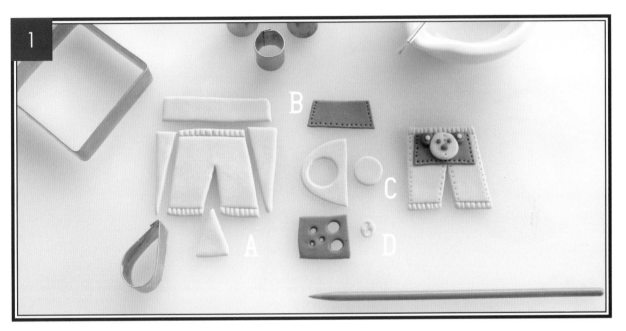

How to:

1. With the rolling pin, roll tan fondant ⅛ inch thick and cut out a large square with the cutter. Use the large teardrop cutter to cut out a triangular shape from the bottom center of the square. Use the square cutter or the rolling pastry cutter to trim off the top and sides to form the baby pants. Use the knife tool to indent the top and bottom of the pants horizontally and then make small vertical lines across for a ribbed effect (**A**). With the rolling pin, roll out brown fondant ⅛ inch thick and trim a rectangular shape to fit on the top of the pants, making sure not to cover the ribbed seam. With the small modeling stick, make dotted indentations around the perimeter of the rectangle (**B**) and glue it to the pants. Roll out tan fondant ⅛ inch thick and cut out a small circle with the cutter for the bear's face. Make dotted indentations vertically across the center of the bear's face (**C**). With the rolling pin, roll out brown fondant ⅛ inch thick. Cut out 2 circles with round tip #10 for the ears (cut off a bit of each ear with the small circle cutter to fit the head), 1 circle with round tip #5 for the nose (shape into an oval), and 2 circles with round tip #3 for the eyes. Glue all the pieces in place. Cut out 2 more pieces of the tan fondant with round tip #3 (**D**). Glue them to the center of the bear's ears. Make dotted indentations for the seams around the perimeter of the pants. Allow to dry thoroughly.

OOH LA LA

Materials Needed

fondant
(pink, black & white)

black & white
gel paste

toothpick

Cutters Needed

⅞-inch circle cutter

2¼-inch scalloped
circle cutter

round tips
#1, #3, #7, #10 & #12

large square cutter

Tools Needed

rolling pin with
⅛-inch guide rings

knife tool

precision knife

small modeling stick

damask embossing mat

Sweet Tips

SIMPLIFY

Omit the hearts on the Eiffel Tower and the buttons on the Onesie.

ACCENTUATE

Use larger circles to make larger poodles, not only on Onesies but also for Parisian glam toppers. Make the Eiffel Tower stand upright on your cupcake by avoiding gluing it to the bottom topper.

PERSONALIZE

Make bibs by using a scalloped circle cutter to cut a piece of fondant and cutting out an opening with a smaller circle cutter. Embellish it with small hearts to match the Eiffel Tower and add the baby's or mom's initials.

EXPAND

Follow the tutorial from the Binky Baby collection (p. 227) to make pacifiers for additional cupcakes. Make the three-dimensional baby from the Baby New Year collection (p. 216), changing the bow to pink.

DECORATE & DISPLAY

Pair pink baby shower decorations with Parisian chic elements for your presentation. Black and white is always a classic color scheme!

Eiffel Tower

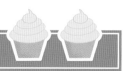

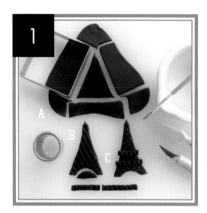

How to:

1. With the rolling pin, roll out black fondant ⅛ inch thick and use the large square cutter to cut out a triangle (approximately 2 inches high) (**A**). Use the precision knife to cut out 2 small pieces at the very top, forming the tip. Use the ⅞-inch circle cutter to trim off the bottom of the triangle, creating the bottom of the tower. With the knife tool, begin making diagonal impressions on the tower and repeat going the other way (**B**). Roll out more black fondant ⅛ inch thick and cut a long strip (approximately ¼ inch wide). Using the knife tool, make reversing diagonal lines. Trim the strip into 2 pieces, 1 longer than the other. Place strips on the tower (**C**). Glue the pieces together.

2. With the rolling pin, roll out pink fondant ⅛ inch thick and cut out 3 circles with round tip #7. Pinch a side of 1 circle. On the opposite side, utilize the knife tool to indent inward, creating a small heart. Repeat with the other 2 hearts (**A**) and glue them onto the tower. Dip the toothpick into some white gel paste and make dots in a pattern from one heart to the next (**B**). With the rolling pin, roll out more pink fondant ⅛ inch thick and spread shortening over it. Place the embossing mat over it and use the rolling pin to impress the pattern on the fondant. Use the 2¼-inch scalloped cutter to punch out a circle (**C**). Glue the tower to the bottom topper. Allow to dry thoroughly.

Poodle Onesie

LEVEL OF DIFFICULTY

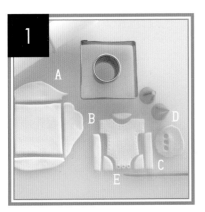

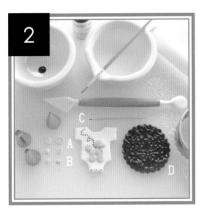

How to:

1. With the rolling pin, roll out white fondant ⅛ inch thick. Cut out a square with the large square cutter (**A**). With the square cutter, trim off two sides of the square, but leaving ½ inch at the top for the sleeves. Use the ⅞-inch circle cutter to trim off the leg holes on the bottom sides as well as a small portion of the top for the head opening (**B**). Use the small modeling stick to make little seam marks on the perimeter of the Onesie (**C**). With the rolling pin, roll out pink fondant ⅛ inch thick. With round tip #7, cut out 3 circles for the buttons (**D**). Glue them onto the bottom of the Onesie and use round tip #1 to indent the center of the buttons (**E**).

2. To make the poodle, with the rolling pin roll out pink fondant ⅛ inch thick. Cut out 2 circles with round tip #12 and 5 circles with round tip #10. Set aside 2 of the smaller circles. With the remaining big and small circles, use round tip #3 to make indentations over the surface of each to create the curls. With the knife tool, indent the sides of the circles to scallop them (**A**). With 1 of the small set-aside circles, pinch a side upward to make the poodle snout (**B**). The other set-aside circle is used for the back section of the poodle's body. Glue all pieces together on the Onesie to form the poodle. Dip the toothpick into some black gel paste and make dots in a leash pattern (**C**). With the rolling pin, roll out black fondant ⅛ inch thick and spread shortening over it. Place the embossing mat over it and use the rolling pin to impress the pattern on the fondant. Use the 2¼-inch scalloped cutter to punch out a circle (**D**). Glue the Onesie to the bottom topper. Allow to dry thoroughly.

BINKY BABY

fondant
(blue/pink & white)

Cutters Needed

⅞-inch circle cutter

round tips
#1 & #3

medium heart cutter

large oval cutter

Tools Needed

rolling pin with
⅛-inch guide rings

2 wooden dowels

small modeling stick

Sweet Tips

SIMPLIFY	Omit the handle on the pacifier.
ACCENTUATE	Cut out simple fondant hearts and circles in coordinating colors to decorate additional cupcakes.
PERSONALIZE	Add the baby's or mom-to-be's initial to the front of the pacifier.
EXPAND	Add elements from the Ooh La La (p. 223) and Beary Sweet Baby (p. 219) collections to the pacifier design for a larger baby shower assortment.
DECORATE & DISPLAY	Utilize pastel-colored cupcake liners and/or wrappers and embellish your presentation with simple baby supplies, such as bottles or clothespins.

227

Pacifier

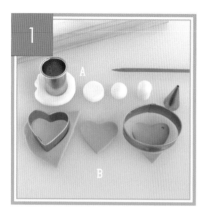

How to:

1. Roll out white fondant thick with the rolling pin and wooden dowels. Cut out a ⁷⁄₈-inch circle with the cutter and roll it into a ball. With your fingers, roll it into a cylinder and narrow the bottom to form the nipple (**A**). With the rolling pin, roll out blue/pink fondant ⅛ inch thick and cut out a medium heart with the cutter. Use the large oval cutter to trim the bottom off the heart and use your fingers to round out the bottom to form the plastic disc of the pacifier. Use round tip #3 to cut out 2 circles on each side of the heart toward the top. Use the small modeling stick to round out the inside of the hole (**B**). Set both pieces aside until they are both fairly hard.

2. With the rolling pin, roll out blue/pink fondant ⅛ inch thick and cut out a ⁷⁄₈-inch circle with the cutter. Use the bottom of a round tip to trim off the top of circle to form the pacifier handle. Use round tip #1 to indent little circles around the handle (**A**). Roll out white fondant thick with the rolling pin and wooden dowels. Cut out a circle with the bottom of a round tip. Round it out a bit and then shape it into a rectangle. Use the small modeling stick to make holes on 2 long sides of the rectangle (**B**). Apply glue to the inside of the holes and around one end of the rectangle. Then insert the tips of the blue/pink handle. As soon as the pacifier nipple and disc are hard enough, glue them together and then glue the handle to the opposite side (**C**). Allow to dry thoroughly.

SHABBY CHIC BRIDAL SHOWER

Materials Needed

fondant
(pink, light blue & white)

raw spaghetti

white shimmer
dust & brush

Cutters Needed

2¼-inch scalloped
circle cutter

round tips
#1 & #12

small & large
flower cutters

rolling pastry cutter

Tools Needed

rolling pin with ⅛-inch
& ¹⁄₁₆-inch guide rings

2 wooden dowels

precision knife

small modeling stick

large ball tool

thin foam mat

flower-forming cup

small spatula

rose embossing mat

Sweet Tips

SIMPLIFY
Make a pearl necklace without the floral and bow embellishments. Or instead of a large rose, follow the rosette tutorial but make larger.

ACCENTUATE
Make a variety of roses in different sizes and color shades for additional cupcakes.

PERSONALIZE
Add the bride's initials to embossed toppers with the same floral pattern.

EXPAND
Follow the tutorial for the bride design from the Going to the Chapel collection (p. 236) to add to your assortment.

DECORATE & DISPLAY
Decorate your cupcakes with pretty frosting using a floral tip and present them in small mason jars adorned with ribbon. Infuse rustic details, such as wood and burlap, to your display.

Shabby Rose

LEVEL OF DIFFICULTY

How to:

1. Roll pink fondant into a ball (approximately ⅓ inch) and shape into a cone to form the rosebud. Insert a raw spaghetti inside the wide end and set it aside to dry (**A**). With the rolling pin, roll out more pink fondant ¹⁄₁₆ inch thick and cut out 3 small flowers and 2 large flowers with the cutters. Use the small spatula to make small slices where each petal connects to make them longer (**B**). Spread a bit of powdered sugar on the thin foam mat and place a flower on it. Pick up 1 petal with your fingers on 1 hand, and with the other hand thin out the edges by slowly turning the ball tool around the petal. Do the same for all the petals to ruffle them. Repeat this step with the rest of the flowers (**C**).

2. Once all flowers are ruffled, spread glue over the center of 1 of the small flowers. In the center, insert the bottom of the spaghetti with the rosebud. Push the flower up all the way to the bottom of the rose bud. Fold up the petals, 1 at a time (**A**). Repeat with the remaining small flowers first and then the large flowers. Use a modeling stick to spread out any of the ruffled edges as needed and place it in the flower-forming cup to dry (**B**). If you can, insert the raw spaghetti through the hole in the cup and pull it out, or break it off. With the rolling pin, roll out light blue fondant ⅛ inch thick and spread a bit of shortening over the fondant. Place the embossing mat over the fondant and use the rolling pin to impress the pattern onto it. Use the 2¼-inch scalloped cutter to punch out a circle and use round tip #1 to make holes around the perimeter of the scallop, creating a doily (**C**). Once the rose is dry enough, glue it to the center of the bottom topper. (**Please note**: Wait for the rose to dry just enough to maintain its shape before gluing to the topper since dry fondant pieces do not stick well to each other.) Allow to dry thoroughly.

Pearl Necklace

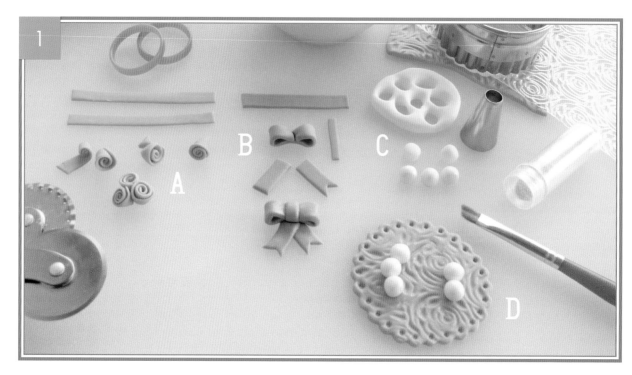

How to:

1. With the rolling pin, roll out pink fondant $\frac{1}{16}$ inch thick and use the rolling pastry cutter to trim 3 strips (approximately $\frac{1}{3}$ inch wide and 2 inches long). To form little roses, start at 1 end of the strip and roll it into itself, pinching the rolling end lightly with your fingers as you roll, while making sure the other end stays loose and wide. Repeat with the other 2 strips **(A)**. You might need to trim the bottoms with the precision knife. Glue them together in a little bouquet. With the rolling pin, roll out light blue fondant $\frac{1}{8}$ inch thick and cut 2 strips with the rolling pastry cutter (approximately $\frac{1}{2}$ inch wide and 2 inches long). Turn 1 of the strips upside down on your work surface and then fold the ends to meet in the center, making 2 loops. Glue the ends and pinch them together in the middle to narrow. Cut the second strip in half and use the precision knife to trim the ends of the bow. Layer one side over the other and glue them together. Cut a final thin strip to form around the center of the bow. Trim it as needed and glue it down. Glue the top of the bow to the ends **(B)**. Roll out white fondant thick with the rolling pin and wooden dowels. Cut out 5 circles with round tip #12. Roll them into balls and brush them with white shimmer dust **(C)**. With the rolling pin, roll out pink fondant $\frac{1}{8}$ inch thick and spread a bit of shortening over the fondant. Place the embossing mat over the fondant and use the rolling pin to impress the pattern onto it. Use the 2¼-inch scalloped cutter to punch out a circle. Use round tip #1 to make holes around the perimeter of the scallop, making a doily **(D)**. Glue the roses, bow, and pearls together on the bottom topper to form the necklace. Allow to dry thoroughly.

GOING TO THE CHAPEL

Materials Needed

fondant
(black, white, desired skin color & desired flower color)

small candy pearls

Cutters Needed

round tip #7

large heart cutter

large scalloped heart cutter

miniature flower cutter

Tools Needed

rolling pin with
$\frac{1}{8}$-inch guide rings

rolling pastry cutter

precision knife

knife tool

small modeling stick

foam block

scroll embossing mat

Sweet Tips

SIMPLIFY	Omit some of the details from the groom's tuxedo and the pearls from the bride.
ACCENTUATE	Punch out hearts in different sizes and colors to accentuate additional cupcakes.
PERSONALIZE	Make additional heart toppers with the couple's initials punched out of fondant with letter cutters.
EXPAND	Follow the rose tutorial from the Shabby Chic Bridal Shower collection (p. 231) to enhance your wedding assortment.
DECORATE & DISPLAY	Utilize pretty cupcake liners and wrappers and enhance your presentation with doilies. Embellish your display with traditional wedding details, such as rings and jewels.

Groom

LEVEL OF DIFFICULTY

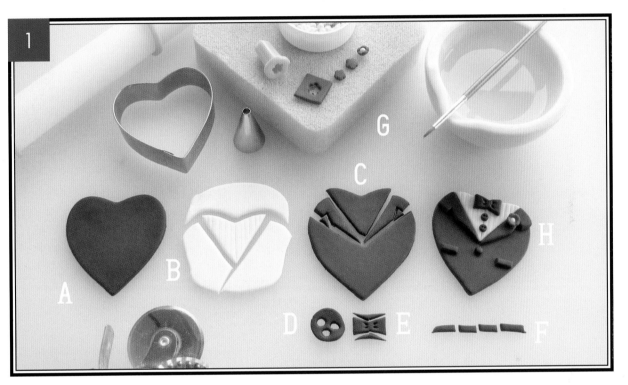

How to:

1. With the rolling pin, roll out black and white fondant ⅛ inch thick. Cut out 2 large black hearts and 1 large white heart with the cutter **(A)**. With the precision knife, cut out a triangular shape from the top center for the white shirt. Use the knife tool to make vertical indentations across the shirt **(B)**. Place it over 1 of the black hearts to use as guide and then trim the lapels of the tuxedo with the precision knife. Cut out a small triangle on the outside of the lapels **(C)**. Glue the white shirt and the black lapels to the other black heart. With the rolling pin, roll out additional black fondant ⅛ inch thick. Cut out 3 circles with round tip #7 **(D)**. Glue 2 of them on the white shirt and 1 below where the lapels meet. Use the small modeling stick to make 2 indentations on the 2 buttons on the white shirt. Cut out a rectangle from the black fondant with the precision knife and trim it into a bow tie. Make small indentations at the center **(E)** and glue it to the top of the white shirt. Cut out 1 last strip of the black fondant with the rolling pastry cutter and use the precision knife to trim small narrow rectangles for the tuxedo pockets **(F)** and glue them in place toward the bottom of the heart. With the rolling pin, roll out fondant in the desired flower color ⅛ inch thick and cut out a miniature flower with the cutter. Press it flat with your fingers and place it on the foam block. Dab on some glue and add a small candy pearl in the center. Press the pearl into the flower on the foam with a tool, like the small modeling stick **(G)**. Glue the flower to the tuxedo **(H)**. Allow to dry thoroughly.

Bride

How to:

1. With the rolling pin, roll out skin-colored fondant ⅛ inch thick and cut out a large heart with the cutter **(A)**. With the rolling pin, roll out white fondant ⅛ inch thick and spread some shortening over the fondant. Place the embossing mat over the fondant and use the rolling pin to impress the pattern onto it **(B)**. Punch out a large heart with the cutter. Use the large scalloped heart cutter to trim off the top to form the dress **(C)**. (If you do not have a scalloped heart cutter, you can simply use the heart cutter for a straight seam.) Glue the dress to the bottom of the skin-colored heart. Form the small candy pearls around the top of the heart in the shape of a necklace and gently press them into the fondant. Once they are in the desired location, pick up each pearl, dab glue on the fondant, and press the pearls in firmly **(D)**. Allow to dry thoroughly.

Displaying,
PACKAGING & SHIPPING

CUPCAKE DISPLAYS

There are countless creative and fun ways to display your fondant-topped cupcakes, including cupcake and cake stands, as well as exciting, unique, and outside-the-box ideas. Whether you are creating a presentation or laying out a dessert table, these are some ideas to enhance your arrangement.

Left: Cupcake, cake, and tiered stands. **Top right:** Plates and trays. **Middle right:** Creative stands. **Bottom Right:** Props and scrapbook paper.

SHIPPING

I'm not going to lie: shipping fondant toppers is not a piece of cake! The more complicated and three-dimensional the topper, the harder it is to package it carefully enough to avoid breakage during shipment. The following are steps you can take for optimum shipping preparation:

- Choose the collection and theme of your toppers and determine whether any changes need to be made to replace or avoid easily breakable details.

- Once completely dry, wrap each individual topper in two to three plastic sandwich bags. Not only are they food-safe, but they will also provide extra cushion for your toppers.

PACKAGING

If you are giving a gift or delivering an order, your packaging and presentation can make a huge difference, both for practicality to ensure they are not ruined during transport, as well as aesthetic purposes. The best boxes have inserts to hold each cupcake in place, but most important are containers with deep built-in openings and tall lids to fit your fondant toppers. Dress them up with ribbons and tags for a final touch!

- Layer your toppers wrapped in sandwich bags inside a box within tissue paper, bubble wrap, and/or foam packing peanuts, making sure you do not leave room for the toppers to move during shipment.

- If your toppers have three-dimensional figures or are extremely fragile, package them inside a smaller box prior to adding to the larger box. Fill the gaps with extra packing supplies and carefully tape the box shut.

- Since the fondant toppers don't have to be refrigerated, shipping them overnight is not required. My packages usually arrive in two to three days, but they have survived a few international trips as well! If you have never mailed toppers, you will have no problem finding volunteers to receive some of your trial shipments!

Resources & CREDITS

FONDANT AND CAKE DECORATING

TOOLS AND SUPPLIES

Wilton
www.wilton.com

Michaels
www.michaels.com

Joann
www.joann.com

Hobby Lobby
www.hobbylobby.com

Global Sugar Art
www.globalsugarart.com

Duff Goldman
www.duff.com

Fat Daddio's
www.fatdaddios.com

Tempting Treasures by Jan
(702) 564-5029 (no website)

Country Kitchen SweetArt
www.countrykitchensa.com

Autumn Carpenter
www.autumncarpenter.com

ShopBakersNook.com
www.shopbakersnook.com

CUTTER BRANDS

Wilton
www.wilton.com

Ateco

FONDANT BRANDS

Wilton
www.wilton.com

Satin Ice
www.satinice.com

FondX
www.fondx.com

Fondarific
www.fondarific.com

GEL PASTES AND EDIBLE-INK MARKERS

BRANDS

Wilton
www.wilton.com

Americolor
www.americolorcorp.com

KITCHEN SUPPLY SHOPS

Sur La Table
www.surlatable.com

Williams-Sonoma
www.williams-sonoma.com

CRAFTS, DECORATING, AND STORAGE SUPPLIES

Michaels
www.michaels.com

Joann
www.joann.com

Hobby Lobby
www.hobbylobby.com

Home Goods
www.homegoods.com

Target
www.target.com

Pier 1 Imports
www.pier1.com

The Container Store
www.containerstore.com

PACKAGING AND SHIPPING

Paper Mart
www.papermart.com

Cuptainers
www.cuptainers.com

BRP Box Shop
www.brpboxshop.com

COLOR MIXING AND DESIGN

Satin Ice Color Mix Guide
www.satinice.com/color.php

Design Seeds
www.design-seeds.com

Fondant Color Blending Chart
www.wilton.com/decorating/fondant/fondant-color-blending-chart.cfm

HEADSHOT PHOTOGRAPHY

Tiny Traits Photography
www.tinytraits.com

RECIPES

Liz Marek's Fondant
Elizabeth Marek, Artisan Cake Company, Portland, OR

www.artisancakecompany.com/tutorials/lmf-fondant-recipe/

Merci Beaucoup!

"Feeling gratitude and not expressing it is like wrapping a present and not giving it."

William Arthur Ward

I believe the same can be said about decorating a cupcake and not sharing it! As I brainstormed ideas and prepared for my daughter's third birthday, I never could have dreamed up this incredible journey I have been on. I would not have survived the surprising twists and turns and all the ups and downs from the last few years without my support system. Therefore, here is my expression of gratitude, my gift-wrapped present, and my fondant-topped cupcake all rolled into one!

TO MY SWEET DAUGHTER, ANABELLE, to whom this book is dedicated—You are my biggest inspiration and my number one reason to celebrate. There has never been a prouder mom. Thank you for your patience and for being my number one cheerleader. I hope all this hard work motivates you to follow your dreams and, most important, to dance.

TO MY HUSBAND, BRAD—My college sweetheart and the most patient man I know! Your willingness to take on new adventures and to try anything at least once is a trait I admire and cherish so much about you. Thank you for supporting and joining me on our latest adventure and for being such an extraordinary husband, father, and party/cleanup assistant! I'm one lucky cupcake.

TO MY PARENTS—I wouldn't be here without you . . . for the obvious reason, but most important, because of the love you have given me, the values you have instilled in me, and the undying support you have offered me. Thank you for believing in me and helping me in any way possible.

TO MY DADDY—Thank you for being my first introduction to party planning and cake decorating; for all you have taught me throughout the years to be a good, true, and genuine person; and most of all, for encouraging me, no matter what I am doing, to have fun.

TO MY MOMMY—Thank you for teaching me the value of hard work, friendship, and loyalty, and though baking and crafting is not quite your thing, the late nights of cutting and gluing and sewing for me and your granddaughter are greatly appreciated, more than you will ever know.

TO MY BROTHER, LES—Since we were kids, I have always admired your artistry and ingenuity, and I am so grateful for the inspiration. Thank you for the love and loyalty.

TO MY GRANDMOTHER VOVÓ—Thank you for being a strong, fearless, and generous role model. Muito obrigada!

TO MY LATE SISTER-IN-LAW, SUZIE—Thank you for being a such a big influence in my life and introducing me to puffy paints and the great big world of crafting. You are missed every day.

TO MY ENTIRE IMMEDIATE AND EXTENDED FAMILY—I consider myself incredibly fortunate to have such a loving and supportive family, from the Norths to the Becketts and to all who have joined along the way. And I love that it continues to grow!

TO MY DEAR FRIENDS, NEAR AND FAR—
Words cannot express my gratitude for your constant support and encouragement. Harriet and the
Katz family—Thank you for believing in me and
supporting me in so many ways. Jessi and Melissa—
I am very appreciative of so many years of friendship and to have you in my life. Meg —Thank you
so much for the gorgeous pics and for the love.

TO MY PARTY AND BAKING COMMUNITIES—
Sweet, sugary kisses to all the amazingly creative
and talented friends I have made since starting
this business. I am so grateful for the incredible
support, encouragement, and camaraderie! Sweet
shout-outs to Mindy Cone of Creative Juice for
the advice and referral and Michele Pentecost of
Intrigue Design Studio for the website and graphic
design magic.

TO MARINA AT TINY TRAITS—A sweet thank
you for your beautiful photography and headshot.

TO CEDAR FORT PUBLISHING—My heartfelt
gratitude to Joanna Barker, Erica Dixon, Casey
Winters, Rodney Fife, and the entire Cedar Fort
team for the support and hard work in helping me
bring my dream to fruition.

LAST, BUT CERTAINLY NOT LEAST, TO THE
SWEETEST READERS, CUSTOMERS, AND
FANS OF ALL TIME—I am truly grateful for
the immense support and love you have shown me
throughout the years. Thank you for constantly
motivating me and being right alongside me on
this exciting ride!

Index

P

pacifier: 227–228

packaging: 238, 240

peas: 161–163

penguin: 149–152

personalize: 2

pig: 56

pirate: 83–87

poodle: 225

popcorn: 38, 116

powdered sugar: 3, 7

princess: 23–25

pumpkin: 191–196

R

rabbit: 171–173

racing: 145–148

rainbow: 167–169

reindeer: 207–210

S

Santa: 205–206, 211–213

school: 153–160

science: 101–104

seal: 71

ship: 86

shipping: 238, 240

shortening: 3–6

shower

  baby: 219–228

  bridal: 229–232

sleeping bag: 36–37

slumber party: 35–38

soccer: 139–143

sombrero: 179

spring: 171–176

summer: 109–113, 187–189

superhero: 89–91

supplies: 3–14, 239–240

surfing: 109–113

sweets: 39–43

T

Thanksgiving: 197–200

tiger: 75, 78

tires: 95, 146, 147

tools: 7–11, 239

tooth: 42

toothpick: 5, 6, 13

toppings: 14

treasure map: 87

turkey: 197–200

tylose powder: 3

V

valentine: 161–166

vampire: 195

W

wand: 25

wedding: 233–236

winter: 201–217

witch: 193

About the Author

After 10 years of working as a buyer in the fashion industry, Lynlee decided to pursue her dreams after her love of decorating cupcakes, planning parties, and crafting culminated into an undeniable passion. As a self-taught fondant decorator, Lynlee quickly transitioned into the party world and began making cupcakes and embellished toppers with unique and creative designs. Since then, she continued to hone her craft by creating the most incredibly sweet and detailed cupcake toppers while providing inspiration and tutorials on her website, in e-zines, and with the launch of her own line of publications. Lynlee and her work have been featured on popular party planning and baking blogs and publications, including Martha Stewart and Disney, among many more! Lynlee currently resides in Las Vegas with her husband and aspiring-baker daughter.

Learn more and be inspired at
WWW.LYNLEES.COM

Praise for

Sweet & Unique

CUPCAKE TOPPERS

"Lynlee's fondant creations are above and beyond anything I've ever seen. Living in Los Angeles, I've had the opportunity to work with what is said to be the best—Lynlee is better than the best! I'm blown away by her talent and would love to work with her on all of my Hollywood celebrity events!"

—SCOUT MASTERSON, TV star, celebrity event producer

"Lynlee's book is the go-to source for fondant decorations! It's full of darling ideas and tips galore for creating the most creative cupcake toppers and treats for birthday parties and other special occasions. It deserves a spot on every party lover's bookshelf!"

—COURTNEY WHITMORE, author, founder of Pizzazzerie.com

"Lynlee's work with fondant is deliciously inspiring! Every design is like a mini work of art, and she breaks each project down into generous detail and imagery for all the aspiring sugar artists out there. These insanely cute creations are guaranteed to be the hit of any party!"

—JENNIFER SBRANTI, founder and editor-in-chief of *Hostess with the Mostess*

"Sugar art is all the rage, and fondant is no exception. *Sweet and Unique Cupcake Toppers* is filled with fun projects for decorators of every skill level. With detailed instructions and ideas for every occasion, no matter what your medium, you're sure to be inspired."

—CALLYE ALVARADO, author, founder of *The Sweet Adventures of Sugarbelle*

"I've never met a more talented cupcake designer. Lynlee has imagination and style, and her creations have such a sense of fun."

—LESLEY WRIGHT, bakery owner and instructor, the Royal Bakery

0 26575 13668 5